THE ULTRA-MAGIC DEALS

Books by Bradley F. Smith:

Adolf Hitler: His Family, Childhood and Youth
Heinrich Himmler: A Nazi in the Making
Reaching Judgment at Nuremberg
Operation Sunrise, the Secret Surrender (with Elena Agarossi)
The Road to Nuremberg
The Shadow Warriors: OSS and the Origins of the CIA
The War's Long Shadow: World War II and Its Aftermath

THE
ULTRA-MAGIC
DEALS

And the Most Secret Special Relationship

1940–1946

Bradley F. Smith

PRESIDIO

Published by Presidio Press
505 B San Marin Dr., Suite 300
Novato, CA 94945-1340

Library of Congress Cataloging-in-Publication Data

Smith, Bradley F.
    The ultra-magic deals and the most secret special relationship,
1940–1946 / Bradley F. Smith.
      p.   cm.
    Includes bibliographical references and index.
    ISBN 0-89141-483-5
    1. World War, 1939–1945—Cryptography. 2. World War, 1939–1945—
Electronic intelligence—United States. 3. World War, 1939–1945—
Electronic intelligence—Great Britain. 4. World War, 1939–1945—
Secret service—United States. 5. World War, 1939–1945—Secret
service—Great Britain. 6. United States—Foreign relations—Great
Britain. 7. Great Britain—Foreign relations—United States.
I. Title.
D810.C88S65 1993
940.54'8641—dc20   92-25749
                                                  CIP

Typography by ProImage
Printed in the United States of America

CONTENTS

ACKNOWLEDGMENTS

A number of colleagues assisted me in the preparation of this volume, and I would especially like to thank Robin Denniston, John Ferris, Charles Burdick, Andrew Lownie, Mark Seaman, Hank Shorreck (of NSA), and Alan Wilt.

Although all documentary research depends on the assistance of knowledgeable and helpful archivists, that is especially true in Washington, and I wish to express heartfelt thanks to the following archivists at the National Archives and the Naval Historical Center. National Archives: Richard Boylon, Greg Brasher, Bill Cunliffe, David Giordano, Tim Mulligan, Tim Nenninger, Ed Reese, Dave Pfaffer, John Taylor, Richard von Doenhoff, and Barry Zerby. Naval Historical Center: Gina Akers and Kathy Lloyd.

Joan Griffin of Presidio Press, precise yet kind, saved me from committing numerous errors of omissions and commission, and my wife Jenny Wilkes Smith, bore well the burden of close association with a befogged researcher.

PREFACE

In the middle phase of World War II (1942 to 1943) the governments of the United States and Great Britain concluded a pair of secret pacts by which they agreed to merge the code- and cipher-breaking (cryptanalytic) operations they were directing against Nazi Germany, Italy, and Japan. During the remainder of the war, Britain and the United States shared with each other most of the cryptanalytic intelligence they secured about their enemies. They also arranged for exchanges of personnel serving within the cryptanalytic organizations of their two countries. Code and cipher breakers of the two North Atlantic powers then worked side by side in Britain and the United States throughout the last two-and-a-half years of the war.

This World War II Anglo-American cryptanalytic partnership was unique. Never before had sovereign states revealed their vital intelligence methods and results even to their closest allies. Once the most secret operations of Britain and the United States had been linked together, however, important consequences followed that extended far beyond an increase in valuable wartime intelligence. When the war ended, British and American officials were understandably loath to give up the secret information that had accrued to them under the wartime agreements. They also knew that each side had learned too much about the other's highly secret activities to make possible a safe return to the earlier condition of total independence in which a constant cryptanalytic war prevailed of all against all.

The Anglo-American partners therefore agreed within a month of V-J Day, amid many general worries about governmental reorganization plans, postwar security, and the rise of the USSR, to extend their cryptanalytic alliance into the postwar era. That decision provided a vital secret basis for the transatlantic special relationship that constituted a major component of the West's security system throughout the nearly half-century-long cold war.

With the cold war at an end, both the British and American governments seem to be thinking again about their close partnership and perhaps about the cryptanalytic links that have bound them so tightly together for so long. As the threat of a worldwide Armageddon recedes, one or both of the Atlantic code- and cipher-breaking partners may be inclined to the view that this most secret special relationship has outlived its usefulness. It is also possible that the people of one or both countries may demand a reassessment of the size, cost, and purpose of their respective "national security" states, and in the end conclude that the military features of the special relationship, including its cryptanalytic core, are no longer necessary.

Yet even though the moment of truth may seem to have arrived for the transatlantic cryptanalytic union, those both in and out of the governments who are eager to weigh its strengths and weaknesses will be hard-pressed to find solid data on which to make a judgment. Not only has all information regarding the current condition and the activities of this union been a closely guarded secret for half a century, London and Washington have also locked arms and minds to prevent release of historical data reaching back as far as the early 1940s. If one may judge by a National Security Agency (NSA) secret history of cryptanalysis in World War II, recently pried out of the agency by a Freedom of Information Act appeal, even NSA's own officials have been so handicapped by secrecy policies that they have had serious difficulty detailing how and why the Anglo-American cryptanalytic partnership came into being, and the processes by which it was continued into the postwar era.

The present volume attempts to meet these difficulties. It traces the developments moving in the direction of a cryptanalytic partnership during the first two years of the war, the negotiation of the agreements in the midwar period, and the implementation phase during 1943–45. It then moves on to examine the process by which the secret union was extended into the postwar era during 1945–46. Throughout, the book is based primarily on documents unearthed in British and American archives, and has been researched and written on the assumption that even the most highly sensitive and intractable issues in the recent history of international relations will ultimately yield at least in part to the traditional methods of scholarship, if enough time and effort are devoted to the search.

Constructing a picture of the Ultra-Magic deals has involved more, however, than simply filing Freedom of Information Act applications and slogging through the files month after month and year after year. The wartime cryptanalytic agreements epitomize a category of World War II history that has tended to be ignored both by popular and scholarly writers, first because it concerns the politics of secret intelligence, and second because it is an aspect of the conflict that clearly pointed forward in time and helped directly shape the immediate postwar era. The Ultra-Magic deals concerned secret matters at least as important for their effects after 1945 as they were for their impact on wartime events. But because the history of World War II has been viewed as a sharply delineated phenomenon, with important causes of the war spelled out in detail but little attention given to the war's causal impact on subsequent decades—aside, of course, from the fact that in some form or another World War II was a contributing cause for the coming of the cold war—the long-term significance of the Ultra-Magic deals has been largely ignored.

The tendency to see the war more as an end than as a beginning has seriously distorted events, and acts as a formidable obstacle to an understanding of the importance of the secret developments that occurred between 1939 and 1945. Even more importantly, this historical compartmentalization has acted as a serious barrier to an understanding of the broad range of historical dynamics that have operated from the midcentury on into our own time.

Between 1939 and 1945, World War II functioned as a mighty engine, producing basic changes that would help shape the world throughout the latter half of the twentieth century. This was a war with vast numbers of participants and wide-ranging zones of operations. It killed and maimed people in far larger numbers than any previous conflict (probably about 40 million killed worldwide) and spread death and mayhem over broader areas—including North Africa and Asia, as well as Europe—than had any of its modern martial predecessors, including World War I and the Napoleonic Wars.

During this, the second and the greater world war, modern military power, for the first time, aimed its lethal force directly at civilian populations. Between 1939 and 1945, ideological killing, enslavement of conquered peoples, blockade, and mass bombing all spread their horrors from the English Channel to the Sea of Japan. This intensive slaughter, when coupled with the need to conduct warfare over vast distances, forced belligerent governments to employ every possible measure to help mobilize their populations for war and to push forward the rationalization and standardization of their productive methods to expand output. Ideology, propaganda, modern communications technology, and coercion were used so extensively by all the belligerents that output rose by leaps and bounds, armed forces were greatly expanded, and by war's end one could for the first time accurately characterize many of the world's peoples as being full members of "warring nations."

All of these developments raised the stakes in warfare and thereby increased every government's concern regarding enemy intentions. Information, especially secret information, about enemy aims and plans was thus even more important in World War II than in other wars. Technology also received special attention from warring governments because they needed new weapons and protective measures for their own forces as well as the means to counter the technological innovations of their opponents. Jet planes and rockets, radar and sulfa drugs, flamethrowers and snorkel submarines, as well as cipher machines and the analytic equipment designed to break them were only a few instances of the vast technological revolution spawned by the pressures, rivalries, and opportunities created by the war.

Even though, upon reflection, it seems obvious that World War II was an enormous innovative force compelling basic change on many levels, in most countries the public has been slow to acknowledge its long-term significance. The emotional carryovers from the war—the pride, pain, sorrow, and enthusiasm it engendered—have tended to fix attention on specific incidents and phenomena, such as the dropping of the atomic bomb, the Blitz, or Hitler's "final solution." The dictates of chronology and national sensitivities have meant also that even the fiftieth-anniversary commemorations of the war have moved reflexively through a series of year-by-year incidents and issues beginning with the outbreak of the war (1939–89), then the fall of France and the Blitz (1940–90), on to the attack on the USSR and Pearl Harbor (1941–91), with El Alamein, D day, and the atomic bomb waiting in the wings. The reexaminations of the war occasioned by these commemorations may have been cathartically healthy, but they also seem to have compounded the prevailing tendency to divide the wartime experience into tight little time periods and nationalistic compartments.

Scholars of World War II also have focused rather narrowly, although much current work successfully transcends most of the nationalistic biases of the wartime period. Even broadly focused studies and surveys, however, have usually begun with the roots of the war and ended with the surrenders of Germany and Japan in 1945. Seldom have even recent works attempted to go beyond V-E and V-J days, with the obvious exception of those scholars specifically concerned with the immediate causes of the cold war.

Governments too have tended to honor the 1945 end line. Many governments reorganized their record systems in the immediate postwar period, and almost all have, in recent years, become less restrictive of scholarly access to records of the wartime era, while remaining extremely tightfisted regarding sensitive materials from later periods. In nearly every archive one chooses to explore, a very restrictive policy immediately shows itself as soon as one seeks to look at events that occurred in September 1945 or the following months and years.

Given the popular, scholarly, and governmental tendency to keep World War II in something akin to splendid isolation, few guideposts exist for those trying to examine any aspect of the war more as a beginning than as an end. This is, of course, especially true of secret intelligence, the realm of the "missing dimension," where information on both the wartime and the postwar periods has been tightly controlled by governments until recently, and rarely studied by serious scholars. Therefore, although the present study will focus on the delicate matter of most secret intelligence cooperation and its effects after 1945, it will do so cautiously, to make certain that the course of wartime and postwar events is not arbitrarily foreshortened, and that effects are not confused with causes.

To do this, it is essential to begin with an examination of that complicated, confused, and confusing subject, vital to every aspect of the secret history of World War II—the state of Anglo-American relations at the beginning of the conflict. Then on to a survey of the even more delicate matter of the state of intelligence collection in the two countries in 1939–40, including an examination of the situation in regard to code making and breaking, and the degree to which Anglo-American intelligence cooperation existed in 1939–40. Once these matters have been laid bare, it will be possible to move onto the track of the Ultra-Magic deals and begin to explore why the most secret special relationship that the war created has survived and thrived for half a century.

CHAPTER ONE
The Anglo-American Setting

Official relations between Britain and the United States were far from cordial during much of the lifetime of those who led the governments and armed forces of the two great western powers during World War II. Every one of the men holding power in Washington and London in 1940 was born before World War I, and the top leaders— Winston Churchill, Franklin D. Roosevelt, Henry L. Stimson, Cordell Hull, Anthony Eden, George Marshall, and Sir Alan Brooke— had all been born in the last third of the nineteenth century. Over the fifty years that extended from the end of the American Civil War to Sarajevo, the oldest of the men (Henry Stimson was born in 1867) had seen their two governments in serious confrontations on a number of occasions, such as the North Atlantic fishing rights controversy of 1888 and the Venezuelan boundary dispute of 1895. So strong was the official American feeling that Britain should be held at arm's length that no U.S. ambassador was actually accredited to the Court of St. James until 1893. Every Fourth of July, official speakers across America ritually echoed Senator Henry Cabot Lodge, who, in the words of the British ambassador in 1906, "was constitutionally incapable of foregoing any chance of an attack on England," twisting the lion's tail, evoking images of the revolution and the War of Independence, and denouncing British imperialism and monarchical rule.[1]

Over the broad sweep of American public opinion prior to World War I, the negative images of Britain may well have outweighed the positive. Although conceding that the Kingdom by the Sea was at least ruled by law and had representative government—unlike the "tyrannies" of central and eastern Europe—most Americans considered Britain to be a class-stratified and hierarchical society with few rights or opportunities for the common man. To many immigrants, and immediate descendants of immigrants (the majority of the American population in 1900), Britain epitomized that from which they had fled, and many of those of Irish descent viewed London as akin to the homeland of the anti-Christ.

For a large number of nineteenth and early twentieth century Americans, the Canadian border still represented the threat of British imperialism. Britain remained the world's greatest imperialist and possessed a powerful navy. Britain was also the biggest commercial creditor, whereas the United States ranked far down the scale among the greatest international debtors. Many forms of economic activity in the United States during this period, from insurance companies to Rocky Mountain cattle ranches, were dependent on capital investment from London. Like most international debtors, these Americans did not like the strings and the charges that came with the money. Consequently at the turn of the century many evil thoughts about London bankers danced through the heads of the American people.

As one moved up the rungs of the American social ladder during the late nineteenth century, one encountered less Anglophobia and greater respect for British institutions, the sophistication of its high society, and the value of its cultural achievements. Here, class, status, respectability, and Americanization played important roles. Many of the new industrial rich—the Harrimans, Vanderbilts, and Rockefellers—looked to the British upper classes as role models, just as the Astors and Mellons had done in earlier generations. All of those who at the turn of the century had been in the United States long enough to have at least one foot on the ladder of success believed that "Americanizing" institutions was essential to tame the immigrant, and the most important such institution was the public primary school, where the English language would act as the lingua Americana, and English literature would tame the savage beast.

By 1900 the industrial production of the United States had shot past that of both Britain and Germany, and American leaders looked out on the world with greater confidence and sophistication. The American government had begun to dabble in regional imperialism and in the joys of naval power politics in the South and central Pacific as well as in the Western Hemisphere. The more expansive and expansionist American leaders became, the more respect they seemed to have for British naval, industrial, and colonial achievements. After a decade and a half in which Cecil Rhodes, Theodore Roosevelt, Admiral Alfred Mahan, and Joseph Chamberlain had proclaimed the virtues of progress, the white man's burden, and the strenuous life, notions of an Anglo-Saxon world stewardship filled the minds of many government officials and leaders of public opinion on both sides of the Atlantic. By the eve of World War I a substantial portion of the American population had come around to perceiving Britain as a strong, but aging, and generally benevolent power.

British pre–World War I attitudes regarding the United States were probably less complex than those that boiled and bubbled across the Atlantic. Generally viewed by the British government as an insular ("self-centered" in the words of one prewar British ambassador) secondary power, filled with "braggadocio" and great potential, the United States held little attraction for the British upper classes during the nineteenth century except for the handful of adventurous enthusiasts for mountains, Indians, and prairies, as well as the occasional noble who sought financial deliverance by means of marriage into the newly rich industrial families. American literature and art made few conquests in Britain except for the works of expatriates such as Henry James and James McNeill Whistler. But respect for Yankee inventiveness was strong in much of the British press and among industrialists, and Mark Twain drew a smile from nearly everyone (he was ultimately given a Doctor of Letters by Oxford).[2]

In much of the British population, the immigration tie to America was probably the strongest bond connecting the two countries. Rare was the British family without at least a cousin or nephew who had gone west, and America remained to some degree in British popular consciousness a land of a second, and perhaps a better, chance in life.

Overall during the early years of the twentieth century, as the British government struggled to keep its footing in a world of colonial rivalry, international instability, and bitter economic competition, dominated by rising German power, concern about America and other secondary states remained in the background. But it is probable that just below the surface of British official consciousness in the twenty years prior to the outbreak of World War I there slumbered the awareness that statistics did not lie and sooner or later the United States was destined to be an extremely powerful nation.

When war broke out in 1914 and the stalemate on the Marne took hold of both the Allies and the Central Powers, only a minimum of insight was required to determine that American production and shipping held the key to Britain's long-term survival and its hopes for victory. Over the subsequent three years there came the well-known British efforts to court American favor and support—the massive purchases, the American commercial loans, the open and covert British propaganda in the Americas—while on the American side, the equally well-known events occurred whereby President Woodrow Wilson adjusted to the British blockade, as well as to a pattern of trade and credit that gradually turned the United States into the world's greatest exporter and creditor, even as it made continuing American prosperity dependent on Allied victory. The resulting intervention in 1917—the first American crusade in Europe—unleashed a wave of war enthusiasm and allowed the U.S. government to play its strong hand—a rapid total war mobilization based on the country's vast human and productive resources. The creation of this large American military machine was probably decisive in tipping victory to the side of the Allies in 1918, but the United States did not actually join the alliance led by France and Britain, self-consciously preferring to remain a pure and unique "associated power," untainted by the dirty power politics of Europe. Of course, during the conflict American forces marched in concert with those of their French and British "associates." There was even limited cooperation on delicate matters such as the sharing of operational intelligence from broken German army codes, and some close personal bonds of comradeship were formed. But at war's end the American dedication to a sense of its own uniqueness, and the possession of a democratic mission, triumphed once again. The Treaty of Paris was rejected by the U.S. Senate; America's armed forces were cut back to the bone; and the country that had just clearly demonstrated its ability to play the part of a near superpower refused to join the League of Nations, which its own president had proclaimed to be the world's best route to lasting peace and stability.[3]

The twenty years that followed 1919–20 were marked in America by the rise of a broad commitment to isolationism and an abhorrence of large standing military forces. The resulting cocoonlike attitude that America had an inalienable right to security was supplemented by the fact that the United States was separated from Europe and Asia by vast oceans and by the retention of a powerful navy. The overall consequence was an increase in Americans' sense of their own uniqueness (man's last, best hope, et cetera), giving the preservation of this special land a nearly mystical significance.

The great American disappearing act of 1919–20 had a very different meaning when viewed from London, Paris, and other foreign capitals during the 1920s and 1930s. The Allies, especially Britain and France, were badly battered by the war, if nominally victorious, whereas the power potential of some of the nominal losers of the great conflict—especially Germany and Russia—had in fact not been broken. The American unwillingness to shoulder a share of the postwar political, economic, and military responsibilities left Britain and France in a position of titular world leadership while much of the real power actually slumbered in the United States or rumbled ominously within Germany, Soviet Russia, and Japan.

In the words of Robert Hathaway, the interwar period was "a time when indifference, suspicion and bitterness" characterized relations between Britain and the United States. The resentments prompted among British leaders by the combination of American power and isolationism were probably reinforced by the irresponsible egoism of American economic policy and the appearance in the United States of the first phase of a mass-media and mass-consumer economic and social system based on cheap automobiles, home appliances, mass advertising, consumer credit, movies, and commercial radio. European societies were soon bombarded by the images and cultural artifacts of this pop cultural revolution, ranging from F. Scott Fitzgerald's Gatsby to the outpourings of Hollywood. Although many Europeans welcomed the arrival of pop Americana, custodians of cultural purity and traditional values immediately raised cries of alarm, and what Stalinists would soon label the "ruling circles" of western Europe generally perceived Louis Armstrong and Mae West as the advance guard of a tide of American barbarism sweeping in from the West.[4]

Then came the great crash and the onset of what virtually all Europeans considered the "American Great Depression." The United States was thereby driven further into impotent separatism, and European leaders

were saddled with many new problems, ranging from massive business failure to catastrophic unemployment, amid an increase in
international instability. Almost immediately after the onset of the
depression the economy of Stalinist Russia began to take off via the
murderous five-year plans for intensive industrialization; then Japan
seized Manchuria (1931) and Hitler came to power in Germany (1933).
Britain and France found themselves swamped by a combination of
their own domestic problems and the rise of the authoritarian expan-
sionists in Moscow, Berlin, Tokyo, and Rome. Little help came from
the United States, which refused joint international measures against
the depression or the expansionist pressures of the Axis powers, Japan, and the Soviet Union. The U.S. government and the American
press were very generous with advice about what Britain and France
should do about aggression, but the United States did not rearm and
took no practical deterrent steps prior to the outbreak of war in September 1939. Cautious discussions on defense preparations were held
with the British,* and the U.S. Navy continued to act as a counterweight
to Japan in the Pacific, but throughout the whole depressing slide into
war during the late 1930s, the United States generally stood aloof, sharing
only one common belief with the Allied governments, namely, the
conclusion that if war with Hitler came, the World War I scenario would
be repeated and a long period of defensive stalemate would ultimately
be followed by victory for France and Britain. This vision gave a measure
of weary hope to the western leaders. It also acted as the only thread
of practical, if erroneous, realism in the American decision to stand
aside. At the start of the conflict in September 1939 a public opinion
poll showed that 82 percent of the American people had wrapped
themselves in the illusion that by the final bell, Britain and France would
have defeated Germany without American intervention.[5]

Therefore there was little American consolation for the Allies, or
love lost between Washington and London, as Europe slipped into war.
No serious military cooperation had taken place between the armed
forces of Britain and the United States prior to the German attack on
Poland. The United States was virtually disarmed (except for the Pacific
Fleet), and the British authorities, who presided over a military estab-

*Regarding prewar intellignce cooperation between the two countries, see pages 19
and 20.

lishment sadly unprepared for the challenge awaiting them, made no energetic effort to secure American aid. Although disastrously wrong in underestimating the dangers inherent in a second war with Germany, the British were absolutely right in assuming that in 1939 the American government and people had little inclination to render assistance, and in any event the United States possessed no immediately useful modern military assets.

Once the fighting began, and Germany gave an initial demonstration of her power by running over Poland in three weeks, a sense of what passed for resigned realism settled in on both sides of the Atlantic. The Anglo-French authorities, bereft of any supportive eastern front by Stalin's nonaggression pact with Hitler, nestled down behind the Maginot line and waited for the blockade to do its miraculous work. In Washington, President Franklin D. Roosevelt succeeded in obtaining modification of the neutrality laws on 4 November 1939, which permitted him to sell war material to the Allies on a "cash-and-carry" basis. This move was obviously intended to provide limited assistance to the Allies and an economic bonus for the late-depression American economy, while avoiding the threats to American flag vessels that had played such an important role in pulling the United States into World War I.

There the balance of German and Allied power, as well as the balance of Anglo-American cautious reserve, remained poised throughout the winter of 1939 and the spring of 1940. The bold and surprisingly rapid success of the Germans in sweeping through Denmark and Norway in April 1940 produced uneasiness on both sides of the Atlantic and began to call into question the comfortable assumption that Germany would allow itself to be ground down in a stalemated war of attrition. Before these doubts could prompt shifts in basic American or Anglo-French policy, however, Hitler struck again. This time the blow fell with such force that the West's victory-through-attrition illusions were completely smashed in a mere forty days.

On 10 May 1940 the Wehrmacht ripped into the Netherlands and Belgium, encircled the main Allied expeditionary force, and brought France to her knees after a lightning campaign that ended on 20 June. In six weeks Hitler had accomplished what the kaiser's armies had been unable to achieve in the years of stalemate and slaughter between 1914 and 1918. By June 1940 Germany controlled central and western Europe.

Great Britain, euphemistically still referred to as "the Allies," stood alone with little consolation except the tattered glory of a successful retreat and evacuation. But with a proper war cabinet finally in place, and the dynamic Churchill having replaced Chamberlain as prime minister, Britain promised to fight on, battened down the hatches, and bellowed defiance at the victorious Germans across the Channel. The British armaments cupboard was nearly bare in June 1940, and its prospects were marginal, but the new tone of Churchillian aggressiveness in the face of disaster was well tailored not only to rally the British people, but also to help prompt a turn in American policy, just when Britain needed it most.[6]

The May–June German triumph in the west had been a staggering blow to American daydreams of easy security in an explosive world. What President Roosevelt on 31 May called "the almost incredible events of the last two weeks"—the fall of France, German control of all western and central Europe, and the possibility that Britain might be forced under, leaving Adolf Hitler as America's all-powerful transatlantic neighbor—revolutionized American public and governmental opinion. What a British Foreign Office official characterized as "a sense of alarm almost amounting to panic" took hold of the population of the United States. By June 1940 the polls showed that the majority of Americans believed that Germany would win the war in Europe. For the first time, most Americans had also swung over to the view that World War II could actually arrive on their doorstep. "Revolution seems not too strong a word," wrote Laurence Greene in the *New York Post* on 7 June, to characterize "the change in American thought" from a belief in security "to a dread of tomorrow." On 1 June, *Time* publisher Henry Luce declared in a radio broadcast that if the United States could "buy an Allied victory in one year for $5 billion," then "we would be the luckiest people in the world."[7]

Isolationist currents were nonetheless too strong, and the legacy of disillusionment from World War I too deep, for Americans to leap immediately into a European conflict. In June 1940 the United States was still psychologically unready for war; lacking large ground and air forces, as well as modern equipment, the country was militarily unready as well. The U.S. Army was actually smaller and less well equipped than the Royal Dutch Army, and General Fedor von Bock had just finished off the Dutch in a mere five days!

Therefore one of the first lessons Americans drew from the events of May–June 1940 was that their country needed to rearm immediately. In the first eight months of the European war, President Roosevelt had been unable to move even modest military appropriations bills through Congress. Then, on 16 May 1940, as the Panzers tore through the Low Countries, the president asked for a billion-dollar defense program, and Congress gave it to him within two weeks, throwing in an extra half billion dollars for good measure. In subsequent months an additional 6.5 billion was approved for defense, and Congress unanimously passed a measure to increase the size of the fleet by 70 percent.

A special enthusiasm for strengthening the U.S. Navy was manifest in the summer of 1940, a reminder that although the United States was engaged in the most extensive peacetime preparedness campaign in its history, many of the old reservations about foreign entanglements and wars, as well as the dangers of standing armies, had not lost their force. Nearly everyone in the United States agreed that a powerful navy was necessary to prevent the United States from becoming a "victim of the dictators," and to stand guard against Japan in the Pacific. But the idea of direct intervention in the war in Europe, or even extending substantial assistance to Britain, was still far from universally popular. On 28 June—after the fall of France—both houses of Congress approved, and the president signed, a measure requiring that no material owned by the U.S. government should be delivered to any foreign country unless it had been certified as surplus by the chief of Naval Operations and the chief of staff of the U.S. Army.[8]

Once aboard the rearmament express, American officials inevitably began to take fresh interest in relations with Britain, since that country was the only Atlantic protective barrier for the United States and, if things continued to go wrong, might soon again become a military partner. The isolationist barriers to foreign aid could be only gradually lowered, however, and the president still needed tact and patience in pursuing a policy of assistance to Britain. One of the most important factors that helped build a bridge from Western Hemispheric defense to one of transatlantic cooperation, and then on to one of transatlantic aid, was the widespread belief in America that the astonishing Nazi triumphs had been caused in large measure by the activities of subversive fifth columns, which allegedly undermined the resistance of Hitler's opponents. The Allied governments and their people took a

much-needed measure of satisfaction from the myth—for myth it was—
that their failure to stop the Panzers had been due less to the Nazis'
supremacy in conventional warfare than to Hitler's supposed mastery
of subversive artistry. The Nazi wizard's "touch from Hell's academy,"
"the splash of colour mixed on the Nazis' fiendish palette," to use General
Edward Spears, exuberant phrasing, received far too much of the credit
for the German triumphs in the minds of many in western Europe and
America.[9]

The American press, like that of the British, was soon laced with
fifth-column stories ranging from simple accounts of civilian snipers
to elaborate descriptions of waves of German paratroops disguised as
nuns leaping from the clouds onto the heads of innocent Allied
civilians. The public everywhere generally accepted even the wildest
of these reports, presumably because the Hitlerian revolution in the
balance of power was too shocking to be explained by ordinary, mundane
causes. The president himself cited fifth-column dangers in an address
to Congress on 16 May, and in a "fireside chat" of 26 May he said:
"We *know* [italics added] of new methods of attack. The Trojan Horse
[which was hardly new]. The Fifth Column that betrays a nation unprepared for treachery. Spies, saboteurs, and traitors are the actors in
this new tragedy."[10] Such alarmist official statements were warmly
received by the American public, which always had a special place in
its heart for a good conspiracy tale. In all of 1939, despite the outbreak of the war in Europe, only 1,600 reports of alleged sabotage had
been made to the FBI, whereas in May 1940, fueled by the new doubts
and fears, 2,900 such reports were received in a single day![11]

When this fifth-column panic had been factored in with the British
government's realization after the fall of France that it desperately required
American assistance, and the newly awakened sense in the United States
that even America might be directly vulnerable to some form of unorthodox "fifth-column" attack, a much better basis for Anglo-American
cooperation was established.

President Roosevelt's ability to assist the British was also enhanced
when in mid-June he broadened his base in a presidential election year
by adding two Republican Anglophile internationalists to his cabinet.
Citing the international emergency as his motive, he appointed the owner
of the *Chicago Daily News*, Frank Knox, as secretary of the navy, and

Henry Stimson, who had served every president since Theodore Roosevelt, as secretary of war. After stormy Senate hearings, which featured angry exchanges between isolationist Republican senators and Anglophile and internationalist Republicans, such as William Allen White and William Donovan, the appointment of Knox and Stimson was confirmed in early July. While putting their main effort into rebuilding American military strength, Knox and Stimson also believed that all possible assistance should be extended to the British; they found a firm ally for this program in Secretary of State Cordell Hull. After discussing the plight of the British with Hull in mid-July, Stimson noted in his diary that the secretary of state recognized "perfectly clearly that they are our last line of defense outside our own powers." This was a far more pro-British sentiment than would have been received from any U.S. government official just six months earlier.[12]

Although such clarity and forthrightness were possible in private discussions and diary entries, it behooved President Roosevelt to move in public with extreme caution on the issue of aid to Britain, since in less than four months an election would determine whether he would serve an unprecedented third term. Privately, he seems to have believed that Britain had a chance to withstand a German attack; he therefore authorized his top officials to send immediately whatever military equipment could be spared, and to bend the bureaucratic rules wherever possible in favor of Britain. This effort was carried out discreetly to avoid alerting the isolationists and Anglophobes, who still possessed considerable power in Congress, the press, and within many blocs of public opinion.

Roosevelt's handling of aid to Britain certainly played a part in opening the door to a half century of presidential extrastatutory initiatives in foreign affairs, but it is difficult to see what else he could have done, given the level of bureaucratic and legislative inertia, as well as the high stakes involved. In any event, Roosevelt carried out this international adventurism with a light heart; his confident and pragmatic approach to executive leadership always seemed to allow him to bounce from one method of implementation to another without being overly troubled about consistency or regular procedures.

Roosevelt's new secretary of war, Henry Stimson, was both shocked and somewhat annoyed by the president's modus operandi, noting in his diary following a cabinet meeting in mid-December 1940 that:

"Conferences with the President are difficult matters. His mind does not flow easily in a consecutive chain of thought . . . it is very much like chasing a vagrant beam of light around a vacant room."[13]

Roosevelt's director of the Budget Bureau, Harold Smith, seems to have been equally aghast in April 1941 when the president offhandedly confided to him that "when he was Assistant Secretary of the Navy during the last war, he got by with murder because there were no rules and regulations in connection with some very important acts, and he thought that there ought to be considerable freedom of action now."[14]

This freewheeling Rooseveltian style, whatever its adverse effects on his colleagues and on the constitutional principle of separation of powers, immediately struck a responsive chord in London. Someone in Washington finally seemed to be doing something to help.

The unorthodox Roosevelt initiatives also received a warm welcome in London, because another energetic innovator had recently taken charge of the British government. The first day of the German attack in the west (10 May 1940) had brought the resignation of Neville Chamberlain and the appearance of Winston Churchill at Number 10 Downing Street. Few British political figures of the modern era have cut as broad a swath through their times as did Churchill, and few have received as much attention from biographers and historians. Most contemporaries seemed quite sure that Churchill's rise to primacy in 1940 was a significant and positive turn in British fortunes, and though a handful of writers have cast doubts on his achievements and importance, not many would contest that he played a major role, first in holding the line, and then in the march to victory. His pugnacious temperament and visceral hostility to many things German and all things Hitlerian seemed to guarantee a fight to the finish, yet his defiant rhetoric helped to rally his fellow countrymen and reassure friends around the world. Certainly his rise to the position of prime minister was of great importance in creating a close relationship with the United States.

Churchill was a "hands-on" prime minister. A man of enormous energy and limitless interests, he quickly developed a detailed grasp of the minutiae of Britain's war effort, often leading his military staff to lament, as General Hastings Ismay did in 1942, that the prime minister knows "where every cruiser is." His first Director of Naval Intelligence, Adm. John Godfrey, later observed that Churchill had "a large bit of everything in his make up." But, like Roosevelt, Churchill had little respect for established routines and the niceties of the chain of command. He loved to hop over the heads of the appropriate authorities to pursue a special issue that had struck his fancy. "Anything unusual or odd or dramatic interested him," remembered Godfrey, including "Q ships, dummy ships, deception, sabotage, etc." Such an unorthodox and innovative approach to supreme command often drove his staff to distraction, and as General Ismay once commented, the prime minister could sometimes "act just like a child who has lost its temper."[15]

But if Churchill's enthusiasm and frequent disregard for customary procedures were a mixed blessing for Britain's wartime government, they were unalloyed gold for Anglo-American relations in 1940–41. His extroverted personality matched that of Roosevelt, and their joint love of the unusual and the unorthodox formed a special bond between them. They both stood on the secure ground of aristocratic cosmopolitanism in their respective societies. Roosevelt was an Anglophile, and Churchill was half American. The two leaders believed that a partnership was necessary in 1940, and they were self-confident enough to believe that they could pull it off against all odds.

During the later years of the war when circumstances would allow freer expression of their differences as well as their similarities, Roosevelt's penchant for liberal causes such as anticolonialism would clash with Churchill's deep devotion to the empire and his determination to defend Britain's postwar position against all comers. In any event, no personal bond between national leaders could have withstood the pressure of conflicting interests in 1944–45 as American power rapidly expanded and Britain's seriously declined. In 1940–41, however, the two men got along extremely well, and their warm personal relationship helped London and Washington transcend the decades of coolness and suspicion to make an effective partnership in the mutual interest of the two countries.

Anything approximating a "buddy theory" of Anglo-American relations must be used with great caution, however. Churchill, though desperate for American aid in 1940, was not prepared even then to play with an open deck or give away the store. Much of the crucial secret data about Britain's war effort was held back from the Americans in 1940–41, and there was little inclination to give way on what the British government saw as fundamentals simply in hope of securing American assistance.

For his part, Roosevelt was prepared to bend over backward to assist Britain, because it was in America's interest to do so once it had been established that Britain had a reasonable chance of withstanding a German assault. But even this step rested on cold calculation, and before the president could take it, he had to secure accurate information about Britain's chances. Unfortunately, in 1940–41 such information was in extremely short supply. The American ambassador to the Court of St. James, Joseph Kennedy, was an Irish-American Anglophobe whose reports to Washington breathed pessimism about Britain's capabilities. The American attachés in London, especially the military attaché, Gen. Raymond E. Lee, were more optimistic about Britain's ability to hold, but they had not been taken very deeply into the confidence of the British authorities. Since the United States did not have even the basic rudiments of a modern intelligence service, the only course open to Roosevelt and Churchill was for the Americans to send special emissaries to London; the British then did everything in their power to convince these official visitors that they were strong, and that although they needed material aid, they had good prospects of resisting a Nazi attack.

Two weeks after the fall of France a procession of official American emissaries therefore began to descend on London. In late June 1940, the U.S. Army Air Corps ordered Lt. Col. (later General) Carl "Tooey" Spaatz to England to examine British and German bombing techniques. In mid-July Col. William Donovan went over on a special survey and liaison mission for the president and the new secretary of the navy, Frank Knox. While Donovan was still in Britain, a high-level U.S. Army–Navy–Army Air Corps "special observers group" arrived in London: Rear Adm. Robert Ghormley (assistant chief of Naval Operations), Maj. Gen. Delos Emmons (chief of the Army Air Corps Plans Division), and Brig. Gen. George Strong (chief of the War Plans Division, and later of G-2, the army's intelligence organization). All of these visitors were warmly received in London and fed a rich diet of optimistic forecasts by the British authorities. They duly reported to Washington that Britain was strong, might well hold out against a German invasion, and was worthy of assistance.

One might quibble with the accuracy of these favorable estimates and forecasts because, with the exception of its fighter defenses, Britain had few powerful, modern military forces in the summer of 1940, and in almost every other aspect of warfare she lagged far behind Germany.

It is only fair to note, however, that much of what was told to the Americans, and much of what was shown to them by the British, was less purposeful deception than lamentable self-deception. Many British authorities actually believed that the Bomber Command of 1940 could wreak havoc in Germany, that the navy armed with asdic (sonar) detection devices would stop the U-boats, and that waves of commando and special operational "dirty tricks" would pry open Hitler's Fortress Europe. Then, it was hopefully predicted, a huge resistance fire on the Continent, and the pressure of the blockade à la World War I, would so weaken Hitler's hold that landings by small British armored forces would provide the coup de grace, and Hitler's Thousand-Year Reich would be no more.

This was certainly a pipe dream, with little more than its starting point—the successful fight against the Luftwaffe by radar and Fighter Command—able to stand the test of time. But it involved little willful misrepresentation. These were the dreams of desperate officials who could not see any other route to victory. Furthermore, despite Britain's weakness in comparison with Germany, almost everything related to the military arts that Americans saw in Britain during 1940 was much more advanced than anything then available in the United States. The Americans did not have to be shown anything especially unique to be surprised and impressed. Even the British Chiefs of Staff system with its supportive committees concerned with planning, logistics, and intelligence looked so modern, sensible, and efficient compared with the organizational autonomy and cannibalism that prevailed in Washington that to the American visitors it appeared little short of miraculous.

All members of the American missions, upon return to the United States, acted as strong advocates of aid to Britain. Donovan, in particular, became an impassioned Anglophile, convinced of British strength and dedicated to persuading the highest officials of the American government that immediate large-scale aid to Britain was definitely in America's interest. In Washington, he became a highly devoted and successful top-level lobbyist for the British cause. He strengthened the president's inclination to aid Britain and intensified the pro-British resolve of Secretaries Hull, Stimson, and Knox, as well as key senators and congressmen. Donovan's main assets were the firsthand knowledge he had gained from his survey trip and his enormous enthusiasm. The British government quickly realized that he was an important factor in pushing through the "destroyers-for-bases" deal in the early autumn of 1940, whereby the Americans swapped fifty overaged destroyers for long-term leases on a number of bases in the Western Hemisphere. Throughout 1941 British officials continued to consider Donovan one of the most useful champions of their cause in the inner sanctum of the American government.

While Donovan's efforts held the limelight, the less visible pro-British activities of the returning American military mission members were also highly important. Within the Navy and War departments, Emmons and Spaatz became crusaders for the idea of aid to Britain. Since every bit of assistance that went to Britain meant that much less for the U.S. Army and Navy, having such experienced advocates inside the service departments—especially at a time of rapid rearmament—was probably nearly as significant in the general development of Anglo-American cooperation as was Donovan's effort with the president and key members of the cabinet.

By the late autumn of 1940 a major shift had occurred at the highest level of Anglo-American relations. Armed with his special emissaries' reports that Britain would stand—reports that were daily and nightly confirmed in September 1940 by the triumphs of the Royal Air Force (RAF) and the grit of the Londoners during the Blitz—President Roosevelt pushed on with his rearmament policy and his determination to assist the British. The first American peacetime draft was instituted in September, and the destroyer-for-bases deal was concluded in August. This two-sided national security policy then triumphed at the polls as Roosevelt was reelected for a third term in November 1940, with strong majorities in both houses of Congress.

Even before this decisive electoral triumph, something approximating a new and special relationship between the governments of Britain and the United States had gradually been forming. In the first phase of the war, Britain and the United States had approached cooperation on sensitive matters, such as secret intelligence, with extreme caution, but in the more intimate and confident atmosphere that emerged in the second half of 1940, the first cautious linkups began to occur between the secret worlds of the two great Atlantic powers.

CHAPTER TWO
The Intelligence Setting

The first steps toward the creation of a special relationship between president and prime minister, made in the summer and autumn of 1940, were not in themselves sufficient to wipe out all the rivalries and suspicions that had clouded official Anglo-American relations since at least 1919. The three main departments primarily concerned with international relations in both governments—diplomatic, military, and naval—were still laced with transatlantic doubts and hostilities.

In the civil sphere of international contact and negotiation, many of the mandarins in both the Foreign Office and the State Department had been seriously marked, and often embittered, by the twenty years of official postwar distancing that had followed World War I. Senior diplomatic professionals, such as Sir Alexander Cadogan in the Foreign Office and Adolf Berle in the State Department, tended to regard all foreign officials as "them" without making special allowance for anything as obtuse as a special connection between distant transatlantic cousins.

Much the same attitude of universal suspicion regarding foreign powers marked the higher military and naval commanders of both countries, with one additional and important naval twist. The Royal and U.S. navies had been placed at the top of the league of naval powers, and granted parity in heavy ships, at the Washington Naval Conference of 1921. From that day onward, even as they checked their wake to make certain that the Japanese, French, and Germans were not gaining on them, the higher officers of the British and American fleets tended to view each other as rivals in the race for naval superiority.

Admiral Harold R. Stark, the U.S. Navy's chief of Naval Operations (CNO) until Pearl Harbor, was uncharacteristically open-minded and generous in his attitude toward Britain (compared with his crusty successor, Adm. Ernest J. King), and the First Sea Lord, Adm. Dudley Pound, could hardly have been characterized as anti-American. But the overarching duty of both these officers was to prepare their country's strongest instrument of power to meet all comers, and it would take considerable retuning before the CNO and the First Sea Lord acquired the new and novel habits of transatlantic partnership.

If the commanders of the two navies tended to eye each other as first-division rivals, top British and American army officers brought to the new and more intimate transatlantic relationship attitudes formed by a long period of scrambling for leftovers. Both the British and American armies had been shrunk, starved, and treated with condescension between the wars, and both still bore the scars of their deprivation and humiliation. In addition, the British army had suffered a pair of disastrous defeats at the hands of the Wehrmacht in 1940, and, though trying to show a brave face, the Chiefs of the Imperial General Staff (Gen. Sir John Dill until 1941, and Gen. Sir Alan Brooke thereafter) were painfully aware that their forces needed drastic reform and modernization, as well as rapid expansion, before they could hope to meet the German army on equal terms.

On the American side, Gen. George Marshall was firmly committed to bringing the miniscule U.S. Army up to mid twentieth century standards, while sharply increasing its size. Many officers in the War Department had mixed feelings about Britain in 1940–41, and a substantial sprinkling of Marshall's staff saw the German army and air force as the best models for emulation, while viewing the British army as a ragged band that had fought too many colonial wars and had been unable to throw off the memories and complexes left from the Great War. This was not a totally absurd or unwarranted point of view, but it certainly clashed with the new spirit of transatlantic partnership present in the White House and much of the country in the autumn of 1940, and also made difficult the creation of a full, and harmonious, Anglo-American alliance.

With such reservations and tensions flourishing in the non-secret branches of the British and American governments in 1940–41, there was little possibility of quick, comprehensive linkups between the secret intelligence activities of the two countries. Intelligence collection is, by its very nature, not only fundamentally secret both in organization and method, but also tends toward universality in its appetite. A good intelligence organization is one that gathers information so broadly and deeply that it can provide valuable assistance to its government whatever twist or turn may occur in international relations and the balance of power. Intelligence professionals therefore do not like to be confined by such transitory categories as "friends" or "enemies."

Bilateral intelligence sharing certainly had occurred during the modern era; wartime allies customarily provided each other with secret information that would help them defeat a common enemy. The ambassadorial, and especially the attaché, systems evolved into their present forms in part because of the recognition by all states that intelligence gathering was so universal and endemic that it might be best formally organized on a reciprocal basis. Some sharing of intelligence between two or more states occurred during both peace and war on many occasions during the first four decades of the twentieth century, and on occasion created strange bedfellows. Between 1936 and 1938, years that bracketed the Sino-Japanese conflict in which Japan was denounced by all the western powers, Britain regularly swapped with the Japanese army secret intelligence regarding the Soviet Union. This exchange, like many other temporary and highly secret arrangements, operated strictly on the principle of quid pro quo. When the quality of the Japanese information regarding the Red Army declined in value, and the Japanese themselves began to loom as a strong revisionist force in Asia, London broke off the secret exchange link with Tokyo.[1]

It is also instructive to note, when considering customary secret intelligence–sharing practices, that in 1937 the American and Royal navies began to exchange secret intelligence about the Japanese navy even as Britain swapped intelligence about Russia with the Japanese army. The Anglo-American naval intelligence exchanges of the late 1930s were prompted less by fears of immediate Japanese aggression than by British nervousness regarding possible Japanese plans to build larger superbattleships, which, if proven true, would have compelled Britain and the United States to begin large, costly, and undesirable naval building programs to maintain the 5-5-3 ratio in capital-ship tonnage, which had been established in the Washington naval treaty of 1921.

Whatever the motivation, in the years 1937–38, the British government was simultaneously sharing secret intelligence with Japan while collecting secret intelligence about Japan from the United States. In fact,

British officials were also exchanging intelligence material regarding Japan with Dutch officials in Batavia during this same period.[2] Although such secret—and not altogether consistent—short-term trafficking in information about other countries may seem offensive to people who believe that something akin to the golden rule should prevail in international relations, it has been a regular feature of modern international power politics. Always based on some sense of enlightened self-interest, such limited arrangements to exchange secret intelligence seldom entailed any special idealistic or ideological affinity between the partners.

Despite the fact that the U.S. Navy did agree to share secret information about Japan with the British in 1937, all countries found intelligence cooperation with Washington unusually difficult to arrange during the interwar period. American sensitivity regarding foreign entanglements was especially strong regarding intelligence matters, which were regarded by much of the population as sordid and dangerous; in 1929 Secretary of State Henry Stimson completely closed down his department's code-breaking section, the Black Chamber. In addition, as will be seen below, the American intelligence system prior to World War II was so small and underdeveloped that effective and equal sharing arrangements with any foreign country, especially with a nation such as Britain, which had a long history of intelligence activities, were very difficult to arrange and implement.

Consequently in 1940 attempts to produce Anglo-American intelligence cooperation had to begin virtually at the beginning. On the British side the prevailing secret department system consisted of a series of traditional intelligence units, which had been expanded to cope with the wartime emergency, and a series of new organizations created to help deal with wartime problems. The traditional British military, naval, and air intelligence organizations paralleled those found in most other countries in peacetime. The naval (NID), army (MID), and air (AID) intelligence of the respective staffs collected data regarding the armed forces of foreign states, and wherever possible obtained information on the likely intentions of foreign governments. In the immediate prewar period, and in the first stage of World War II, British concern regarding the details of the German, and then the Italian, armed forces rapidly intensified. The armament and order of battle of German and satellite armies and air forces became matters of vital importance, as did German armament capabilities, technical development, and strategic and tactical procedures. Above all, determining the intentions of the enemy was of vital concern to British naval, air, and military intelligence sections. Following June 1940, when Britain stood alone and was completely on the defensive, all aspects of military intelligence collection, especially that related to German and Italian intentions, became the most important single concern of the British government.

In the peacetime years until 1936 the individual British military intelligence branches were forced to depend on whatever secret information each of them could collect on its own initiative, as well as what it could wangle from its intelligence colleagues in other services and from relevant civilian intelligence-producing organizations. In prewar Britain three such traditional nonmilitary organizations were important primary intelligence creators, namely the Foreign Office, through its overseas outposts; the Secret Intelligence Service (SIS, reabbreviated MI 6 during World War II), which was a nominal Foreign Office dependency; and the Security Service (abbreviated as MI 5 during the war, when, although not a subunit of the Foreign Office, through much of the period Anthony Eden, the foreign secretary, also served as the cabinet minister in charge of its activities).[3]

The British government was sufficiently alarmed by the events of 1936, which featured Hitler's reoccupation of the Rhineland, the Italian occupation of Ethiopia, and the beginning of the Spanish Civil War, to install a formal coordinating mechanism into the free flow of intelligence information. A Joint Intelligence Committee (JIC) was then set up in Whitehall, which brought together representatives of the three military services and the Foreign Office. The major function of the JIC was to create a forum in which consensus estimates on the intentions of foreign states, especially those of the Axis, the Soviet Union, and Japan, might be prepared, and the differing interpretations produced by the various intelligence services and departments might be reconciled. Although the JIC never achieved the degree of success originally hoped for in advancing consensus or making intelligence assessments, it continued to function throughout the war and acted as a pillar of support for the efforts of the Chiefs of Staff Committee to create coherent and consistent strategic policies.[4]

Organizations devoted to promoting liaison and cooperation between the various British intelligence services and departments were especially useful because internecine conflict was always especially bitter regarding intelligence. In the course of the war emergency British organizations with intelligence functions of one kind or another emerged so rapidly that an American historian, turned wartime intelligence officer in London, once spoke of Britain's "57 varieties of MI [military intelligence]." The reproductive capabilities of British intelligence did not quite reach that total, but specialized units on air reconnaissance, prisoner interrogation, and the like did rapidly expand the size and scope of the military intelligence empire. In addition, organizations outside the military services, such as the Ministry of Economic Warfare, the Special Operations Executive (devoted to supporting resistance movements in enemy territory), and the Political Warfare Executive (which, after 1941, covered the field of propaganda) all had at least some wartime intelligence functions.[5]

The activities and command structure of the organization at the heart of Britain's regular intelligence system, the Secret Intelligence Service (SIS, MI 6), also engendered serious conflict. In November 1939 the longtime head of SIS/MI 6, Adm. "Q" Sinclair, finally retired. Churchill, then the First Lord, who always relished a good bureaucratic fight and took a special interest in intelligence matters, sought to have his personal favorite, Rear Adm. John Godfrey, made "C" (the code name for whoever was head of the British Secret Service). But the cabinet and departmental chiefs were wary of increasing Churchill's influence in Whitehall, especially on intelligence matters. Throughout the 1930s Churchill had retained his own personal intelligence adviser, Maj. Desmond Morton, to provide sensitive information that could assist in Churchill's attacks on the "appeasement" policies of Neville Chamberlain. Churchill had retained Morton's services even after he entered the cabinet in September 1939, but in November 1939 Whitehall officialdom and the remainder of the cabinet drew the line on Morton and Churchill extending their influence to the top of MI 6.

Godfrey was not made "C"; that post went instead to "Q" 's extremely well-connected and politically astute long-term deputy, Sir Stewart Menzies, who, in November 1940, took over MI 6 and also became titular head of the British cryptanalytic organization, the Government Code and Cipher School. Menzies' pleasure at his new appointment was probably short-lived, because in the summer of 1940 Britain faced a desperate intelligence situation as well as the threat of German invasion.[6]

Despite the great number of British wartime departments concerned with intelligence, and partly because of the coordination problems engendered by them, the British government was far from rich in reliable intelligence in the period following the fall of France. Air reconnaissance units were not then functioning effectively, few prisoners with valuable intelligence had been secured by the retreating British expeditionary forces, and MI 6 had been so completely surprised by the speed of the German advance that it had neglected to make effective preparations for the creation of a stay-behind network of agents in the event that British forces had to flee. Consequently agent intelligence from the Continent stopped almost completely in the summer of 1940. Every office in Whitehall concerned with the defense of the island therefore turned to MI 6 in desperation, and in vain, when they sought to secure vital information regarding German plans and intentions.

Complaints about the failings of MI 6 soon spread throughout the British government, culminating during March 1941 in a virtual ultimatum from the directors of military and naval intelligence that Menzies either reform the system and increase intelligence output or someone else would be made "C." Menzies managed to weather this storm, but his position remained far from secure in 1941, and it was not made easier by the fact that, while the British government was trying to ease its way into a special relationship with the United States during this period, one of MI 6's top officials, Sir Claude Dansy, harbored an intense dislike of America and Americans.[7] Thus, for Menzies and MI 6, as well as the British nation and the Allied cause, it was indeed fortunate that in late 1940 and on into 1941 the British code and cipher breakers at Bletchley Park, who fell under Menzies' overall authority, were beginning to chalk up significant successes in their battle against German codes and ciphers.

Modern governments had long used secret methods to transmit confidential messages. Carrier pigeons, secret ink, codes (which substitute one word for another), and ciphers (which substitute letters within words) had all been employed by governments for confidential communications throughout the nineteenth and early twentieth centuries. But in the 1930s and 1940s technology had revolutionized all forms of rapid communication, which in turn required the development of more sophisticated methods of encoding or enciphering messages. The fundamental change was the widespread use of radio communication. During World War II the combatant governments flooded the airwaves with messages in a volume and variety that dwarfed the wireless communication flow of World War I and of the 1930s' "run-up" conflicts in Ethiopia and Spain. Between 1939 and 1945, endless streams of radio messages passed back and forth between the military, air, and naval authorities in the belligerent capitals as well as to and from their formations overseas. Supply departments, shipping organizations, intelligence units, and a host of other formations bombarded the ether with directives and reports. The closer one came to zones of actual combat, the busier became the airwaves as fighter pilots, tank drivers, artillery spotters, and anyone else who could hold a microphone added his rapid-fire chatter to the general radio din.

The broad scope of military and naval operations, ranging from the North Atlantic to the central Pacific, and from Alaska to the Cape of Good Hope, was a primary cause of this enormous flow of messages, because radio was the only communications medium that could cope with such vast distances of land and sea. The large number of combatant nations, each with its own maze of government departments, was a second major cause of the great explosion of radio traffic, because coordination, both within each government and between governments, entailed constant reporting, clarification, and the issuing and reissuing of orders. New methods of waging war—such as Nazi blitzkrieg tactics, which required close cooperation between air and tank forces, or the Allied submarine-killing tactics, which bound together air and naval operations—also forced fighting units to utilize extensive and rapid operational radio systems.

This great increase in the volume and variety of radio messages produced a parallel rise in the importance of cipher-and-code security. In earlier eras when important government messages had been transmitted by post, telegraph, or courier, the amount of encoded or enciphered information that came under the eyes of an opponent was severely limited. But in the new era of radio war, a vast quantity of information from the other side was constantly flowing past the ears of every belligerent. To meet this danger, and to cope with the greatly expanded volume of radio communication that needed cipher-and-code protection, nearly every combatant in World War II employed some form of machine encoding or machine encipherment. Although the machines varied greatly in format, and in the complexity and security of their enciphering systems, they all "scrambled" clear texts so that, to the uninitiated ear, messages seemed to be merely meaningless jumbles of letters or numbers. The authorized recipient of such a scrambled message would, of course, be able to decipher it, usually by means of a properly adjusted machine comparable to the one that had dispatched the message originally.

These enciphering machines used various mechanical switching or electrical rotating devices to turn clear messages into jumbles in order to protect them during their passage through the ether. The switching or rotating mechanisms then could be reset, on the basis of some daily or weekly list of settings, to turn a jumble back into clear text. The more complex and sophisticated the switching or rotating devices, the greater the level of security of the system. If the settings of a highly complex system were changed frequently, if the radio operators and code clerks did not make serious errors, and if extra care was taken at all levels of operation, then the enciphered messages had a high level of security. During World War II, the highest grade American and British machine ciphers, and the actions of their operators, met all of these requirements, and none of the top-level western machine ciphers was broken by the Axis powers (although the Germans did better against the old-fashioned Allied naval codes used in the North Atlantic as well as against various State Department codes).

The German, Italian, and Japanese authorities were not so fortunate. As is now well known, the British made a highly successful attack on the German Enigma enciphering machine, and the Americans had comparable success against the diplomatic machine cipher of the Japanese. These, and other British and American cryptanalytic successes, were not primarily the result of "stolen codes," or comparable bits of espionage sleight of hand, as had taken place occasionally in an earlier era when secrecy depended on cryptic notes and faceless figures huddled in doorways. Cryptanalytic success came in the 1940s by a detailed understanding of the nature, workings, and weaknesses of the enemy cipher machine, especially the scrambling mechanism, and discovery of methods to recover or infer which setting the enemy was using on any particular occasion. Capturing individual enciphering machines, as well as the tables listing the daily settings in current use, played a significant role, especially in British successes against the naval Enigma. Sloppy work by German, Italian, and Japanese operators (and their superiors) produced many giveaway errors called "cillies" or "sillies," which helped their opponents to "break in" to particular machine settings.

In the case of highly complex systems such as the German four-rotor naval Enigma (Triton), regular successful break-ins required "cribs" as well as "cillies." A crib was a giveaway error in which a low-grade enemy cipher, such as a weather cipher, regularly repeated the same information that was contained in very complex ciphers, such as the U-boat cipher Triton. Once cryptanalysts established that information was being repeated routinely in different ciphers, they would first find the duplicated information (such as a daily weather forecast) in a low-grade cipher message that could be easily broken, and then search out the parallel portion in the higher-level cipher. As soon as this duplicated information had been located, the door would be open for a full-scale attack on the current setting of the high-grade cipher.

At the foundation of nearly all successes against sophisticated machine ciphers lay the development of a mechanical, and then electrical, analytic machine—the so-called "bombe"—capable of determining which settings were *not* being used at any particular time by the enemy cipher-machine operators. The mechanical, and later electrical, ability to survey the nonsense messages and quickly establish which of the countless settings of the enemy cipher machine could not have made a particular pattern of enciphered jumble often allowed Allied "code breakers" to narrow down rapidly the number of settings that were capable of actually producing the jumble at hand. Then, by various processes of trial and error, the "possibles" would be eliminated one by one until the setting currently being employed by the enemy was accurately identified.

With its long tradition of intelligence activity, and the singular successes it had scored against German codes and ciphers during World War I, Britain was well placed to meet the challenges posed by machine enciphering during the late 1930s. In the interwar period the British government had put an end to the duplicative and inefficient practice of allowing each of its separate departments and services to mount attacks on foreign codes and ciphers, concentrating its complete cryptanalytic effort in a single centralized organization that served all high-level military and civil authorities cleared to receive it with decrypted (and in most cases with "elucidated," that is, annotated) foreign radio traffic. This organization, located throughout the entire war at Bletchley Park, near what would later become the "new town" of Milton Keynes, bore the innocuous name of the Government Code and Cipher School (GC & CS) until 1942, when it was renamed the Government Communications Headquarters. Charged with developing Britain's codes and ciphers, as well as cracking those of other countries, GC & CS was always a relatively large establishment, employing roughly eight thousand people in the latter stages of the war.

The GC & CS was one of the few organizations in the British government well prepared to deal with the challenges posed by World War II. On 1 August 1939, a month before the outbreak of the conflict, the military service sections of GC & CS had moved into the new setting at Bletchley Park, with the commercial and diplomatic sections following fifteen days later. There, they still faced a formidable challenge. While continuing their efforts against the diplomatic, commercial, and military codes and ciphers of a host of countries ranging from Japan to various neutral countries, which might contain useful information related to Germany's war effort, the cryptanalysts had to concentrate their attention on the most important constituent portions of the mysterious outpourings of Enigma messages from Germany. Each branch of the German military forces used a different Enigma system, and as the wartime months and years went by, German organizations as diverse as the police, the weather services, and the railroads would use their own Enigma variations.[8]

Greatly assisted by the pioneering work done on the Enigma by the Poles and the French, the Bletchley Park cryptanalysts, then under the direction of Cdr. Alistair Denniston and his deputy, Cdr. Edward W. Travis, scored some early successes against portions of the German cipher system during the Norwegian campaign, opening up the main enemy cipher used for that operation (dubbed "Yellow" by the staff at Bletchley Park). But the decipherment had been produced by relatively slow hand methods, because no electric bombe calculator then existed, and most of the information it yielded appeared so late in the day that it had little operational value. The breaking of Yellow was nonetheless a major achievement, signifying above all else that the German ciphers were far from inviolable, and providing the British government with the first important deposits in its bank of inside information on German operational methods and tactics.[9]

In the course of the disastrous campaign in the west during May–June 1940, Bletchley made additional important cryptanalytic progress toward offsetting Germany's technical and military superiority. Soon after Italy entered the war in June 1940, the cryptanalysts of GC & CS broke into the main Italian air force cipher being used in the Mediterranean area. This achievement substantially lessened the value the Germans had hoped to garner from the appearance of Italy as a full-blown belligerent.[10]

A spring-summer break-in with greater long-range significance was the penetration of a German air force operational combat cipher (called "Red" by the British). Unfortunately, this breakthrough also involved long delays, and though the first penetration coincided with the beginning of the German attack in the west in May 1940, Bletchley was unable to attempt its first general summary of German air strength and deployment (order of battle) based on Red until 5 August 1940.

The successful break into Red may have been accelerated by the appearance at Bletchley Park of the first British-manufactured bombe during May 1940 (although some Bletchley veterans contend that it did not go into operation until August 1940). At whatever point in the summer of 1940 this mechanical analytic machine appeared, it allowed GC & CS to make a great leap forward in machine-based cryptanalysis. Though the immediate operational benefits of the development were few, the advantage in the secret wizard war had started to shift in favor of Britain, even as Germany was achieving its most important and dramatic victory in France and Flanders.

That Britain could simultaneously score one of the war's great secret technological successes and lose a decisive battle may at first glance appear quite paradoxical. But three basic facts related to cryptanalysis explain it.

The first factor was the problem of delay in decryption, discussed above in relation to Yellow during the Norwegian campaign. The introduction of the bombe did not miraculously permit simultaneous decryption. Identification of the daily settings was still a long and laborious process, and Red yielded very few instantaneous German secrets either during the French campaign or in the Battle of Britain, which followed.

The second limiting factor affecting Red was that it was an operational, rather than a strategic, command cipher. It carried mainly nuts-and-bolts traffic on Luftwaffe operations and battle coordination; yet no one in British intelligence then knew enough about German military and air matters to ferret out of Red clear clues regarding the German command's overall intentions.

The third fundamental problem that impeded the effective explication of the information available from Red was that even in relation to immediate battle usage, this cipher yielded a bewildering array of code names, abbreviations, references to standing orders, and so forth, all of which were complete mysteries to the British. Many months of cryptanalysis *and* the buildup of a comprehensive body of data on German organization, procedures, and operational terms would be required before ciphers such as Red could produce a generous harvest of immediately useful secret information.[11]

Nonetheless, it was obvious in the inner recesses of Whitehall that Bletchley was on the high road to a very good thing. Under various code names, such as "Boniface," which ultimately settled into the security classification "Most Secret Ultra," bits and pieces of deciphered and elucidated material from the German Enigma began to arrive in the highest government offices during the summer of 1940, and with increasing frequency during the autumn of 1940 and the spring of 1941. The arrival of these materials, which for simplicity's sake will henceforth be referred to as items of Ultra intelligence, must have appeared to Sir Stewart Menzies as something akin to treasures from heaven. The director of MI 6, and the espionage organization he commanded, actually knew little about Bletchley's operations and had played no significant part in its triumphs, except that "C" had stressed that GC & CS be run on the basis of interservice cooperation. As the titular head of GC & CS, however, Menzies was able to control much of the early distribution of Bletchley's most secret Ultra product, and he thereby reaped important benefits for the prestige of his tarnished organization.[12]

Another of the early recipients of Ultra intelligence was the prime minister, who found this material both fascinating and extremely useful. Winston Churchill desperately needed developments to indicate that a victory might be waiting at the end of the tunnel of British endurance. In addition, cryptanalysis, especially machine cryptanalysis, was just the kind of innovative, technical, unorthodox, and secret endeavor that would appeal to the new prime minister. Possession of Bletchley's crop of decrypts gave the prime minister another weapon with which to confound, and dominate, his staff and military advisers. Consequently as early as September 1940, even though he had been receiving some decrypts direct from Bletchley, Churchill demanded to be shown all Enigma messages daily. He never actually saw all such messages (the volume and complexity of Bletchley's output quickly exceeded the capacity of any single individual to screen everything), but he prized and protected the "golden eggs" he did receive, and his interest and occasional supportive intervention guaranteed Bletchley Park a favored place in nearly all the battles over resources and personnel, which continually raged within a badly stretched British government. This was especially important because Bletchley was an enormous amalgam of army, navy, RAF, and Foreign Office interests and personnel. Such a complex phenomenon produced interminable jurisdictional conflicts, and a sympathetic patron at Number 10 Downing Street was therefore essential for its survival and success.[13]

In addition, although in mid-1940 no one in the British government seems to have dreamed of sharing this embryonic secret with the Americans, possession of Ultra gave the prime minister a number of highly secret informational and technical aces to hold up his sleeve while he alternately fenced with, and begged from, President Roosevelt and his aides. Such vital intelligence assets were especially important to Britain in late 1940 and early 1941, because its bargaining power was very weak, and intelligence was one of the few areas in which Britain, despite the failings of MI 6, was in a much stronger position than the United States.

Intelligence in the United States during the late 1930s and early 1940s epitomized the lackadaisical attitude the country had adopted toward world affairs in the interwar years. No secret service or central intelligence agency existed, rigid compartmentalization of intelligence collection was endemic, and there was precious little rigor or sophistication present either in the collection or processing of intelligence material. The traditional branches of government concerned with foreign affairs—state, war, and navy—collected bits and pieces of information from around the world by use of consuls and attachés, then filed them away on the basis of geographical or subject headings. Little collation of such material with information from open sources occurred, and very few interchanges took place between the intelligence and operational branches of any department.

With a minimal sense of threat or danger from the outside world during the 1920s and much of the 1930s, there had been little urgency associated with the acquisition and processing of intelligence material. Security was also extremely lax. When a crisis occurred in a part of the world in which any branch of the U.S. government took a special interest, emissaries, such as those who had gone to Britain in 1940, were dispatched to the scene in hopes of getting the facts. The resulting information was then simply sent back to select senior officials, who "took note" of it and then buried it in the files. None of the information required decisive action, since only in the rarest of circumstances did the U.S. government do more than file a diplomatic protest outside the Western Hemisphere in the fifteen to twenty years following World War I.

Order-of-battle estimates made by the U.S. Army were hopelessly out of date by 1940, as were most of the evaluations of military technology of foreign armies. Pieces of relevant information existed in the files of G-2 or other branches of the U.S. Army, but they had not been pulled together and evaluated to serve as a foundation for making policy decisions. Without a secret intelligence service, there was little basis even to speculate about the intentions or probable actions of any foreign army or air force.

Naval intelligence was somewhat more sophisticated because the U.S. Navy held an exposed position in the Pacific, and because naval order of battle was a far clearer and more easily defined activity than trying to gauge the intentions of foreign countries or guess what might happen if a particular country ordered a mobilization of its ground and air forces. Yet even in regard to naval intelligence, the United States did not have a modern or efficient system for acquiring, organizing, and distributing important information. When in early 1941 Admiral Godfrey, the British DNI, was allowed to survey the U.S. Navy's intelligence arrangements, he was shocked to discover the extent of the inefficiency and irrelevance that prevailed in the American Office of Naval Intelligence (ONI).[14]

During his survey, Godfrey was impressed by only one aspect of the intelligence-gathering activity of the American departments—the cryptanalytic work on Japan being done by the U.S. Navy and Army. Like the British, and most other governments, the United States secretly carried on radio interception and cipher- and code-breaking work during the interwar period. Americans customarily emphasize not only their predilection for efficiency, but also the relative openness of their government's institutions, and in this connection historians and political commentators have frequently stressed the fact that in 1929 President Herbert Hoover's secretary of state (the same Henry L. Stimson who would preside over the War Department and much of the country's cryptanalytic activity between 1940 and 1945) closed down the Black Chamber in the State Department. This action seemingly took the U.S. government out of the radio interception and cryptanalytic business, but in fact by the late 1930s and early 1940s at least six traditional American government organizations were engaged in intercepting and breaking secret radio messages—the Federal Bureau of Investigation (FBI), Coast Guard, State Department, U.S. Army, U.S. Navy, and Federal Communications Commission (FCC). As soon as the war emergency and the fifth-column scares emerged in 1940–41, this number was increased by the code- and cipher-breaking efforts of newly created emergency organizations, such as the Office of the Coordinator of Information.

Most of the rash of American cryptanalytic activities in the late 1930s and early 1940s—which in its duplication and interdepartmental rivalry embodied precious little of the efficiency of which Americans were so proud—was directed at clandestine (alleged espionage and subversive) radio traffic, and therefore belongs mainly to the history of the fifth-column panic and its effect on civil liberties in the United States. But U.S. Army and Navy cryptanalysis, although it too engaged in a large amount of work on clandestine radio, also focused on the secret military and diplomatic traffic of foreign countries. In this sense the United States had, in the late prewar period, joined in "the secret game" just like the European and Asian countries whose secrecy policies were generally reviled by the American press and public.

Of the cryptanalytic services operated by the two American service departments, that of the U.S. Navy had the most clearly delineated and realistic mission. As the first line of American defense against the growth of Japanese naval power and possible expansion in the Pacific, the U.S. Navy needed to acquire all possible information regarding the strength, disposition, and movement of the Japanese fleet. With naval bases on the West Coast of the United States, Alaska, and the Panama Canal Zone, and across the Pacific from the Hawaiian Islands through Wake, Guam, and Midway to the Philippines, the authorities directing the American high seas fleet had ample opportunities to intercept large quantities of Japanese naval traffic. The U.S. Navy also had a full-blown cryptanalytic branch, named Op-20-G, which, on the basis of an informal agreement with the U.S. Army concluded in the autumn of 1939, could concentrate on the ciphers and codes of the Japanese navy. The U.S. Army cryptanalysts were authorized to work on nonnaval Japanese traffic as well as the traffic of Germany, Italy, and the Latin American republics, with emphasis in the latter category on the codes and ciphers of Mexico.[15]

Although the navy was carrying the responsibility for the American cryptanalytic attack on the communications of its largest and most dangerous rival, the Japanese Imperial Navy, Op-20-G's total manpower consisted of only sixty officers and men as late as January 1941. This pitifully small force, spread out from Washington, D.C., to Hawaii, nonetheless had fulfilled much of its vital mission during the 1930s. The Japanese navy during this period employed five major code and cipher systems—administrative, merchant shipping, material (logistical and technical), operational, and intelligence. Op-20-G ignored the code system for intelligence, because it was infrequently used by the Japanese navy and did not have a direct bearing on fleet movements. Two of the other general Japanese crypto systems—the material and operational codes—were yielding to the attack by Op-20-G in the second half of 1940. The director of the U.S. Navy's cryptanalysts predicted on 4 October 1940 that they would be broken within six months. The merchant code was then already "99 percent readable," and intelligence from the administrative code—the most important of the five systems, since it carried operational traffic—was being obtained from nearly "all intercepted messages."[16]

Despite these successes, all was not smooth sailing for the U.S. Navy's cryptanalysts. In late 1939 and the first months of 1940, the major Japanese naval crypto systems had undergone radical changes, and "a temporary reduction in the intelligence obtained by cryptanalytic means" had been the worrisome result. Therefore, although the miniscule staff of Op-20-G was rightly proud of its achievements against Japan—the cutting edge of American security concern—it was not smugly complacent in late 1940.[17]

The mood that prevailed in the even smaller cryptanalytic service of the U.S. Army was much closer to astonishment than optimism. The Signals Intelligence Service (SIS) of the U.S. Army Signal Corps was the real Cinderella of the underfunded interwar American army. This tiny unit had a total staff of only eight in 1938, but under the direction of the eccentric cryptanalytic genius Dr. William Friedman, and with the strong support of the chief signal officer, General J. O. Mauborgne, the microscopic U.S. Army cryptanalytic service managed to hang on during the difficult years of the depression era. Beginning in 1932, the Signal Corps operated six widely scattered radio intercept stations in New Jersey, Texas, California, Hawaii, Panama, and the Philippines, but the intercept material provided to the cryptanalysts by these stations was not very satisfactory because no formal order authorizing cryptanalytic work had been issued, and the operation of Army SIS had to be disguised as a training exercise. Finally, in March 1938, at the time of Germany's seizure of Austria (*Anschluss*), General Mauborgne and G-2 persuaded the then U.S. Army chief of staff (Gen. Malin Craig) to issue an order on 30 March authorizing the Signal Corps "to maintain and operate in time of peace under strictest provisions to insure secrecy, such radio intercept and cryptanalytic services as are necessary for training and national defense purposes."[18]

During the eighteen months between the issuance of this order and the outbreak of war in Europe on 1 September 1939, the staff of Army SIS increased to eighteen. Unable to secure a steady flow of high-quality intercept material from the Atlantic area, and hobbled by the continuing shortage of staff, SIS chose to concentrate its cryptanalytic attack on Italian commercial traffic, the radio messages of the Mexican army, and the diplomatic ciphers of Japan. No cryptanalytic units were stationed outside the continental limits of the United States, and no attempt was made to break, or even intercept, any German Enigma traffic, or any of the army or air force radio traffic of Japan.

Enciphered Japanese diplomatic messages were a highly important target for SIS cryptanalysts in 1939–40 because of the continuing Sino-Japanese war and the increasingly bellicose attitude adopted by Japan. The problems posed by Japanese diplomatic ciphers were, however, formidable in the extreme. In 1939 the Japanese government had introduced a new machine cipher, dubbed "Purple" by the American cryptanalysts; this cipher carried much of the high-grade diplomatic traffic between the Foreign Office in Tokyo and Japanese diplomatic missions abroad. Purple therefore had to be the primary national-defense target for the Army SIS cryptanalysts, even though few resources or personnel were available to tackle the job. The SIS had no analytic bombe equipment, comparable to that being developed at Bletchley, to assist its cryptanalytic attack. Consequently Friedman, Frank Rowlett, and a small group featuring only one individual who could read the Japanese language, a civilian named John Hurt, toiled on through much of 1939 and the first half of 1940, attempting to break Purple purely by hand methods, depending heavily on cillies and especially on cribs, as Japanese cipher clerks struggled to make the transition from older secret communications systems to Purple. This was a battle against great odds. As Dr. Abraham Sinkov, one of the small band of SIS cryptanalysts, later remarked, it was a "coup de dictionaire."[19]

Despite the enormous obstacles, Friedman, Rowlett, and their colleagues pressed on, and by an all-out effort began to break into Purple during August 1940. James Bamford, an author with solid in-house American cryptanalytic sources of information, asserted that the first decrypted Purple message was produced on 25 September 1940. According to Friedman himself, as well as a recently declassified NSA history, it was in October 1940 that the Purple cipher was completely broken. To achieve this feat the SIS cryptanalytic team had constructed a copycat Purple machine; the design was acquired not by theft, which was the common method used in the secret world, but by logical deductions drawn from the form and patternings of the Japanese messages. Once in possession of their handmade Purple machine, the cryptanalysts of SIS were able to test various possibilities related to the setting and encipherment pattern being used by the Japanese. Henceforth, the intelligence gained from the Purple copycat apparatus was generally referred to as "Magic," produced by a "Magic" machine.[20]

The Magic triumph scored by SIS was obviously a major contribution to the national-defense arsenal of the United States. It also gave Washington a potentially valuable bargaining counter at a time when the British and American governments were moving closer together and considering just how far to go in sharing their national-defense secrets. In this context it is important to emphasize that in the autumn of 1940 the only important intelligence assets possessed by the United States were the Magic machine and the U.S. Navy's achievements against the ciphers and codes of the Japanese navy. All the other intelligence activities, from attaché reports to the cryptanalytic work against Italian commercial codes, could be of only marginal significance to the authorities in both London and Washington.

Yet, in respect to their cryptanalytic achievements against Japan, there was little love lost between the U.S. Army and Navy. In contrast to the system at Bletchley Park, the cryptanalysts of the American armed forces worked in isolated compartments and viewed those serving in other branches of the service with extreme suspicion. Secrecy, competition, and rivalry were the dominant themes, not only concerning possible foreign enemies, but in respect to the cryptanalytic intelligence personnel of any department of the U.S. government except one's own.

This competitive isolationism, which affected secret activities in every branch of the American political system, did not, paradoxically, improve American security precautions. In 1940 all U.S. government departments had notoriously lax security. In October, when Magic began to arrive in the office of the chief of staff of the U.S. Army, Gen. George C. Marshall, the G-2 notified his superiors "that very secret papers, such as reports of Japanese diplomatic conversations, were being circulated in this office on an ordinary buck slip." Consequently security in the chief of staff's office was tightened somewhat, with special leather folders labeled "Secret Documents" being employed for the distribution of Magic intercepts to Marshall's staff.[21]

But these measures were still far removed from the kind of tight security system that modern governments customarily employ even in peacetime. The U.S. government, for all its rearmament efforts and worries about possible threats from abroad and fifth-column dangers at home, was still a country at peace, with strong feelings of aloofness and virtue standing between it and the need for rigid security precautions. This attitude, together with the small quantity of valuable secret national-security assets aside from Magic and the achievements of Op-20-G, would seriously impede extensive intelligence cooperation between Britain and the United States in 1940–41.

The first cautious moves to arrange some limited forms of Anglo-American intelligence cooperation indicated that such efforts probably would not have a bright future. In late 1939 the British government sent William Stephenson to the United States to oversee protective measures designed to safeguard war material that the British were purchasing from America. In May 1940 Stephenson took on the additional, occasional, duty of slipping to top U.S. officials an item or two of intelligence based on "Most Secret" sources, and cooperating with the American authorities in controlling German (and then Italian) agents in the United States and Latin America. Initially, Stephenson and his secret organization, British Security Coordination (BSC), seem to have cooperated effectively with local police forces, and during the first phase of his tenure in the United States he apparently formed a reasonably harmonious subversive-hunting partnership with J. Edgar Hoover and the FBI. Such antisubversive cooperation was relatively easy for Stephenson to arrange because it was not a new feature of Anglo-American secret relations. Information on security suspects had long been exchanged between the FBI and MI 5 through the American embassy in London. The war emergency and the fifth-column scare merely had moved the exchange process to the United States, increased the range of cooperation, and substituted BSC for MI 5.

The pursuit of security suspects by a British organization on American soil was, however, a very sensitive matter, as was any Anglo-American crusade against Axis agents elsewhere in the Western Hemisphere. From the beginning, the American armed forces kept Stephenson at arm's length, and though BSC worked closely with William Donovan after the establishment of the Coordinator of Information office in late 1941, and the Office of Strategic Services (OSS) in 1942, relations with the FBI, the attorney general's office, and the State Department deteriorated steadily. By March 1942 top representatives of State, Justice, and the FBI carried their grievances about BSC directly to Ambassador Lord Halifax, demanding that the British government put an end to BSC's secret operations within the United States. As a result, during the last three years of the war, BSC's major importance lay in its control of the most secure cable connections that linked New York and Britain, as well as San Francisco and British colonies in the Pacific. Over those lines passed top secret communications between British missions in the United States and their superiors at home and in the colonies, and, in addition, a good portion of the secret intelligence that British and American military authorities shared during these last years of the war.[22]

The fact that BSC retained long-term significance as guardian of the secret cables does not alter the fact that its importance as an intelligence partner with regular American organizations such as the FBI was of short duration. The British hope that the American armed services might be able to provide useful information on Germany and Italy from conventional intelligence sources was dashed even more quickly. In the summer of 1940, Secretary of the Navy Knox had ordered William Donovan during his survey trip to London to raise the possibility of intelligence cooperation between the Admiralty and the American ONI. On 15 July Donovan met with the DNI, Admiral Godfrey, and did indeed deliver the message from Knox. In addition, Donovan offered upon his return to Washington to urge intelligence cooperation with Britain, to recommend direct liaison between the British DNI and the American ONI, and to try to arrange for British officials to receive the reports being sent home by American consular officers, especially those "in French ports." True to his word, once back in Washington, Donovan sold the president on the idea of sharing intelligence with the British. On 5 September 1940 a presidential order was issued authorizing the British attachés in Washington to receive copies of all State Department and consular reports that contained information of value to them. This move seemed to indicate that the two countries were at last moving down the main road to a full partnership, including secret intelligence.[23]

During that same first week of September 1940 the Luftwaffe also unintentionally did its part in driving Britain and the United States together. On 7 September Hermann Goering unleashed the Blitz with a crushing thousand-plane raid on London's East End, followed by a heavy night attack on the same area. For the next seven weeks the mass bombing of London became the central focal point of German offensive operations, British defensive efforts, and America's changing attitudes toward the war and assistance to Britain. Fighter Command and the grit of the Londoner succeeded in thwarting Hitler, who realized by 17 September that the Blitz had failed to reach its primary objective. Goering's Luftwaffe had not secured the necessary air control over the Channel and southeastern England, and the Führer therefore secretly postponed Operation Sea Lion. Sharp attacks continued on London for an additional two weeks, and sporadically throughout the following winter, but as early as 1 October Britain had won the first really decisive defensive battle of the war.

The enormous drama of the Blitz was played out before the eyes and ears of the world's press as no other conflict had ever been. Throughout September a host of American reporters, news photographers, and cameramen stationed in London blanketed the newspapers, magazines, and newsreels of the United States with tales and images of the Blitz. Every evening Edward R. Murrow and his colleagues broadcast the sounds of the onslaught, and every morning newspapers across America poured out wire-service stories on the brave Londoners who were standing up heroically to everything the Nazis could throw at them.

The actual Blitz, and the media blitz that reported on it, did more than anything else that occurred between the fall of France and the attack on Pearl Harbor to bring the war home to the American people. The Blitz experience and the response of the British population and the RAF dramatically elevated Britain and her people in the eyes of most Americans. American opinion therefore became more sympathetic toward aid to Britain, and even the military reverses that occurred elsewhere in the world during the same period—such as the bungled British operation against Vichy-controlled Dakar, or the failure initially to stop the Italian army's sixty-mile advance into Egypt—did nothing to dampen this enthusiasm.

Anglophile enthusiasm spreading across the country may well have made it easier for President Roosevelt to navigate the first American peacetime draft through Congress. This new public mood may also have helped to embolden the American naval observer in London, Admiral Ghormley, to push forward rapidly in making arrangements for Anglo-American naval cooperation in the Pacific. In a meeting with Admiralty officials on 23 September, Ghormley opened the door to such cooperation, agreeing to the creation of a common U.S.–U.K. naval communications code-and-cipher system for use in the Pacific and Indian oceans. Then, on 4 November, the American chief of Naval Operations, Admiral Stark, urged Secretary Knox and the president to initiate Joint U.S. Army–Navy defensive planning for the Pacific, and also recommended that secret staff talks with the British and Dutch be held in Singapore.[24]

This proposal for Anglo-American cooperation in the Far East encountered serious obstacles regarding intelligence. The British had been shocked to learn during October meetings in London that the American navy had no overseas intelligence centers ashore, and that any intelligence the Americans possessed regarding Japan could be made available to the British only in Washington, or through the good offices of the various U.S. naval commanders at sea.[25] An American naval observer was soon assigned to Singapore, and a British officer representing the commander in chief of the British China Squadron also became "resident" in Manila, but these postings did not immediately produce a large-scale interchange of high-grade intelligence regarding the Japanese in late 1940 or in the first part of 1941.[26]

By January 1941 both governments showed signs of retreating from their earlier enthusiastic rush toward secret cooperation. With the Blitz battle won, and little chance of a German invasion materializing before spring, the American government was not as desperately eager to render assistance. The American armed services, sensing that the most threatening moment for Britain had probably passed, and facing the need to arm a vast conscript army and navy, were less enthusiastic about sharing their precious stock of modern equipment with Britain.

On the eastern side of the Atlantic, second thoughts also arose among those officials who had hoped for large returns from the secret aspects of Anglo-American cooperation. In mid-January Adm. H. Pott, the British naval attaché in Washington, reported to the Deputy Director of Naval Intelligence in London that the intelligence material from the State and service departments that had been offered to the British by the presidential order of 7 September had turned out to be extremely disappointing. No useful liaison meetings had occurred with American officials, who themselves seemed to be lost in an assortment of data, unable to gauge its significance or reliability. Consequently neither the State Department nor the Office of Naval Intelligence had offered the British naval attaché an opportunity to examine their files, and the only thing approximating intelligence information that Pott had received had arrived "on unsigned, unheaded, slips of paper," with no indication of its source or estimate of the information's reliability.

Faced with disappointments such as these, as well as the prospect that both the course of the war and securing assistance from the United States would be very long journeys, Anthony Eden minuted on 15 January

1941 that in his view the United States, which he characterized as "that vast country," would never "organize itself effectively for war until it is at war."[27] On one level, that judgment appeared to be accurate, at least insofar as the strengthening and modernizing of the U.S. armed forces was concerned, because when the Japanese finally struck on 7 December 1941, the American forces were caught totally unprepared. In regard to assistance to Britain, however, the U.S. government ultimately did better than Eden had expected. The Lend-Lease Act, passed in the spring of 1941, opened wide the coffers of American production to assist the United Kingdom. So even Eden's sage and pessimistic observation did not precisely hit the mark.

The 1940–41 era was a time of undulating hopes and disappointments regarding Britain's needs and chances in the war, as well as a period of ups and downs in American willingness to provide assistance. Despite these uncertainties, and the rapidly changing circumstances, a first attempt was then made to arrange an Anglo-American cryptanalytic partnership at the most secret level. That effort too had a complex, but highly significant, history, because it was to be the overture to the creation of the most secret special relationship.

CHAPTER THREE
Broken Deal, 1940–41

On 31 August 1940 an American army officer made the first serious move toward the formation of a transatlantic cryptanalytic partnership. In a meeting between the British Chiefs of Staff and the American Military Observer Mission (Emmons, Ghormley, and Strong), ostensibly devoted to the question of arms standardization, the U.S. Army representative, Brig. Gen. George Strong, noted that "it had recently been arranged in principle between the British and United States Governments that periodic exchange of information would be desirable." What Strong was referring to in this rather vague opening phrase may not have been altogether clear to his British listeners because various Anglo-American cooperative noises had just been made at every level from the heads of government to the various special missions. But Strong then went on to give the expression "exchange of information" a much more pointed and highly significant turn. According to the official British record of the meeting, the American brigadier voiced the belief that "the time had now come" when the exchange of information should be placed on a regular basis, and he outlined "certain methods by which the sources of information at the disposal of the United States might be placed at the disposal of the British Government."

Strong's statement as recorded in these minutes may, on its face, still not appear to have made a clear offer to exchange cryptanalytic information. But the reference to "certain methods" related to "the sources of information at the disposal of the United States" was suggestive. The British response as recorded in the minutes increases the suggestiveness, for as soon as Strong completed his statement, Air Marshal and Chief of the Air Staff, Sir Cyril Nevall, immediately undertook "to take this matter up with the Prime Minister."[1]

Any doubt as to whether General Strong offered the British some form of cryptanalysis cooperation covering highly secret sources on 31 August 1940 has now been removed by the official *History of British Intelligence in the Second World War*. F. H. Hinsley and his colleagues state that on 31 August 1940 the "Army representative" on the American team of military observers, General Strong, told the British Chiefs of Staff about "the progress his Service was making against Japanese and Italian cyphers and formally proposed to the Chiefs of Staff that the time had arrived for a free exchange of intelligence."[2]

These pieces of evidence clear up the long-standing uncertainty over who made the initial move toward Anglo-American cryptanalytic cooperation, and when it was made. Strong definitely did it in London on 31 August 1940. But even with the basic facts now firmly established, a pair of significant mysteries remains that cannot be answered on the basis of the currently available documentation. The first of these concerns timing. General Strong revealed the "Purple-Magic" secret to the British at a very early point in its development. He did it before the Purple break-in was complete and well before Friedman and Rowlett had produced their crowning, and still astounding, achievement of building an exact replica of the Japanese Purple machine. Why Strong would tell the British about Magic at such a crucial, and relatively early, point in its development is difficult to imagine. But whatever the reasons for his action, the early date of Strong's revelation to the British constitutes a far bolder and more generous overture to Anglo-American cryptanalytic cooperation by the U.S. Army than even the most enthusiastic champion of such intelligence sharing has dared to suggest.

The second peculiar aspect of General Strong's 31 August 1940 approach to the British Chiefs of Staff was that he was the only person on that day who made a cryptanalytic overture. The British offered nothing in return, nor did the U.S. Navy lay any of its code- and cipher-breaking achievements on the table. The U.S. naval observer, Admiral Ghormley, was present at the meeting but, according to the available accounts of the session, he said nothing about cryptanalysis. Consequently there was not a general American proposal to share cipher-breaking information with the United Kingdom, only an offer by the U.S. Army.

Since the U.S. Army and Navy were accustomed to going their separate ways even on vital matters such as cryptanalysis, this would not have been seen as unusual or offensive behavior within military circles in Washington. The army and navy had divided up various cryptanalytic targets in the world, and by that partition the army authorities felt that their navy colleagues would not contest their decisions on the distribution of Magic. Indeed, one of the most aggressively territorial of the top cryptanalysts, Capt. Laurance F. Safford, then the head of Op-20-G, declared after the war that "the army had solved the Purple system and therefore was free to dispose of it as they saw fit."[3] But the meeting of 31 August had not occurred in Washington, and it was not simply an American interservice gathering. This had been a meeting with the British Chiefs of Staff who reported directly to the prime minister. From the British point of view the meeting with the American observer mission was self-evidently an official bilateral gathering with significant political overtones. Even when seen from the American side of the table it was clearly much more than an episode in the interminable Washington struggles over status and turf. Yet General Strong had felt able to go it alone in offering cryptanalytic cooperation to the British, without the U.S. Navy having to follow suit.

General Strong's action was hardly an individual aberration or indiscretion, for although he was a bit headstrong and eccentric, George Strong was also a highly respected and seasoned staff officer, slow of speech but quick of mind. As an old cavalry commander he was also notorious for doing everything by the book. So even though Strong most probably was acting under orders, there is no available evidence to suggest who could have issued such orders. If the president had decided to initiate cryptanalytic cooperation with the British at that moment, he surely would have committed his naval staff to the partnership as well as that of his army. If the president had not issued, or approved, a cryptanalytic cooperation order, then one of two individuals who stood between Strong and the president in the War Department chain of command would have to have done so. But it is very difficult to imagine that either George Marshall or Henry Stimson would have taken such a step entirely on their own initiative.

So a mystery remains regarding George Strong's offer of 31 August: why it was made and at such an early date. What is clear is that the offer was unprecedented. Never before had a major power in the modern era offered to reveal its secret cryptanalytic methods to another government. Once out of the bottle, the genie of cryptanalytic cooperation could not easily be recorked. Both London and Washington therefore spent much effort and anguish over the subsequent four years trying to control and tame the powerful spirit that had been released by General Strong.

The response of the British authorities to the American cryptanalytic initiative was quick and positive. On 5 September 1940 General Strong cabled Washington, asking General Marshall whether the U.S. Army "would agree to full exchange with the British of German, Italian, and Japanese code and cryptographic information" (in 1940 the word *cryptographic* often referred to code-and-cipher breaking as well as the making of code-and-cipher systems), because the British were prepared to move ahead. Apparently either at this time, or shortly thereafter, Admiral Ghormley jumped on the cryptanalytic-cooperation bandwagon as well, and sent a similar query to the U.S. Navy Department, because within a few weeks both American services were busy trying to decide just how far, and how fast, to move toward cryptanalytic union with the British.[4]

In late August and early September 1940 Anglo-American cryptanalytic cooperation became intertwined with the issue of the sharing between the two countries of scientific and technical information related to radar and radio communications equipment. The British embassy in Washington had sought since at least May 1940 to arrange such an interchange, but the proposal initially had been vetoed by the prime minister. Shortly after the fall of France, however, Churchill reversed himself; on 8 July 1940, in a conversation with President Roosevelt, the British ambassador, Lord Lothian, had offered an immediate openhanded exchange of information "in the ultra short wave [radar] field." Lothian proposed that there should be no bargaining on this matter, and declared his country ready to reveal everything it had on a reciprocal basis, with no strings attached.[5]

The initial reaction of American military and naval officials to the Lothian offer was one of cautious skepticism. The U.S. Navy was, as usual, especially reserved. A week after Lord Lothian's initiative, a memorandum prepared by the navy's technical-research authorities raised the possibility that the main purpose behind any such show of British openhandedness might be an effort to gain access to the "full resources of the radio industry" of the United States in order to tie the production "in this country" to Britain's needs. Ten days later, the director of the U.S. Naval Research Laboratory, H. G. Bowen, declared that he was very doubtful that the British were far ahead of the United States in regard to the use "of radar in air warfare."[6]

Franklin Roosevelt, on the other hand, chose to dismiss all doubts. He ignored the fact that this initiative was clearly an effort to curry American favor while the British still held a technical lead on radar. The president treated Lord Lothian's proposal as simply an openhanded offer by a generous friend, and ordered his service cabinet members— Secretaries Stimson and Knox—to open up all the American radar cupboards and not permit obstruction by the U.S. Army and Navy.

British technical wizard Prof. Henry Tizard arrived in Washington in late August. On 29 August the American navy was given a briefing on the main British submarine detection device, asdic. U.S. Navy officials seem to have been impressed with asdic, just as U.S. Army Air Corps officers looked with pleasure and interest on the special radar equipment that was soon shown to them. The range and quality of the British disclosures were so great that by early October one of the top U.S. Army technical specialists, Alfred Loomis, assured Secretary Stimson and General Marshall that through the Tizard mission the Americans "were getting infinitely more from the British than we could give them." Though the U.S. Navy had initially held back more than the U.S. Army, it too had swung around by mid-October and was ready to acknowledge that it had received substantial benefits from Tizard and his team.[7]

Like the various American missions sent to London in the summer of 1940, the Tizard mission thus did a good deal to build up confidence in Britain's strength and ability, both in the White House and within the service departments. It also began to tie the two countries together in the realm of highly secret technical equipment. Such cooperation was an indispensable foundation for collaboration on intelligence matters, especially in the area of modern cryptanalysis, which had become so highly technical due to the challenges posed by the extensive use of machine ciphers.

It should be noted, however, that the Tizard mission had not been intended to concern itself with cryptanalysis. Before the mission left Britain, Ultra had specifically been excluded from its brief. On 26 July 1940 the air minister, Sir Archibald Sinclair, assured the prime minister that the British authorities had no intention of allowing discussions with the Americans on radar to slip over into the zone of cryptanalysis. Churchill reinforced this point by warning Tizard's group "not to discuss with the Americans the German radio method of navigation [that is, the central direction from Adm. Karl Doenitz's headquarters] and our method for dealing with it."[8]

Therefore the exaggerated claims, first made in the 1970s and frequently repeated since, that the British and American cryptanalysts began toiling hand in glove from the time of the Tizard mission's arrival in Washington have no basis in fact. But it does appear possible that a more restrained suggestion could be correct, namely that another germ of cryptanalytic cooperation was seeded during Tizard's visit. We know that on 27–28 August Tizard met with General J. O. Mauborgne, who was in charge both of the U.S. Army's radar activities and its cryptanalytic operations. Although Mauborgne's discussion with Tizard focused on what was referred to officially as information on "munitions, devices, or processes of manufacture owned by the US Government," as well as British technology, it is also true that during the Tizard visit official American approval was given for dissemination to the British of some form of intelligence that had been "gained abroad." A document of 9 September 1940 prepared by the G-2, Gen. Sherman Miles, requested authority to include "cryptanalytic information" among the items that could be exchanged with the British.[9]

There is no evidence now available to shed light on the "cryptanalytic information" that Miles wanted to exchange, nor on the intelligence "gained abroad" that was on the agenda of General Mauborgne. What the British were told, and by whom, remains a mystery. All that can be said is that some offer regarding cryptanalytic intelligence exchange seems to have been made by the U.S. Army in September 1940, and it is likely that either General Mauborgne or General Miles was the one who made it.

In any event, despite the gaps and queries left by the current security and withholding policies of London and Washington, it is possible to outline the main steps the two countries took in pursuit of a cryptanalytic deal in the last three months of 1940. The first available document relevant to this process refers to an event that occurred in London on 22 October. On that day the American naval observer in London, Admiral Ghormley, met in Whitehall with the DNI (Admiral Godfrey) and Brigadier Menzies ("C"), the overseer of both MI 6 and Bletchley. The document does not specify the subject of this highly unusual meeting, but it obviously concerned intelligence, for some arrangement related to the sharing of secret material was discussed, and in the course of the talk, Ghormley emphasized that the exchange should occur "in Washington" rather than in London.[10]

The security surrounding what was to be exchanged, in itself, raises the possibility that cryptanalytic cooperation was the subject of this meeting. That possibility is enhanced by a postwar memoir written by Laurance Safford, Op-20-G chief in 1940. Safford was blindly opposed to cryptanalytic cooperation with Britain, and after the war repeatedly reproached the U.S. Army for having opened the door to a general agreement on such matters. He also condemned Ghormley, claiming that Ghormley had agreed in London, without securing prior approval from the Navy Department, that a cryptanalytic deal should be made.[11]

Safford indulged his great capacity for excited exaggeration in this postwar memoir, but there seems to be at least some substance behind many of his accusations. The presence of Ghormley in an *à trois* meeting with Admiral Godfrey, and especially with Menzies, on 22 October 1940 certainly raises the possibility that this is the start of general Anglo-American cryptanalytic negotiations. That likelihood is confirmed by the fact that on the following day, 23 October, there occurred in Washington the first high-level meeting in the United States related to a possible Ultra-Magic deal for which any contemporary account has survived. Secretary of War Henry Stimson recorded in his diary a tangled story of his dealings with Secretary of the Navy Frank Knox on 23 October as the two men attempted to press forward to cryptanalytic cooperation with the British. Stimson wrote in this diary entry that the matter at hand was the sharing of information regarding "the code methods of the Germans." He made no mention of sharing information on either Italian or Japanese codes or ciphers, but he did indicate that British officials concerned with the code-exchange question were already in Washington.[12]

The security authorities of Britain and the United States have managed to keep secret the identity of these British officials, but it is probable that they were not men of the highest influence or authority regarding questions of cryptanalysis. In the opening phases of all subsequent cryptanalytic negotiations between the two countries the British sent to Washington men of very high position, such as the director of the

Government Code and Cipher School. But Bletchley's director at this time, Cdr. Alistair Denniston, was not in Washington, and would not make his first trip to the American capital until August 1941. It is also clear from the meeting between "C," Godfrey, and Ghormley, which had occurred on 22 October, that both Godfrey and "C" were still in London. So we are left with a mystery regarding the identity of the British officials, but that mystery may provide a hint that Whitehall did not attach supreme importance to these discussions. The British government would have sent lower-level officials to Washington only if it viewed an accord with the United States on such a sensitive matter with considerable reserve.

Stimson's diary account of his meeting with Knox contains another indication that the Americans were operating under illusions regarding British eagerness for a cryptanalytic deal. Stimson wrote in his diary that the British emissaries had come to Washington prepared "to sell" what they knew about German ciphers. Unless the secretary meant that short phrase metaphorically, he could not have been farther from the truth, because not only were the British not going to sell, in the final analysis they would even pull back from trading cryptanalytic secrets with the Americans in 1940–41.

Stimson, however, was not easily deterred either in his diary or in life. On 23 October 1940 he worked hard to establish the basis for a cryptanalytic agreement. First he talked over the sharing issue with Assistant Secretary of War John J. McCloy, Gen. Sherman Miles (the G-2), and Gen. J. O. Mauborgne, the head of the Signal Corps. The account of the army's cryptanalytic achievements provided by McCloy, Miles, and Mauborgne so impressed the man who had earlier closed down the Black Chamber in the State Department that Stimson decided it would not be wise to record the "wonderful progress" even in his diary. When this chat was finished, Stimson and his three War Department colleagues went over to the navy building—still on 23 October—to meet with Secretary Knox, Adm. Leigh Noyes (the navy's chief communications officer), and Adm. Walter Anderson (the chief of Naval Intelligence). Admiral Harold Stark, the chief of Naval Operations, was called in during the meeting and strongly supported the idea of cryptanalytic cooperation with Britain. By the end of the discussion all those present—six senior U.S. Army and Navy officers, the two cabinet secretaries, and Assistant Secretary of War McCloy, but *no* cryptanalysts from either service—did likewise, subject only to the proviso that the president and Secretary of State Cordell Hull should "know about it."

On the following day, Stimson cleared the sharing proposal with Hull and then called the White House to notify the president. Shortly thereafter, Roosevelt's military aide, Gen. "Pa" Watson, telephoned Stimson to say that "the President was perfectly satisfied to rest upon the judgement of Knox and myself in this matter and approved of what we proposed to do." This is the only recorded occasion on which President Roosevelt was asked to consider Ultra-Magic cooperation during World War II, but in the administratively relaxed atmosphere that prevailed in the Roosevelt White House it was not uncommon for such casually given authorizations to legitimize important aspects of U.S. government business year after year.

In any event, with presidential authorization and the approval of the secretaries of state, war, and navy, it might seem that the American side of a deal had been done. But Safford's postwar memoir contends that sharp opposition to the idea still simmered, especially in the "working echelon" of the navy's cryptanalytic section, and Safford's view of events was partially seconded by a confidential letter written by Friedman in November 1954. Here again Secretary Stimson's diary provides additional evidence for Safford's contentions. On 12 December the secretary was compelled to assist Secretary Knox in beating back the opposition to a deal that still existed within the U.S. Navy. Stimson accused the navy staff of having "gone back" on the October understanding that code- and cipher-breaking information would be shared with Britain; a "sheer repudiation," he called it, and mused that "some of the Naval officers are a good deal more stubborn[,] and verging on insubordination[,] than anything I have struck in the War Department."[13]

Indeed there was deep resistance within Op-20-G to the sharing of cryptanalytic information with any foreign government, even at a time when navy cryptanalysts were struggling to catch up with the changes the Japanese were making in their naval code-and-cipher system. When in June 1940 T. V. Soong of the Chinese Nationalist government sought to arrange an exchange of information regarding Japanese naval cryptographic systems with the U.S. Navy, he had been roughly handled. Navy officials told Soong that the American government would be glad to receive anything the Chinese were prepared to give, but were unwilling to provide anything in return. Soong temporarily dropped the subject, but in early November, shortly after the meeting described in Stimson's diary, between American officials and the cryptanalytic emissaries from Britain, Soong tried again. This time he offered to show the Americans the Chinese cryptanalytic operation in Chungking and provide them with all Chinese decoding work on the Japanese navy, while emphasizing that the Chinese were asking for nothing in return. Only on that basis, all take and no give, was the U.S. Navy willing to talk with the Chinese. In mid-November 1940 Maj. J. M. McHugh, U.S. Marine Corps, was sent to Chungking to study Chiang Kai-shek's cryptanalytic operations.[14]

Op-20-G was almost as cautious about sharing cryptanalytic information with the U.S. Army as it was with foreign governments. When Friedman's team completed its full break into Purple and had built its first Magic machine, in the autumn of 1940, it was then hobbled by the lack of secure army facilities in which to manufacture more such machines. The U.S. Navy came to the rescue and produced six more Magic machines in its secure laboratory facilities, but for its services it insisted on being paid off in the form of two Magic machines for its own use, and for much of the next year the two American services ran parallel operations against the Japanese Purple cipher.[15]

Nonetheless, by mid-December Secretaries Stimson and Knox had succeeded in driving the naval staff into line regarding the need for cryptanalytic cooperation with Britain. Although the precise terms of the final Anglo-American agreement cannot be established, Safford's bitter remarks in his postwar memoir contend that, after haggling, a group of higher British and American officers agreed in December to share *all* the information they possessed on German, Italian, and Japanese code-and-cipher systems, and that they sealed this deal by signing a one-page agreement to that effect. Only one additional copy of that paper was made, according to Safford, in order to maintain maximum security while providing each country with written proof of the terms of the deal.

Safford's account of this phase of the story is certainly not lacking in errors and exaggeration. One of his obviously inaccurate contentions is the claim that the American naval negotiators strongly pressed the British to provide them with an example of a German naval Enigma machine. According to Safford the U.S. Navy had learned from intelligence reports that Britain had recovered a number of such machines from sunken U-boats as well as from a raid on the Lofoten Islands. But no informed British negotiator would have listened to such demands even for a minute: In December 1940 the Royal Navy had not yet recovered a single complete naval Enigma machine, and the Lofoten raid as well as other capture operations lay four months in the future.[16]

One cannot therefore accept as correct everything Safford wrote after the war regarding the Anglo-American effort to reach an understanding on cryptanalysis in the winter of 1940. But the captain's claim that a written agreement was concluded between the two countries is again confirmed by an entry in Secretary Stimson's diary. The relevant passage was written five months after the November 1940 entries and arose from Stimson's discovery that Secretary of State Cordell Hull was unable to remember that "way back last winter we arranged with the British to exchange secrets on this matter [cryptanalysis] and did so." In order to convince Hull, Stimson "had in Sherman Miles [the G-2] and *got* [out] *the record of the arrangement* [italics added] which was made, of course, with the consent of the President," and proved to Hull that nothing had been agreed with the British that would weaken American code-and-cipher security.[17]

So there was a written record, and that record set forth the terms that had been agreed upon with the British, not just the understandings that had been reached between the U.S. Army and Navy. What had troubled Hull in the spring of 1941 was not interservice rivalry but the possibility that the agreement with the British might jeopardize State Department code security, which was very vulnerable, as will be seen below. Apparently one look at the text brought out by General Miles was enough to convince Hull that no British threat to State Department codes existed. Therefore the written text must have set out the terms of a British-American agreement to share with each other information on the codes and ciphers of other countries, most probably Germany, Italy, and Japan.

The text of this Anglo-American pact on cryptanalysis, concluded in December 1940, still has not been made public. However, the sequence of events that followed shows that this understanding opened the way for the immediate dispatch to the United Kingdom of a joint American army-navy secret mission, charged with delivering America's current cryptanalytic treasures to Britain in anticipation of receiving in return some of Britain's important code- and cipher-breaking secrets.

The mission, unfortunately, was plagued by bad luck from the beginning. The original plan called for dispatch of a four-man team composed of two young navy cryptanalysts, plus two army specialists, including the dean of American code and cipher breakers, William Friedman himself. But shortly after New Year's Day 1941, Friedman suffered a nervous collapse, apparently caused by overwork, and was unable to make the journey. The revised team was still composed of four competent men: Robert Weeks and Prescott Currie for the navy, and Leo Rosen and Abraham Sinkov for the army. All of them had considerable cryptanalytic experience to their credit. Sinkov, for example, was one of Friedman's bright young men and had been a lecturer in the army's main cryptanalytic training course as early as the middle 1930s. In 1936 he had been sent to Panama on a special mission to set up a radio intercept system in the Canal Zone, and in subsequent years he had evolved into an expert on Italian commercial codes.

But in England little if anything was known about the achievements of these men, and to compound the difficulty, the mission was decidedly junior in rank. Sinkov, the senior member of the team, was only a temporary army captain, and the others in the group also had temporary military ranks—Rosen an army first lieutenant, Weeks an ensign, and Currie a naval lieutenant, junior grade. The lack of stars and eagles on the shoulders and collars of these four young men would compound the difficulties facing them when they arrived in Britain.[18] Another major obstacle to the mission's success was its timing. January 1941 found the Atlantic so populated with important British and American missions that the significance of Sinkov and his associates could be lost easily in the traffic.

On 15 January a team of senior British military and naval officers arrived in Washington to begin the first round of staff talks on combined planning for possible hostilities in the Pacific. These "ABC-1" discussions lasted until March and were looked upon as highly important by both governments. London saw them as a major step toward direct American involvement in the war, and the U.S. authorities were eager to secure all possible assistance in erecting barriers against Japan in the Pacific.

ABC-1 would, alone, have greatly overshadowed the Sinkov mission. In addition, during January, Franklin Roosevelt's special emissary, Harry Hopkins, made his debut visit to the United Kingdom. Though not everyone in Whitehall immediately grasped his importance, enough did to lay the basis for Hopkins' future role as the indispensable facilitator of high-level Anglo-American cooperation. Hopkins soon formed a close bond with the prime minister, and as long as he remained in the country he was the object of virtually all British high-priority initiatives aimed at snuggling closer to the United States.

On the lower level of Anglo-American cooperative efforts, in early 1941 Sinkov and his colleagues also faced competition from another American mission concerned with codes and ciphers. J. Edgar Hoover sent agents Clegg and Hince to London in January to secure general information on the methods used in Britain for "handling cryptography in all its aspects." Their attention was focused mainly on Britain's own cipher-and-code procedures, but these two agents, or their immediate successors, were soon attached to MI 6. In the words of the official *History of British Intelligence*, this opportunity was taken "to advise the United States that the Government Code and Cypher School's work on Axis cyphers was leading to an increased output of intelligence." This vague notification, passing as it did through FBI channels, seems not to have reached the American army-navy cryptanalytic authorities with full force, if at all; therefore, the FBI–MI 6 contacts apparently increased, rather than decreased, the misunderstandings between the code- and cipher-breaking authorities of the two countries.[19]

In this context of important comings and goings during January 1941, the arrival on 7 February of four junior American officers was unlikely to make British officialdom sit up and take notice, even though the Americans did come across the Atlantic on the shakedown cruise of the new British battleship HMS *George V*, and bore with them some of the principal achievements of American cryptanalysis. The team's baggage held various cryptanalytic papers, including materials on Italian commercial codes, and, if Safford's postwar memoir is reliable on this point, the keys to the Japanese navy's merchant-ship code (which was certainly being read by Op-20-G in October 1940) plus "two [Japanese] fleet codes with current keys and techniques of solution."[20]

Even more significantly, Sinkov and his colleagues brought a complete American Magic machine as a present for the British government. Since the end of World War II, tales have circulated that the mission brought anywhere from two to four such machines and that one of these was quickly sent on to Singapore by the British. Friedman himself claimed in a confidential letter written in the mid-1950s that the mission bore two Magic machines. Sinkov carried only a single Magic machine, however, and since the official *History of British Intelligence* shows that this machine was soon being used to crack Japanese diplomatic messages in Europe and the Middle East, it seems obvious that no Magic machine was immediately sent to Singapore. Yet the gift of even one Magic machine was an act of enormous generosity on the part of the neutral United States, and if Safford's account of the number of American naval cryptanalytic treasures handed over to the British is even close to accurate, this mission constituted one of the most generous initiatives in the history of modern cryptanalytic relations.[21]

The British response was far less open and forthcoming, though courteous. The Americans were welcomed and treated kindly by the head of the army section at Bletchley, Brig. John Tiltman. Tall, rangy, cheerful, and outgoing, Tiltman was an able cryptanalyst of the old, premachine, school. He liked cryptanalytic shoptalk, and he definitely made a big hit with the American team. But he was not a very suitable person to introduce the Americans to the technical-scientific side of the Bletchley operation, because he was not high-tech oriented and had never felt at home with machine ciphers.

During the Americans' visit to Britain, the mission received the first tour of Bletchley accorded any Americans. They were given a lecture on the general cryptanalytic methods used by the British, and the four Americans were able to engage in a good bit of code-breaker shoptalk. Sinkov, for example, discussed Italian codes with his British counterparts and was surprised to learn that they held a copy of the Italian commercial codebook which he had long been struggling to break.

The visit was also sufficiently extensive and detailed for the American team to grasp the importance of the Bletchley "hut" system for producing finished intelligence and providing "auxiliary information" to assist the cryptanalysts. The British had already organized their navy as well as their army and air force Enigma operations in the form of a two-hut process (Huts 8 and 4 for navy, 6 and 3 for army and air force). In the spring of 1941 important and immediately breakable Enigma material was arriving primarily in "Red," which was passed from the intercept stations to Hut 6. There it was first grouped on the basis of the various cipher keys used by the Germans. When possible, the German originators and receivers of each message were also identified. The

Hut 6 watch then determined which group of messages was to be given top priority in the day's breaking process, and the Hut's cryptanalysts, using a broad range of analytic methods and equipment, searched for clues to which settings the Germans had employed on that day. Whenever a setting was found, the Hut 6 team broke every high-priority message they could find in that setting.

The raw broken messages were then handed on to Hut 3, where German-language specialists arranged the streams of letters into German words and then attempted to determine the meaning of each message and judge its importance. In February 1941 the evaluation side of Hut 3's work had not progressed very far, because the workings of the German military system—its internal code words, procedures, and personalities—could not be mastered quickly. The valuable intelligence acquired from this process was therefore limited. In addition, at that time Hut 3 was rarely able to provide Hut 6 with much specific information useful in the cipher-breaking process.[22] But at the time of the visit by Sinkov and his colleagues, it was already obvious inside Bletchley that over time the expertise of Hut 3 personnel, plus the value of their files, would wring ever more valuable intelligence from the raw decrypts produced by Hut 6, and would also provide the cryptanalysts with an ever larger volume of data about German manners and mores to help them in their cipher-breaking efforts. The hut system was one of the most important dimensions of the "Ultra secret": Sinkov and the other members of the American mission saw enough of it to grasp its importance, and explain it to their superiors in Washington, who presided over systems based on stultifying compartmentalization of cryptanalytic and intelligence functions.[23]

It should not be imagined that the survey visit of Bletchley given to the Sinkov mission was seen as a brush-off in British eyes. Even the new director of Military Intelligence, Gen. F. H. N. Davidson, was given only a quick day tour of the Park on 28 January 1941, though he was the highest ranking intelligence officer in the British army. This short outing was considered to be all the firsthand experience that even the DMI required to grasp the methods and workings of the Government Code and Cipher School.[24]

The American team was of course not given an Enigma machine nor provided with a magic wand to reveal the secrets of the various forms of German enciphering methods. The British had captured some naval Enigma rotors in the late winter of 1940–41 and had reconstructed portions of the enciphering processes of the naval Enigma machine, but they were still far from a complete solution of its mysteries and, aside from Red, had made only limited headway on other German army and air force keys.[25]

Therefore the claim made by Sir Stuart Mitchell in 1971 that Sinkov and his colleagues were let in on the methods used at Bletchley to provide "quick identification of the key changes" the Germans made in the Enigma machine probably greatly overstates the situation. In any case, this was too complicated a process to be demonstrated effectively during a short survey. Similarly, Admiral Godfrey's December 1941 statement that "the American officers when they were over here were informed of all our methods and shown our machines" grossly misstates the case. Sinkov and his group were told only "in a general way" about British decryption processes; they were not allowed to see a bombe, or even told of its existence. The American team therefore had no hard evidence to prove the importance of analytic machine methods in the British cryptanalytic effort, even though they suspected that some machine-calculation method was being used at Bletchley.[26]

The Sinkov mission was given a sample of the latest British high-speed DHF (high-frequency direction finder) equipment to take back to the States, and the navy members of the team may have been given a paper diagram of the structure and wiring of the German three-rotor naval Enigma machine, plus some key lists. But, overall, the Sinkov mission seems to have fallen through the cracks of the British liaison system. It had arrived at a moment when the usual British reservations about security were compounded by a belief that too much had already been given to the Americans, and that now circumstances had changed sufficiently so that increased circumspection was possible.

The corner had not been turned from defeat to victory, but some of the dangers that had loomed large the previous summer were now dissolving. The Blitz had failed and the threat of German invasion was receding, although the Chiefs of Staff would not officially declare it "no longer imminent" until April 1941. Near the end of 1940 the British had struck hard blows against the Italian fleet in the Mediterranean and launched a counterattack against the Italian army invading Egypt, which was so successful that by early 1941 it had netted 130,000 prisoners against a loss of 155 British battle dead. In the course of this operation, the offensive capability of Mussolini's African army had been destroyed.

Britain was still very dependent on American supplies and goodwill, but it had few illusions left about the immediate effective power of the American armed forces, although it retained a healthy respect for the U.S. Navy in the Pacific. The Tizard mission had also destroyed most of the fantasies that had existed in London regarding the state of American military technology. Not surprisingly, therefore, clear indications emerged in late autumn and early winter 1940–41 that the British government was having second thoughts about the policy of openness toward the United States. In the van of those calling for a clampdown on the quantity and quality of information being provided to the Americans was the prime minister. On 29 October 1940 in a meeting of the Defense Committee, Churchill declared that he was "inclined towards a stiffer attitude than we had recently adopted" in making available to the Americans information about British production. Three-and-a-half weeks later during a cabinet discussion of the general issue of openness with the United States, Anthony Eden, the war minister (who turned foreign secretary a month later in the shakeup that sent Lord Halifax to Washington following the death of Lord Lothian), favored keeping the door open as much as possible, but Churchill would have none of it and carried the cabinet with him in favor of more caution and circumspection.[27]

On the following day (22 November 1940), when he learned that the American military attaché, Gen. Raymond Lee, had recently received a British intelligence report that included some "wrapped-up" information derived from Ultra (wrapped-up refers to information given with the source disguised or not indicated), Churchill left no doubt that he was strongly opposed to any openhandedness toward the Americans regarding most secret intelligence. "This report and others like it should be steadily dampened down, and its circulation restricted as far as possible," the prime minister minuted to Sir Edward Bridges. "The reports given to the American attaché should not be broken off suddenly but should become less informative and padding should be used to maintain bulk." Then, as if to leave absolutely no doubt about his feelings regarding the need to hold tight to Ultra and other vital secrets, Churchill added, "This is not through any lack of confidence in him [Lee] but because wild scattering of secret information must be curbed." Nor should this British decision to tighten up on intelligence sharing have come as a great surprise to Washington: Herschel Johnson of the U.S. embassy in London was already lodging complaints about it with the Foreign Office as early as December 1940.[28]

In light of the British turn toward caution, as well as the American services' notoriously poor security precautions, it was probably inevitable that Bletchley would treat the Sinkov mission with considerable circumspection. It should be noted additionally that in early 1941 the British cryptanalysts still had not secured the broad and deep successes against the German Enigma that would later stun even the most experienced secret visitors from across the Atlantic. The German army and navy ciphers continued to elude the most determined efforts of the British cryptanalysts, whose main successes at that time came from Red. Occasions did occur when decryptions were made of German "orders of the high command" and when "the objectives of planes" had been determined in advance by Bletchley, just as Sinkov and his colleagues were told during their visit to GC & CS. But the great breakthroughs that ultimately led to much of the German Enigma traffic being read currently and in great depth simply had not happened in February 1941.[29]

British officials at Bletchley seem to have provided little information regarding the what, how, and why of their operations, while overselling their successes. The American cryptanalytic visitors therefore failed to secure a clear picture of what was going on at Bletchley and why. To the men of GC & CS this may have seemed a safe and sane exercise in transatlantic secret relations at a time when the Ultra secret was absolutely vital to Britain; supplying general Ultra information to the United States could not possibly be fitted into the "need-to-know" principle.

That was not the way it came to be viewed by the cryptanalysts in Washington, however. Sinkov and his colleagues arrived back in the United States in April 1941 with little to show in exchange for their strenuous efforts except general impressions of Bletchley and British intelligence practice as well as evidence of British bonhomie. Some American officials, including William Friedman, seem to have been content with the results of the mission, but others in the U.S. Army and Navy cryptanalytic sections who had approached cooperation with Britain cautiously at best—and in the case of Op-20-G in a mood of sour suspicion—viewed the gifts borne home by the prodigal sons as meager indeed. Cries of betrayal by perfidious Albion, and outrage toward their cryptanalytic cousins, echoed down the halls of Op-20-G.

Within the American cryptanalytic services the villain of the piece was assumed to be the British Foreign Office, that center of alleged intrigue and duplicitous behavior that always tormented the traditional Yankee soul. But the Foreign Office actually exercised no direct day-to-day authority over Bletchley in early 1941, and at a time when Lord Halifax and then Anthony Eden were anxious to court Americans, it is highly implausible that the Foreign Office would have gone out of its way to stonewall a highly secret American mission.[30]

Sir Stewart Menzies, perhaps reinforced by Churchill himself in his new mood of restraint regarding the sharing of secret information with the Americans, was a more likely candidate for the man who took the lead in holding the Sinkov mission at a distance. As noted above, the only real political and military ace Menzies held in the Whitehall political battles of early 1941 was his titular authority over Bletchley, about whose operations he knew very little. He was not a cryptanalyst and did not have close personal relations with either the older generation of Room 40 veterans, such as the director of Bletchley, Commander Denniston, or the young technical and mathematical wizards, such as Alan Turing. Temperament, class, and the fact that his primary concerns were in the political battles in Whitehall meant that in regard to Bletchley, Menzies was the epitome of the absentee landlord—remote, uninformed, quick to tout successful activities but deeply worried about possible losses. "C" simply could not take any chances with the security of Bletchley, not only because what went on there was vital to Britain's chances of survival, but also because "the golden eggs" from the Park were the only valuable intelligence assets he had to use in the Whitehall battles that threatened his position and that of MI 6.

It is possible therefore that "C" was the one who decided that the Bletchley door should not be fully opened to Sinkov and his colleagues, and that by stressing the vital need for security he carried the Chiefs of Staff with him. Certainly, ten months later, as can be proved by archival documents, when once again the question arose of opening up more of the Ultra secret to the Americans, it was the Foreign Office representative who broached the possibility in a Chiefs of Staff meeting, and it was "C" who adamantly refused to permit it (see below, p. 102).[31]

If, for any reason, "C" had not ordered a go-slow policy toward the Sinkov mission, the director of Bletchley Park, Alistair Denniston, probably would have taken that course on his own. Denniston was a kindly man and an able cryptanalyst of the old premachine cipher period, but he was far removed by class and experience from the rough and tumble of high-level Whitehall maneuvering or the roaring go-ahead atmosphere of wartime Bletchley. He tended to look inward, trying to mind the shop in the ways of peacetime, sticking with familiar ways and fully trusting only familiar people. By early 1941 he was already out of his depth in the new world of permanent crises, large organizations, bureaucratic maneuvering, and high-tech machine cryptanalysis. His basic inclination toward rigid secrecy was therefore intensified into a near obsession, which would have made openhanded sharing with a low-ranked mission from across the sea extremely difficult.[32]

When the "C" and Denniston factors are thus added to the importance of Ultra to Britain, the improvements in the British position in the war, and the legitimate British worries about American insecurity, it is easy to understand, if not to justify completely, why the British failed to carry out their side of the December 1940 sharing agreement, and why the American mission was held at arm's length during February 1941. But the consequences of this rather offhanded British action were serious. Rosen, Sinkov, Weeks, and Currie had not learned enough at Bletchley to be able to explain to their superiors at home why Britain did not, and could not, provide the Americans with a cryptanalytic wonder weapon analogous to a Magic machine. Bletchley was like a huge problem-solving corporate enterprise, which sent out door-to-door investigators every day to see what headway could be made. To do this the Bletchley staff used bombes, hand methods of cryptanalysis, a sharp eye for cillies and cribs, intelligence and technical hints from Hut 3, plus any brainstorms that offered hope of providing potentially useful information. If they made headway on any occasion against the daily setting of any particular cipher or ciphers, well and good, but the next day the settings would be changed again, and the whole game of needle-in-a-haystack would begin all over again.

The British code- and cipher-breaking system was so multifaceted and complicated that no one could have brought back a sample of anything from Bletchley in the early spring of 1941 that would have convinced the higher officials of American SIS and Op-20-G that they had received fair value for money. The first round in the battle for effective Ultra-Magic cooperation therefore ended in abject failure during early 1941, and it left behind a legacy of such misunderstanding and suspicion that it would long delay, and make much more difficult, the next attempt to produce a partnership between the secret worlds of the United States and Britain.

CHAPTER FOUR
Edging Closer in 1941

**Phase I: From the Sinkov Mission to Operation Barbarossa
(January–June 1941)**

Events more than affection, or secret shenanigans, were the driving
force that moved Britain and the United States closer together regarding
cryptanalysis in 1941. During the first six months of that year, Hitler,
not the Allies, called the shots. First he played cat and mouse with
Britain and her friends, then gave them a series of devastating lessons
on the value of speed and effective coordination of operations. In February
1941, just as Britain launched its long-anticipated offensive against
the Italians in East Africa, Field Marshal Erwin Rommel and the Afrika
Korps made their first appearance in the Western Desert. The British
high command failed to grasp the seriousness of the danger posed by
Rommel and went off on a series of hastily improvised operations in
the Balkans and the Middle East.

London's optimism about these offensives stemmed in part from
continuing British triumphs against the Italians. The offensive in East
Africa, which had been supplied with excellent signals intelligence from
Bletchley, moved forward at considerable speed during the early spring,
taking Addis Ababa by April 1941. This success provided a welcome
fillip to morale at home and soon gave the British complete control
of the western side of the Red Sea.

The British authorities were also driven into an offensive posture
by their apprehension regarding German intentions in the Balkans.

Mussolini had invaded Greece in October 1940, but had stumbled to a halt due to rugged terrain, harsh weather, and determined Greek resistance. By February–March 1941 London learned from Red and other intelligence sources that formidable German forces were moving into the upper Balkans. So large were these German troop concentrations that London concluded a major thrust was being prepared that might drive through the lower Balkans and Greece, and then continue on into the Middle East, threatening the oil fields and rolling up the whole British position in the region. Grasping a rather desperate hope, large elements of the British North African army were moved in to stiffen the Greeks and help deter the German forces from striking south by southeast. Hitler failed to cooperate with this blocking operation, however, and in late March and early April his armies struck simultaneously at the Western Desert Force in North Africa and against the Yugoslavs, the Greeks, and the British expeditionary force.

In North Africa, Rommel had broken the British line by the first week of April and driven the Western Desert Force as far east as Benghazi. Although British troops, surrounded deep in Rommel's rear, heroically defended Tobruk, the offensive by the Desert Fox recovered most of the territory the Italians had lost in the 1940 campaign. It was a crushing blow to British power and prestige. A weak British counteroffensive launched in June only made matters worse, as the combination of superior German firepower, excellent battlefield signals intelligence, and Rommel's generalship inflicted so much damage on the Western Desert Force that the balance of power in northeast Africa was tipped decisively in Germany's favor.

The results of the German attack in the Balkans were at least as devastating. By mid-April, Greece and Yugoslavia had surrendered to Hitler, and for the third time in World War II a British expeditionary force had been driven from the Continent. In the follow-up operation against Crete, the British defenders—this time well supplied with intelligence, including Ultra—inflicted heavy casualties on the German invaders, but they could not prevent a German triumph, or avoid yet another forced evacuation.

In spring 1941, small British forces did succeed in crushing pro-Axis forces in Iraq, and two months later seized Syria, thereby preventing possible pro-Axis moves by the Vichy French units stationed there. These minioffensives managed to create a real, if very thin, protective shield against a further German advance into the Middle East. Since, due to excellent signals intelligence, the British forces had covered much ground at low cost, the operations seemed at the time to be well earned, and badly needed, offensive triumphs. But even these attacks were actually showy diversions, peripheral to the main course of events. Hitler had decided against an immediate thrust into the Middle East in favor of an all-out assault against the Soviet Union. On this occasion, too, Bletchley Park, along with more conventional sources of intelligence, provided advance warning. Churchill tried to alert Stalin that the Wehrmacht would soon march eastward, but the Soviet leader paid no attention to warnings from Churchill or anyone else in 1941. In any case, Britain was in no position to back up its prophecies by providing military forces to help defend the USSR.

The German offensive of 22 June was quickly recognized as a major turning point. While initially inflicting horrific casualties on the Red Army and the Soviet people, Operation Barbarossa would also create the basis for the East-West coalition that would ultimately destroy Nazism. Yet at the time of the attack, Hitler was, for the last time, completely in charge, determining the form and momentum of the whole great conflict that, under his direction, was spreading across Europe and North Africa.

The first phase of Operation Barbarossa thus stands as a fitting end line for the war period that stretched from January to June 1941. Throughout those five months the Nazi leader repeatedly demonstrated that he, not Britain, was in the driver's seat. By energetically recovering the initiative he had briefly let slip during the Battle of Britain, Hitler proved to the British government that it did not have a realistic hope of winning the war on its own. Only massive assistance from another country could provide the means to realize the dream of Allied victory. With the USSR as yet unable to demonstrate much capacity to play the role of savior, all of Britain's hopes had to rest on the United States.

Ever since the days following Dunkirk, the realization that Britain's fate probably lay in the hands of America had hung over Whitehall, but it had been a wispy dark cloud, partly dispersed by the triumphs achieved by Fighter Command and the grit of the Londoner during the autumn of 1940. In the spring of 1941, however, the reality of Britain's ultimate dependence on the United States was made crystal clear by the failures in the eastern Mediterranean. The British would continue to worry about future domination by the United States and grumble about the slowness, blindness, and inefficiency of the Yanks. London would also trumpet its bravery and achievements in order to increase its prestige in the United States. But once the Americans opened the door and offered to place a sizable portion of their productive capacity at Britain's disposal, London had to bend toward America in order to secure the supplies it desperately needed.

The Lend-Lease Act, passed by Congress and signed by the president on 11 March 1941, formalized Britain's wartime dependence on the United States and transformed the political, as well as the supply, relationships between the two countries. The legislation was one of the crowning achievements of Franklin Roosevelt's innovative wartime administration. In one stroke the president made possible massive assistance to Britain without at the same time opening the door to a repetition of the costly war-debt problems that had accompanied the cash loans made during World War I. "Loaning" goods rather than money was easier for a worried yet hesitant American public to accept in 1941, and at war's end no one in the United States would be likely to cry out for the return of empty shell cases or other litter of war remaining from Lend-Lease. In addition, massive shipments of material to Britain, coupled with American rearmament, would also finally write paid to the American Great Depression and jolt the economy into full employment.

As soon as Lend-Lease became law, the number and size of British supply missions in the U.S. capital rapidly increased, and in June 1941 a Joint Staff Mission (JSM) also was established there under Adm. Sir Charles Little. The JSM was intended to serve as the unifying body through which all British service department dealings with the U.S. Army and Navy could be carried in an orderly manner. Although most of its initial functions concerned equipment coordination, such as that related to the standardization of arms, from the earliest days of its existence the JSM also sought to encourage the American services to bring modernity and order into all aspects of what the British perceived to be the factious and uncoordinated American military system.

Since Admiral Little was a reasonable man, and his successor, Field Marshal Sir John Dill, was an especially sensitive individual who liked the United States and formed a close working relationship with General Marshall, the British Military Mission had considerable latitude in the American capital. From the spring of 1941 until the bombing of Pearl Harbor, British officials in Washington punctuated their supplications for aid with suggestions for bettering American defense arrangements. A number of valuable innovations, such as the creation of the American Office of Scientific Research and Development in June 1941, owed a good deal to British encouragement and advice. Many elements copied from the more centralized war machine that Whitehall had been forced to develop since September 1939 gradually found their way into the American War and Navy departments.

These peculiar circumstances, which made the British Joint Staff Mission a band of both advisers and beggars, inevitably contributed at least a different tone to the thorny question of Anglo-American intelligence cooperation. The British Mission was eager to nudge the many independent intelligence organizations of the United States into effective coordination with each other. A miniature Joint Intelligence Committee (JIC) was actually formed within the Mission in a vain hope that this model might encourage the U.S. Army and Navy to develop a comparable joint intelligence organization of their own.[1]

The FBI and the U.S. Navy actually did begin to trade pieces of foreign coded material between April and June 1941: The navy gave J. Edgar Hoover one German diplomatic code and one Japanese navy code that had come into its hands. In return the FBI promised soon to provide the navy with information regarding some Vichy French codes that Hoover's men had recently broken.[2] But in regard to the endemic intelligence, and especially cryptanalytic, rivalry between the U.S. Army and Navy, little had altered by the summer of 1941, despite coaxing by the British and much American wringing of hands regarding the chaotic situation. As a postwar study made by NSA would observe with succinct precision, "the method of processing the [Magic] diplomatic messages," used in the pre–Pearl Harbor period, as well as the handling of other cryptanalytic materials, remained both "duplicative and unseemly."[3]

Jealousy and bickering between the American services lessened their efficiency and also continued to hamper all forms of Anglo-American intelligence cooperation. The U.S. Army and Navy could not even agree that the limited low- and medium-level intelligence exchanges that did occur in London should be carried out through parallel offices of the two services. The U.S. Army insisted that the only conduit for such exchanges with the British related to army matters should be its military attaché, Gen. Raymond Lee, and that under no circumstances should such information pass through the U.S. Army Observer Mission in London. The U.S. Navy was equally adamant that no intelligence exchange should occur through its London attaché, and that all naval intelligence information must pass back and forth through Admiral Ghormley of the Naval Mission in London. Not surprisingly, as soon as the British Joint Staff Mission was adequately staffed in Washington, it attempted, with marginal success, to short-circuit this absurd jurisdictional problem by arranging for British material to be teleprinted across the Atlantic, so as many exchanges as possible could be made in Washington rather than London.[4]

Even in dealing with the British authorities on such relatively simple matters as possible cooperation in the use of common enciphering systems, the two American services could not see eye to eye. In May 1941 the U.S. government had begun to take code-and-cipher security more seriously when an army–navy–FBI team led by Commander Safford discovered that State Department codes were old-fashioned and that the department encoding procedures were only moderately secure. This investigation did not prompt the State Department to make basic reforms, however, and its codes continued to be vulnerable to foreign governments, especially Fascist Italy until 1943, and Nazi Germany until at least the winter of 1944–45.[5]

The U.S. Army and Navy persisted in a similar mood of anarchic independence when they came to face the question of establishing secure methods of communicating with British military and naval units. In June Admiral Ghormley in London initiated Anglo-American encoding cooperation by showing British officials the American ship and aircraft identification codes. The Admiralty then responded by instructing a member of the U.S. Naval Mission in the operation of the Royal Navy's electric cipher machine.[6] But on 10 May 1941 Col. Clyde L. Eastman, acting chief signals officer of the U.S. Army, strongly rejected an RAF proposal for "a general exchange of cryptographic [encoding] systems" between the air forces of the two countries, citing "considerations of supply, distribution, training, and security" to justify his refusal.[7] Eastman did agree, with Commander Safford's concurrence, that the RAF should be given samples of the U.S. Army's Air-Ground Liaison Code, Fire Control Code (which was then no longer classified as a code), and the

U.S. Army Air Corps' Contact Code and Strip Cipher systems "on a reciprocal basis."[8] But Eastman stressed that in the event of America entering the war, communications between military units of the two countries should be carried out only by means of liaison officers, not through common code-and-cipher systems. When, three months later, such an American liaison officer was actually attached to the RAF on a trial basis, he concluded that not even uncoded (en clair) voice communication between British and American personnel would be possible. Citing "the differences of the English and American languages combined with normal radio distortion," Maj. George Price concluded that if, and when, America entered the European war, air units of Britain and the United States would have to operate completely independently, each with its own ground-control system functioning in its own "language" and with its own codes.[9]

The U.S. Army found it relatively easy to take this position of splendid isolation regarding secret communications with the British, because, unlike the U.S. Navy, the American army was not deeply embroiled in the anti-U-boat campaign during 1941. On the other side of the world, however, once Japan made its sortie into Indochina in July 1941, all branches of the British and American armed forces were compelled to consider what to do if full-scale war broke out in Asia, for they then might actually have to carry out large joint operations. This possibility began to nudge Britain and America closer together regarding communications, intelligence, and related matters in the Far East. The "ABC-1" talks had determined in March that British, Dutch, and American forces should conduct further talks regarding the defense of the Pacific. In April, military and naval discussions between the three countries took place in Singapore, focusing on the strategic defense arrangements for the containment of Japan. Two months later the U.S. Army attaché in London was allowed to sit in on the War Office's daily general intelligence briefing on Far Eastern matters as well as the one on European developments.

ABC-1 had also concluded in paragraph 19 that although Britain and the United States would "retain the independence of their respective intelligence agencies," they would also "maintain close [intelligence] liaison with each other . . . [regarding Japan] not only through the Military Missions [in Washington and London] but also between all echelons of command in the field."[10] This was a far-reaching, if rather vague, commitment, and in early May the Admiralty suggested to Washington that the DNI, Admiral Godfrey, should journey to the American capital to give "full effect to paragraph 19, ABC-1." By the second week of May, both the U.S. Army and Navy had agreed to Godfrey's visit, and the DNI spent most of late May and June studying the American intelligence situation and trying to work out a method of coordination between the two countries.

Godfrey was not impressed by what then passed for an American intelligence system, especially its lack of coordination. His negative impressions increased Whitehall's reluctance to take chances with the security of special high-level intelligence, such as Ultra, by sharing it with the leaky and disorganized American intelligence community. Godfrey did conclude, however, that the United States produced bits of potentially valuable information on Vichy France, French North Africa, and South America. Only in regard to the Pacific, however, did the admiral see any serious prospect of gathering large amounts of useful information from American sources, because "Japanese Special Intelligence" was the only source of important and highly secret information that Washington possessed.[11]

That SIS and Op-20-G were producing valuable cryptanalytic intelligence on Japan, and indirectly on other countries due to the information contained in secret Japanese diplomatic messages, came as no surprise to Bletchley Park or the intelligence branches of the British government. British intercept stations blanketed most of Europe, North Africa, and the Middle East, and the Magic machine that Sinkov and his associates had brought to Britain in February 1941 was churning out a substantial flow of secret information for Bletchley. In April, May, and June, the GC & CS definitely acquired vital data about pro-Axis groups in Iraq from this source, and in early June a considerable volume of information regarding German aggressive intentions against the USSR had been garnered from Magic intercepts of messages made by the Japanese ambassadors in Moscow and Berlin. In fact, it was the Magic intercept of a 4 June message made by Ambassador Hiroshi Oshima in Berlin to the Foreign Office in Tokyo that finally "convinced the [British] JIC that Germany intended to turn on Russia."[12]

The information the British obtained from Magic about developments in Europe and the Middle East, together with what they had secured about Japan from this same source as well as from Op-20-G, left London in no doubt that America had high-level intelligence assets in the Pacific. Indeed, the U.S. Navy had taken another step forward against Japanese navy codes during May 1941 by stealing a bag of "official Orange [Japanese] naval codes, training manuals, and various documents containing instructions to merchant ships" from a Japanese merchantman in San Francisco, photographing the documents, then returning the bag to the merchant ship without being detected.

Since Britain could monitor Japanese diplomatic and naval radio traffic only in Hong Kong, the South Pacific, and Southeast Asia, whereas the American monitoring stations in the Philippines were much closer to the Japanese heartland, close Anglo-American cryptanalytic cooperation in the Pacific was mutually beneficial. It could also sit alongside a system for exchanging lower-level intelligence about Japan, which had been operating even before Admiral Godfrey's visit to Washington. As early as April 1941, the two countries had been exchanging agent and informant reports acquired by their various secret contacts operating in Japan and in Japanese dependencies. These reports were concerned with such matters as shipbuilding and details of the deployment of naval units, but did not extend to the level of such top secret matters as Japanese strategic plans and intentions.[13]

Then in mid-June 1941, the U.S. War Department gave Far Eastern intelligence cooperation an additional push forward by formally requesting a broad exchange of British and American army and air force intelligence regarding the Far East. London welcomed this approach and authorized its service attachés in Washington to carry out such exchanges of routine Far Eastern materials, but not on "information from SIS" sources, or information related to the activities of the British Special Operations Executive (SOE). It appears highly likely that the British attachés were barred from special, that is, cryptanalytic, exchanges as well. Foreign Secretary Anthony Eden emphasized in a 13 June message to Ambassador Halifax that the British government wanted as many of these intelligence exchanges as possible to be carried out directly between the American and British operational centers in the Far East, especially those exchanges concerned with highly secret information. Since London already had one good ear cocked for the sounds of Japanese plans and intentions due to its possession of the Magic machine—a copy of which may well have gone to Singapore by this time—its primary objective by mid-1941 seems to have been the securing of an additional flow directly into its Far Eastern Intelligence Bureau at Singapore of American cryptanalytic intelligence on the Japanese navy as well as the Magic intercepts secured from the American tracking station in the Philippines.

In June 1941 the two countries secretly agreed that intelligence on Japan would henceforth pass between Singapore and the U.S. military authorities in the Philippines, as well as to and from the U.S. Pacific Fleet. This made possible a broad exchange of finished cryptanalytic intelligence, including, apparently, information on the main Japanese naval cipher, JN 25. Even these exchanges did not, however, concern information on cryptanalytic methods.

So intelligence was exchanged, just as operational coordination definitely took place. But from July 1941 onward, following the Japanese seizure of all French Indochina and the imposition of an embargo on oil and scrap-metal sales to Japan by the ABC countries (America, Britain, and the Netherlands), the western powers were still consistently wrong about Japanese plans and capabilities.[14]

Compared with what happened in the Pacific, Anglo-American efforts to cooperate on cryptanalytic intelligence in the North Atlantic during the spring and summer of 1941 were less complex but also much more successful. The passage of the Lend-Lease Act and the resulting great increase in the flow of American goods to Britain immediately generated concern in both Washington and London that defenses had to be strengthened to protect the flow of goods crossing the Atlantic. The British government initially hoped that the United States would assume direct responsibility for the convoy protection of its Lend-Lease shipments, but President Roosevelt refused to go that far, fearing that such a move coming immediately on the heels of the Lend-Lease Act would pump new life into isolationist opposition to aid for Britain. Instead, the president took two immediate halfway steps, which enhanced the protection of the shipments and also created conditions under which the armed forces of the two countries would be drawn into closer operational and intelligence cooperation.

On 9 April 1941 the U.S. government concluded a formal agreement with the Danish ambassador in Washington, granting "landing fields and other defense facilities" in Greenland to the United States for the duration of the war. The agreement was made in part because

Roosevelt feared that Germany might try to seize this territory, thereby threatening the security of the central and western Atlantic. By taking control of Greenland the American government prevented any westward forays by the Nazis and also acquired an essential stopover point for short-range aircraft being ferried to Britain. An additional important reason for stationing American forces in Greenland was the creation of a central Atlantic platform upon which a huge protective umbrella could be opened to shield Lend-Lease shipments destined for Britain.

Two days after the Greenland-occupation agreement was concluded, the president notified Churchill that he had decided to redraw the north-south security line that the United States had laid down early in the war to prevent German submarines from carrying out attacks near the East Coast of the United States. On 11 April 1941 Roosevelt pushed the line far to the east to a point running southward from the eastern portion of Greenland. American air and naval forces would henceforth patrol west of the new line (25 degrees west), to ensure the safety of neutral vessels and help protect them from attack by U-boats. In addition, the United States confidentially informed London that the American patrol forces west of the 25-degree line would provide British naval units with all intelligence they could gather regarding the identity, location, and course of any ship of the "aggressor nations" operating there.

This decision meant that the American patrols in the central and western Atlantic would function not only as thinly disguised associates of Royal Navy antisubmarine operations, but also would be close partners of Britain in operational intelligence collection. Within two weeks of the president's letter to the prime minister informing him of the new patrol arrangements, the U.S. Navy had developed a system for conveying all sighting information to the British. The U.S. patrols were ordered to send such information to the Navy Department in Washington, whence it would be teleprinted to the American embassy in London, and then passed on to the Admiralty. Although this was an awkward and slow procedure for dealing with something as split second in its importance as U-boat sightings, it was the best that could be done in early 1941. The American authorities had decided that for the time being, due to "political reasons," that is, the fear of a possible political-isolationist reaction if such an arrangement became public, it was impossible to use a more rapid communication method such as U.S. vessels radioing directly to the Royal Navy commanding officer for America and the West Indies. But the cipher-and-code publication necessary for this kind of communication had already been prepared, and it would go into operation later in the year.[15]

On their own, the U.S. forces in the Atlantic were then in a poor position to do much effective reconnaissance. Not only did they lack experience in U-boat tracking, but no coordination machinery existed to link together the information-gathering activities of the U.S. Army Air Corps with those of the U.S. Navy's Atlantic command. In mid-1941, no American aircraft carrier was operating in the Atlantic, and American naval patrol vessels had little modern direction-finding equipment. To top off the list of U.S. inadequacies, Op-20-G had as yet made no headway against the German naval Enigma.

In order to gain maximum benefit from the tracking efforts of American patrol vessels in the western Atlantic, it was therefore in the interest of the Royal Navy to provide the Americans with all possible relevant British information regarding the strength and disposition of German U-boats and raiders in the area. This pressure on the British to share information with the U.S. Navy was enhanced by the longer-term advantages of creating a combat partnership between the Royal and American navies.

The need to protect the security of their intelligence sources certainly set limits to what the British could offer, especially to a peacetime America with little security-control machinery in place to protect sensitive information. It is also important to emphasize that although the British were in a much better position than the Americans, the British intelligence situation regarding the Atlantic was far from ideal in April–May 1941. An indication of the seriousness of the difficulties is provided by the fact that it was not until February–March 1941 that the "Y" (interception) Board had drawn clear organizational distinctions between interception and cryptanalysis, with MI 18 finally being given full authority over the former, and Bletchley Park complete control over the latter. But this was still not enough to settle the Admiralty's difficulties over the organization and expansion of "Y" and the intelligence gathered therefrom. Not until July did the navy formally petition the Treasury for authority to carry out a full reorganization of signals interception and intelligence, and only on 8 August

1941 was the Admiralty Signals Department reorganized to include a deputy director of signals (Y) in the person of Capt. H. R. Sandwith.[16]

In the meantime Bletchley Park had been working assiduously to break into a broad range of German secret communication systems, but its initial successes came on secondary codes and ciphers. In February Bletchley had broken into the German railway administrative code by using hand decoding methods. In that same month the cryptanalysts, this time aided by bombes, started to work their way into the German weather ciphers. These ciphers were important in part simply because some of the information they carried was of operational value. Since the British authorities were frequently without good weather information of their own for such areas as central Germany or the coast of Norway, the decrypted German weather traffic helped fill the gaps. More important, the weather ciphers were a prime source of cribs, because weather reports were frequently repeated in many daily messages of the German army, navy, and Luftwaffe. The probability of finding duplications that could offer a way into a high-level cipher was therefore greatly enhanced once the texts of the original weather messages became available.[17]

The series of February breaks made by Huts 8 and 4 into the weather ciphers used by the U-boats were especially important because they coincided with a series of captures of naval Enigma machines, rotors, and logs, which gave Bletchley the opportunity to read completely a series of naval Enigma messages. On 4 March 1941 the Lofoten Islands raid netted considerable cipher material from the German armed trawler *Krebs*. On 7 May the capture of the weather ship *München* produced more cipher material, as did the seizure of U-110 two days later. Through these and other captures, as well as the general work on the naval Enigma, which had been uncovering small clues over the preceding eighteen months, Bletchley broke into the February 1941 German naval cipher traffic with a month delay, and that of April within a week or two.[18] Such delayed decipherment obviously did not provide much operational information that could be applied in the fast-moving battle conditions prevailing in the North Atlantic. But even the delayed decrypts did give the Admiralty a treasure trove of information on German naval equipment, operational methods, and tactics, which was of value in combat.

The importance of the information acquired from delayed and current decrypts was enhanced by the unusual organization within the Admiralty, which drew together informational fragments from all sources that might be useful in combat and applied them to the immediate circumstances prevailing at sea. This Operational Intelligence Centre (OIC) used large plotting boards to register the position, and trace the probable movements, of German submarines as well as surface warships and raiders. It derived its information from reconnaissance reports, Y traffic analysis, DHF fixes, and whatever cryptanalytic material it received from Bletchley via a direct liaison link provided by Cdr. Malcolm Saunders. On top of that, the Centre depended on the informed intuition of its staff. After the retirement of Paymaster Capt. Ernest Thring in early January 1941, the OIC Submarine Tracking Room was run by a gifted amateur turned reserve officer, Cdr. Roger Winn, later seconded by another amateur, Patrick Beesly. Their labors and successes always bordered on the mythic because they were required to produce conclusions about the enemy that went beyond the sum of the hard data they had at hand, and to do it for a naval milieu of which they had no direct experience. Winn was apparently appointed to the post because his name had been mixed up with that of a veteran submariner, but in actual fact neither Winn nor Beesly had any direct experience with submarines or combat at sea. Nonetheless, even in periods when Bletchley was nearly completely silent regarding German naval matters, the OIC had achieved some dramatic successes, including a highly creditable supporting role during the pursuit and final destruction of the *Bismarck* on 27 May 1941.[19]

Therefore it should come as no surprise that in late spring of 1941, two weeks after President Roosevelt established his new patrol system to the west of the 25-degree line, the British naval attaché in Washington, Rear Adm. H. Pott, would approach the American DNI, Capt. Alan G. Kirk, with some Admiralty "estimates" that Pott thought might be relevant to the American escort and patrol system used in the western Atlantic. The material in question, dated 30 April 1941, consisted of only a vague and general estimate of Axis submarine disposition, declaring that on the previous day sixteen German and five Italian submarines were thought to have been at sea. But even this seemed to be near gold to the intelligence-starved officers of the U.S. Navy Department, and when Pott inquired whether Kirk would prefer to receive such estimates weekly or daily, Kirk immediately replied "daily." Even more important, after Kirk relayed the material to Op-20-G together with the query as to whether that organization wanted to see this kind of British summary daily, the reply came back, "Cdm. Safford says yes!" Clearly, in that period, Op-20-G was so far at sea regarding German operations in the North Atlantic that the U.S. Navy was heavily dependent on Britain for any intelligence regarding the situation there.[20]

It is important to emphasize that this was not an instance of Ultra cooperation in the sense that information derived from currently decrypted naval Enigma was being circulated to the Americans. Pott's estimates were very general totals of enemy ships at sea, probably prepared by the OIC, at a time when Bletchley was *not* currently reading the German naval ciphers. But these reports were nonetheless highly sensitive documents that the British on no account wanted inadvertently leaked to the Germans, because the reports indicated the kind of achievements being chalked up by the OIC puzzle solvers. That the reports were sent unsolicited to Kirk, and then relayed on to an appreciative Op-20-G, meant that although a naval cryptanalytic partnership had not begun, the two navies were for the first time moving in that direction. Once again the basic principle had manifested itself that joint operations and common interests were more important than affection or secret machinations in pointing the two countries in the direction of a partnership on highly secret matters.

There are additional hints from the spring and early summer of 1941 that the Royal Navy wanted to get closer to Op-20-G, whose higher officers still needed considerable nursing and gentle care. Deep resentments lingered there among Safford and his colleagues, who believed that the British had been guilty of foul play at the time of the Sinkov mission, and who were always prone to suspicious thoughts about their transatlantic rivals. The arrival in Washington of an officer from Halifax who was cleared to liaise on "special intelligence" may have been part of a British reconciliation process. It is known that by mid-July 1941 the Admiralty had sent at least one most secret message directly to Safford, although it is not currently possible to determine the subject or authorship of this message.[21]

In any event, a far more favorable situation existed by June 1941 for sharing highly secret naval information than had existed five months earlier. The two Atlantic fleets were engaged in something very close to joint operations, and some secret information about the deployment of the navies of the "aggressor nations" was being shared. Then, just as this operational and informational relationship began, new achievements by Bletchley laid the basis for an even closer and more secret partnership.

The naval Enigma material that had been captured in March and May had by June 1941 become part of a high-priority effort by Bletchley to produce current readings of the German naval cipher. This attack was reinforced by a steady expansion of the bombe supply. By late June six bombes were working on various forms of the Enigma, and at least one was always reserved for use against the main German naval cipher. In addition, a broad and concerted attack was being made against an assortment of low- and medium-grade German codes and ciphers such as the air-sea rescue code, the lightship codes, and the principal German dockyards' cipher.

By carefully studying the results of this wide-ranging naval cryptanalytic work, Bletchley personnel learned a great deal about German code-and-cipher practice. This knowledge, in turn, revealed patterns in naval Enigma traffic that indicated where and when information now easily read in low-grade codes and ciphers was likely to be repeated in the high-grade German naval cipher, which was as yet unbroken.

The break-in potential of these cribs dramatically increased in value during May 1941, when it was discovered that the German naval meteorological cipher carried some weather reports that had originally come from U-boats in the Atlantic. These reports had first been sent by the U-boats in the main naval high-grade cipher; this provided Bletchley with the ultimate crib, because it arose from a fundamental flaw in German message transmission practice—the systematic repetition of the same information in a high- and low-grade cipher. The appearance of portions of the daily U-boat transmissions in low-grade weather messages gave Bletchley a head start in defeating each new high-grade cipher setting. Once the cryptanalysts learned of the telltale signs of the vulnerable weather portion of U-boat messages, they were well on the way to a quick daily break-in.

Bletchley skillfully combined the lessons learned from the successful captures of high-grade February–March traffic with the cribs revealed by the weather and other low-grade codes and ciphers, and with the mistakes made by the German cipher clerks (such as repeating standardized openings), so that from June 1941 the bombes were able to do their work with a very high level of effectiveness. Though Hut 8 had to find the daily setting anew every single day, the three-rotor naval Enigma was read currently through the last six months of 1941, and then for every single one of the remaining 1,200 days of the European war.[22]

As soon as the Admiralty began to receive the great outpourings of currently decrypted German naval Enigma from Bletchley, it grasped that the very nature of the intelligence side of the war against the German navy had been transformed. To regularize this radically new situation it abolished the old and irregularly used security designation "Hydro," which had been stamped on the occasional items of immediately useful operational information that had heretofore come from Bletchley. Henceforth all the naval intercepts would, for the first time, bear a new security classification stamp, "MOST SECRET ULTRA," and only those officers who came within a stringently regulated need-to-know category would be permitted to see this Ultra material.[23]

In the second half of June 1941, just as the Germans tore into western Russia and Japan prepared to plunge deeper into the heartland of the Far East by seizing all of French Indochina, Britain clearly had scored one of the most significant cryptanalytic successes of the entire war. The securing of current naval Enigma dramatically increased Britain's success rate against the U-boats and thereby made far safer the supply line from the United States to both Britain and the Soviet Union.

In June 1941, however, the Admiralty had not yet faced the question of how much of its newfound, and fragile, Ultra secret should be shared with its American naval partners in the battle of the North Atlantic. That problem would be dealt with only in tiny incremental steps during the final six months of 1941, and then with much greater urgency, in the new era produced by the great disaster of Pearl Harbor.

Phase II: From Operation Barbarossa to the Aftermath of Pearl Harbor (July 1941 to January 1942)

The six months that followed July 1941 have usually, and rightly, been seen as a steady progression toward two of the truly decisive events of World War II—the defeat of the German army before it reached Moscow and the Japanese attack on Pearl Harbor in December. These two occurrences, each in its peculiar way, bound together the Grand Alliance and set the stage for ultimate Allied victory.

To the ordinary mortals who lived through the last six months of 1941, Moscow and Pearl Harbor came as shocking surprises. Few people anywhere—certainly not the authorities in London and Washington—believed that Japan would have the fallacious gall to attempt such a surprise attack. Immediately after 7 December, the astonished U.S. Army leaders sought some solace and satisfaction from the fact that the German embassy in Washington had been as badly fooled by the Japanese "sneak attack" as they were. The all-pervading disbelief was what had made Admiral Yamamoto's strike possible, but after the event, when shock was transformed into anger and determination, the American people were instantly committed to all-out war, and that fact would ultimately doom the Axis powers.

The Soviet victory came as a comparable surprise, not only to the Germans but to virtually all army, navy, and political leaders in the West. Although most of the western press, as well as government spokesmen, had chorused their faith in the USSR—"anyone who marches against Hitler is our friend"—few western military officers actually believed that the Soviets could stop the Wehrmacht. The British and American records are laced with defeatist prophesies by generals and admirals, many of whom were strongly anti-Soviet with no confidence in Russia's capacity to fight a modern war, or Stalin's ability to rally his country. Therefore, although trickles of supplies went to the USSR from both Britain and the United States after 22 June 1941, such aid was not given high priority in the summer and autumn of 1941. The Soviet Union was not even cleared for Lend-Lease assistance until November, five months after the German attack, and just a month prior to the Red Army's triumph at Moscow.[24]

A comparable lack of urgency characterized the Anglo-American measures taken against Japan. No serious effort had been made to gauge the possible Japanese response to the crushing embargoes on strategic raw materials that the British, American, and Dutch governments imposed in July 1941. Even when the danger signs increased in late autumn, little was done to put the western forces in the Far East on a war footing, or to give them special training to cope with a Japanese offensive.

Racist belittling of Japan partly explains the Anglo-American blindness and indifference regarding the rising Far Eastern dangers, just as ideology played a part in the undervaluing of the capabilities of the USSR. But western timidity regarding these two zones also was caused by the fact that the British and American authorities had their eyes focused mainly on other areas and other dangers. London, North Africa, and the Middle East were still the primary worries, made more severe by the ominous possibility that after crushing the USSR, Hitler might smash into the Middle East from the north as well as the west, annihilating Britain's position there. London also looked on the Atlantic and the battle against the U-boat as a truly decisive campaign, because if Britain lost there, the flow of supplies from the Dominions and the United States would stop, and all would be lost.

In the American capital too, worries about the Pacific, as well as about the Middle East, usually took a backseat to concern about the U-boat and the threat its attack posed to Atlantic shipping, especially once Lend-Lease supplies began to be shipped to Britain. Most of the overt military and political moves made by the United States during this period occurred in the Atlantic rather than the Pacific. In early July 1941, the U.S. government extended eastward the policies that had begun with the occupation of Greenland: The line was now pushed on to include Iceland. In September, after the destroyer USS *Greer* was attacked by a U-boat off Iceland, Washington retaliated by ordering its patrol vessels in the western and central Atlantic to shoot German submarines on sight. When this policy resulted in the torpedoing of the USS *Kearney* in mid-October, and the sinking of the USS *Reuben James* two weeks later, President Roosevelt ordered the arming of all merchant ships engaged in the Atlantic crossing.

During this "undeclared war" between the U.S. Navy and the U-boats in the North Atlantic, America's president and Britain's prime minister met face to face. The meeting occurred appropriately aboard U.S. and Royal Navy ships in a quiet corner of the Atlantic off the coast of Newfoundland in August 1941. In addition to smoothing out details of aid, trade, and convoy relations between their two countries, the two leaders announced their support for the Atlantic Charter. This document, which set forth the Four Freedoms and promised no British or American postwar territorial annexations, would normally have been considered a statement of war aims, but because the United States had not formally declared war, it was advertised as a joint expression of views by close friends. Whatever the legalistic hedges, since the charter was signed in the North Atlantic where the two navies were fighting side by side, both the charter and the meeting itself emphasized how close the two countries had come to joint belligerency in this region.

Not everything went smoothly for this Atlantic partnership in the summer and autumn of 1941. The German cryptanalytic organization, the B Dienst, made things difficult by breaking into Naval Cipher Two during September 1941, continuing to read it on through January 1942. In addition, powerful currents of American opinion indicated desperate fear that President Roosevelt was courting war in the Atlantic, and more than a few government officials also believed that the heavy emphasis on Europe was leaving America dangerously vulnerable in the Pacific. When the one-year selective service bill came up for renewal by Congress during August 1941, it cleared the House of Representatives by only a single vote—an obvious indication that, just three-and-a-half months prior to Pearl Harbor, the American national defense posture was still far from universally popular across the United States.

The policymakers in Washington nonetheless continued to cling to their national-defense vision emphasizing Atlantic defense and aid to Britain. Precautionary measures in the Pacific were not taken, opening the way for the Pearl Harbor disaster. Regarding cryptanalysis, little progress was made toward comprehensive and effective Anglo-American cooperation in the Pacific during this critical period. Though a U.S. Army observer was added to the U.S. delegation in Singapore by at least October 1941, no significant headway against Japanese army or air force code-and-cipher systems had been made by either country, and the American signals intelligence personnel working in the Philippines were not even attempting to intercept Japanese army and air force radio traffic.[25]

Equally serious was the lack of any U.S Army, or Army Air Corps, cryptanalytic unit in the Hawaiian Islands prior to the Japanese attack, and the failure of the U.S. Navy to keep the local army commander, General Walter Short, abreast of the cryptanalytic situation regarding the Japanese fleet. Indeed, even a week *after* the attack on Pearl Harbor, the adjutant general in Washington refused Short's request that an army cryptanalytic unit be stationed in Hawaii, citing a shortage of personnel and the fact that the army was still only breaking the Purple cipher and had made no headway against any Japanese army or air force cryptographic system. The War Department then advised Short that he should liaise with the navy's "cryptanalytic section now operational at Pearl Harbor" because "navy traffic is of most value to [the] Hawaiian Department." But it was not until 1 February 1942, seven weeks after the Japanese attack, that the American army command in Hawaii finally established a liaison arrangement with its naval counterpart regarding cryptanalytic matters.[26]

These pre–Pearl Harbor deficiencies had been compounded by the fact that British and American rivalries in the region remained strong. Washington was cautious about being identified with "British colonialism." London was so fearful of American encroachment that in September 1941 the British Dominion's Office seemingly warned the Australian authorities not to give information from most secret sources to Americans, because the British government wanted to control the flow through the Far East Combined Intelligence Bureau in Singapore.[27]

For its part, Washington was so reserved that it even balked at establishing radio communications between the armed forces of the two countries. On 24 October 1941 London proposed that an emergency transmission network be created in the Far East and Pacific area, to make possible communication between British and American army commanders as well as communications linking the two armies with London and Washington. The War Department strongly rejected the proposal a month later—just thirty days before Pearl Harbor—on the grounds that any direct contact between American armed forces and London was undesirable. In any event, since the U.S. Army in the Far East had no rapid communication system of its own, outside the Philippines, the War Department concluded that there was surely no reason to arrange one with the British. This negative and blind response, coming on the eve of Pearl Harbor, foretold much of the story of that disaster. The Anglo-American intelligence preparations in the Pacific were, if not a shambles, at least far removed from efficiency, undercutting the argument of those who believe that a conspiracy in high places would have been required to enable the Japanese to succeed at Pearl Harbor.[28]

Neither Washington nor London, much less Singapore or Pearl Harbor, was prepared for the boldness of the Japanese move on 7 December. The president even confided to the British ambassador on 6 December that he was not as convinced as the secretary of state that the Japanese were about to undertake an aggressive action somewhere in the Far East. But even if the president and all of his aides had been more alert to the danger, the Anglo-American governments had failed to create the broad, deep, and well-coordinated intelligence and detection screen necessary to foil the attack. A sobering corrective to the widely held belief that Pearl Harbor must have been the result of treachery is the fact that one year *following* the attack, and six months after the American victory at Midway, U.S. Navy intelligence again completely lost the Japanese fleet. Secretary of the Navy Frank Knox told Henry Stimson and Cordell Hull on 29 December 1942 that "the Japanese main fleet had disappeared . . . our Navy didn't know where it was." If that could happen in the Pacific under the battle-hardening conditions of late 1942, anything was surely possible in the intelligence and command chaos of 1941![29]

The muddle that prevailed in the Pacific during the last six to twelve months before the United States was forced into the war also explains why in 1941 positive moves toward Anglo-American cryptanalytic cooperation had to come in the Atlantic rather than the Pacific. The increasingly active role played by American forces in the Battle of the Atlantic from July to December 1941 took place at a time when Bletchley was frequently producing a current daily decryption of much of the U-boat radio traffic, and other agencies of the British government were gaining additional valuable information from taps on the conversations of German U-boat crews who had been captured. From the beginning of this period the procedure was already in place for the daily reports of the Submarine Tracking Room to be sent to the American Naval Mission in London for relay to the Navy Department in Washington. Captain R. M. Wraugham oversaw this process for the Admiralty, including relations with the U.S. Naval Observer Group. No significant change occurred in this system during the period, although it is possible that occasional U-boat location messages were also passed to the Navy Department by the British Admiralty Mission in Washington.[30]

The initial messages sent from London—those for July 1941—seem to have been quite patchy, perhaps because the Submarine Tracking Room was having startup troubles while learning to integrate the new current Ultra flow with its more traditional forms of intelligence on the U-boats, such as "Y" information and aerial reconnaissance. But the spasmodic flow of messages also may have been due to division and indecisiveness in Whitehall. Again, "C" opposed giving the Americans Ultra in any form, even though they were now participating in the Battle of the Atlantic, and time may have been required to overcome Menzies' opposition. On some days during July only one or two U-boats appeared on the U.S. Navy's daily situation maps for the Atlantic, while on immediately adjacent days the number of located German submarines jumped to between ten and fifteen. In August 1941 the daily situation maps began by showing six or seven submarines, and then rose steadily to fifteen to seventeen by midmonth, and to thirty to forty by month's end.[31]

As if to make certain that there should be no doubt that this detailed and increasingly comprehensive plot of U-boats in the Atlantic originated from the British Submarine Tracking Room, a note on the map of 25 August 1941 said, "Submarine position as estimated by Admiralty for 24 August."[32] The U.S. Navy's "U Boat Estimate and Situation Reports" for autumn 1941 contain additional confirming notes. That of 6 October 1941 said regarding four submarines located off Brest, "estimated by the British and are doubtful," whereas that of 16 November was headed "Admiralty U Boat estimate."[33] Buried in the records of the Pearl Harbor hearings is a complete set of British U-boat estimates for the Atlantic covering the months of November and December 1941, each report headed "ALUSNA [American Naval Mission] LONDON to OPNAV [Chief of Naval Operations] Washington."[34]

Therefore the British official *History of British Intelligence in the Second World War* is right on target when it states that in September 1941 the U.S. Navy was routing and rerouting convoys in the western Atlantic on the basis of information supplied by the Admiralty. The U.S. Navy also was acting on the basis of such information in August, and perhaps as early as July 1941.[35] It must be noted, however, that none of the available reports from the Admiralty to the U.S. Navy contained raw German U-boat messages. They were simply the daily locational plots of German submarine positions. When they are compared with an OIC report of the "U Boat situation on 15 December 1941," the earliest such report seemingly available in open records, the form and content are nearly identical.[36]

Even at the time, great efforts were made to disguise the source of the detailed information which actually had been supplied by the Submarine Tracking Room. In order to help conceal the source, a note in the U.S. Navy's "Eastern Sea Frontier War Diary" for July 1942 stated that "the British had developed the use of RDF [radio direction finding] to such an extent that the Admiralty was able to furnish daily reports of submarine movements to the U.S. Navy Department in Washington even before our entry into the war."[37] With all due respect to RDF, which did play an important role in the Submarine Tracking Room's successes, along with air reconnaissance and other intelligence sources, the handful of navy individuals in the know on both sides of the Atlantic were aware in late 1941 that much of the credit belonged to Ultra. On occasion, even on the U.S. Navy operational maps, a slipup would occur, revealing that the information in the submarine plots went beyond anything that possibly could have been provided by traditional intelligence sources. A map for 18 September 1941 contained a penciled-in square east of Greenland with a note: "Estimated 10 subs *will* [italics added] operate in this area." Obviously, such a detailed reference to enemy intentions points directly to cryptanalysis as the only possible source.[38]

This disguised but highly important cooperation between Britain and the United States regarding most secret intelligence in the U-boat war inevitably helped tuck the Americans into other corners of British and Dominion secret activities. In October 1941 the U.S. military attaché in London noted that a dispatch he was sending to Washington regarding the Russian campaign contained information from the "British Intercept Service," and therefore needed to be kept secret "even from the British Mission." In November 1941 the U.S. Army received copies of the British "K" administrative code, which Royal Navy vessels used to identify themselves to friendly ships and planes, and henceforth U.S. Army Air Corps planes were able to provide more efficient close-in support in antisubmarine operations.[39] In the same month, the Canadian government, which bore much of the convoy-protection responsibility in the western Atlantic, offered American authorities "free access" to the results of Canadian monitoring activities. This material seems to have consisted mainly of RDF bearings, but at least some information on German clandestine activities in the Western Hemisphere was also included.[40]

A far more significant move toward full, high-level, cryptanalytic cooperation between the United States and the British Commonwealth occurred on 3 July 1941, when American authorities were informed that the first senior representative of Bletchley Park would be coming to Ottawa and Washington for an extended visit. The visitor was the director of Bletchley, Cdr. Alistair Denniston, who arrived on 10 August 1941, perhaps symbolically, in light of the increased cooperation between Britain and the United States, aboard an airplane of the U.S. Army Air Corps. Denniston spent 10–23 August in the United States, splitting his time between Washington and New York, followed by two weeks in Canada for observation and staff meetings, and another quick visit to New York squeezed in at the end of August.[41]

The top American code-and-cipher men were pleased to discover that Denniston was not only a highly experienced cryptanalyst but a friendly man, for whom personal relations and mutual trust were all-important. During his visit to Washington, although no formal deals were made between Bletchley and U.S. Army SIS or Op-20-G, a good measure of professional respect was produced and warm personal bonds were created, especially between Denniston and Friedman. At one point during the visit, Friedman drove Denniston to New York in his own car. This personal and professional bonding lasted well beyond the visit and even the end of World War II. Denniston was surely right when he wrote to Friedman in June 1945, "I like to think that I, the first to visit you, had a hand in founding an efficient and successful cooperation which had fine results in every field of operation."[42]

Indeed, though Denniston seems to have left America harboring personal doubts about the war readiness of the United States, his visit may well have allayed some of the worst suspicions and resentments regarding arrogant and perfidious Albion that had long boiled in Op-20-G and various corners of Army SIS. In this same period, isolated pieces of intelligence derived from Ultra were occasionally slipped to high American officials, and by October 1941 the U.S. Army had acquired enough information about the British "Y" service to prepare a secret report describing its major features. These instances of British openhandedness undoubtedly helped create increased American confidence in the cryptanalytic policies and performance of the United Kingdom, but it must be underscored once again that Ultra transmissions to the United States were very rare events in late 1941.[43] Wild tales of wholesale handouts from Bletchley during the pre–Pearl Harbor era are definitely false, and it is also incorrect to view every British item of information from secret sources that came to the United States as ipso facto an Ultra product, because material ranging from photoreconnaissance to agent reports was also handled with high security. The only wrapped-up, and generously blended, Ultra definitely being provided regularly during the last half of 1941 was the U-boat information from the OIC, and only a tiny circle of high-level U.S. Navy officers saw that.

It is also understandable why the British were so reluctant to provide a bountiful supply of Ultra information to the Americans during 1941. The need-to-know principle, i.e., that if someone did not require a piece of information to perform assigned duties successfully, then it should be denied to them on security grounds, indicated that aside from the U-boat war it wasn't operationally necessary, and on the political front Britain was so weak and vulnerable compared to the United States that it was in no position to fritter away its most valuable assets without securing some important quid pro quo. Whitehall therefore saw no reason to break with the traditional principle that one held tight to one's own intelligence assets. The appalling lack of security and war readiness that prevailed in Washington—and was played out every day before the eyes of British, as well as Japanese, German, and Italian observers—merely intensified Whitehall's determination to hold fast to its valuable secrets. Even American civilian officials frequently were shocked by the easygoing attitude of the American armed services. A State Department report of 7 July 1941, surveying the lax security arrangements in the War Department, summed up the entire shameful situation in a single incident. After citing the chronic inadequacy of the War Department's nighttime alert system, the author of the report noted a recent occasion when a State Department official found the War Department duty officer "by a remarkable feat of guessing, in a locker room of the Columbia Country Club, although persons at his home did not know where he was other than that he might be playing golf somewhere."[44]

A powerful nation floating along in this relaxed condition during the middle phase of a world war was not only a poor candidate to be a cryptanalytic partner, it was also asking for a good, sharp shock. That jolt came, of course, in the form of the Japanese attack on Pearl Harbor on 7 December, followed by declarations of war on the United States by Hitler and Mussolini. By the second week of December, America suddenly found itself in a two-front, highly technical war, allied with China, Britain, and the Soviet Union against Germany, Italy, and

Japan (though Moscow did not enter the Pacific war until the late summer of 1945).

Devastating defeats for the western powers quickly followed in the Far East. Singapore fell in February, the Dutch East Indies and Rangoon surrendered in March, and the Burma Road into China was cut in the same month. Americans received some solace from the fact that they held out longer than the others—with Bataan not falling until April 1942 and Corregidor in May—and because Jimmy Doolittle managed to tweak the nose of the Japanese a bit with his mid-April raid on Tokyo.

The response of the American people to these shocking, and generally sobering, events was a great upswing of patriotism and a new-found willingness to sacrifice in order to expand the armed might of the United States and help bring Allied victory as quickly as possible. The U.S. government did its best to tighten security and take on the appearance of a serious modern military power, while trying to hold the line as much as possible in the Pacific and Atlantic, and drastically expanding the size of its armed forces and the production of war material.

The British public's response to Japan's advance across the Far East was much more measured. The defeats in the Pacific were regrettable and embarrassing, but not as threatening as those inflicted by Hitler. Since the process that had produced the defeats in the Far East had also brought the United States into the war and drastically expanded American production, for most Britons the trade-off seemed a reasonable bargain—except for the Japanese treatment of British prisoners, which remained a matter of unusually deep resentment for a generation. Churchill allegedly mumbled a small prayer of thanks after Pearl Harbor and then, accompanied by his top military and civilian colleagues, quickly journeyed to Washington to hammer out joint strategic decisions and to link together as closely as possible the war production and military organizations of Britain and the United States.

The resulting Arcadia Conference, held in Washington from 22 December 1941 to 14 January 1942, took place in an atmosphere both confusing and threatening. The HMS *Repulse* and the HMS *Prince of Wales* had been lost to the Japanese before Churchill left London, and the defense of Malaya began to crumble while he was in Washington. The British attack in the Western Desert was then moving forward quite successfully and took El Agheila, but, once again, the Western Desert

Force had suffered high equipment losses, and a week after Arcadia ended, Rommel drove east once more, wiping out the British gains. Only in the USSR were the Allies clearly and decisively triumphant: The Red Army had not only stopped the Panzers before Moscow but had immediately launched a winter counteroffensive that drove the battered and frozen German units far to the west of the Soviet capital.

Neither the victorious Soviets nor the battered Chinese were present at Arcadia, however, so the British and the Americans were able to make their plans and arrangements with a minimum of disagreement or rancor. The basic strategic decision of the conference was that of "Europe first," with the Pacific once again relegated to second place, even though the Japanese were just getting into their full offensive stride. The conferees went on to propose and discuss various scenarios for invading the European continent, all of which would be canceled during the remainder of 1942 and on through 1943.

The "Europe first" strategy was a British proposal. Churchill and his aides won that point and thereby carried the United States into a system of joint strategic planning. One of the most important results of this development was that the American War and Navy departments were compelled for the first time to create a mechanism for preparing interservice position papers on strategic, supply, and command matters, to balance those produced by the British Chiefs of Staff Committee. The U.S. conference delegation met this problem by creating the Joint Chiefs of Staff (JCS), an arrangement that subsequently was made official and permanent by presidential order. The JCS henceforth acted as the centralizing instrument for American army-navy policy-making. Although the independence of the U.S. Army and U.S. Navy was not thereby ended, or in most day-to-day matters even affected, the JCS did provide a means through which common solutions could be found to common problems, and some of the suicidal interservice rivalry that had seriously weakened American military power could be blunted.

Once the JCS was in place, it was a simple matter to go on and create a Combined Chiefs of Staff (CCS), so the military leaders of the United States and Britain could create a series of consensus agreements necessary for joint action. Since much of the critical work of the CCS was to be focused on overall strategic planning, and establishment of the production and manpower programs to make the plans fulfillable, it was decided at Arcadia that the CCS would be sited in Washington with the Joint Staff Mission, now under Field Marshal Sir John Dill, acting as the proxy equivalent of the British Chiefs of Staff Committee.

The creation of the JCS and the CCS system was vitally important for the future development of Anglo-American cryptanalytic cooperation, although the image of hierarchical efficiency merely papered over many bitter rivalries between, and within, the two countries. For the first time the military chiefs of the two nations had a mechanism through which they could work together on a regular basis, and in the CCS they could also take each other's measure, gradually building up confidence while creating combined committees to facilitate their collective work. At the same time, the creation of a Joint Chiefs of Staff in the United States would make a permanent change in Washington; the JCS ultimately would be a central element in the structure of the postwar national security system.

Among the most important of the auxiliary organizations created by the JCS was an American Joint Intelligence Committee in which the strategic intelligence of the two U.S. services could be hammered into an American consensus. Beyond the JICs of America and Britain, a Combined Intelligence Committee (CIC) was also established, which sought to reconcile the intelligence conclusions that each country's JIC had prepared regarding important strategic questions. Here again, these innovations of early 1942, which were intended to facilitate cooperation with Britain, helped provide the U.S. government with an instrument useful for superpower status, because the JIC would ultimately be one of the organizations that evolved into the Central Intelligence Group (CIG) and then the National Security Council (NSC) after 1945.

But whatever the long-term significance of these developments, one can easily overemphasize the effectiveness and efficiency of the system in the early 1940s, for the JICs and the CIC were never as strong or as important in either country as they appeared to be in the organizational charts. The joint intelligence structures limited the damage caused by interagency rivalry and made possible consensus on some important issues, but these did not become all-powerful intelligence supremos, because the individual information-collection agencies in the two countries—such as MI 6, the State Department, and the military intelligence departments—continued to fight for their points of view both outside and inside the JICs.

While struggling to support their respective intelligence estimates, both the British and American JICs had to use the best possible intelligence they could find. Inevitably disagreements between them arose in the CIC, which led to questions about the intelligence data base supporting their respective positions on issues ranging from enemy intentions to the quantity of men and material Germany or Japan would be able to make available at any particular time and place. This, in turn, would make it impossible for Britain or America to keep completely secret the intelligence sources. They needed to reveal these sources in order to win inter-Allied arguments for themselves. These committees therefore indirectly spawned a mechanism that sooner or later would require the sharing of cryptanalytic information, at least to the degree that such information bore on strategic policy questions.

In addition, it is highly possible, as some have suggested, that during the Arcadia Conference Winston Churchill revealed the broad range of the Ultra secret to the president. It is definitely clear, in the words of Churchill written to the president a month after Arcadia, that "one night when we talked late," the two leaders had engaged in an extended discussion of ciphers and cipher security. In that context a general discussion of Ultra and Magic would have been difficult to avoid. But even if, by some peculiar chance, the two leaders managed to dodge full cryptanalytic frankness on that occasion, powerful historical forces ranging from the disaster in the Far East to Arcadia, and then on to the creation of the JCS and CCS systems, were pushing the American services and Bletchley Park toward the necessity of changing the ways they dealt with cryptanalysis, and with each other.[45]

Of the American services, the U.S. Navy was the most resistant to overall reform, even though it had suffered the greatest damage from Japan's successful surprise attack. Op-20-G clung to its existing position in the naval organizational setup and continued to maintain its chief "overseas" outpost at Pearl Harbor. In the face of the Japanese advance, Op-20-G's Philippines units had to be evacuated to Australia, but no fundamental reorganization resulted from this move, and navy and army cryptanalytic activities in the region remained hermetically sealed from each other. In the Atlantic, the U.S. Navy was satisfied for the moment to receive whatever wrapped-up U-boat intelligence it could obtain from the Admiralty, and it continued the cumbersome system of using the Naval Observer's Office in London as the conduit through which these reports reached the Navy Department. Furthermore, the U.S. Navy still refused to curtail the varied cryptanalytic activities of its close associates in the Coast Guard who continued to intercept and decipher "clandestine" traffic in the Western Hemisphere outside the United States.[46]

The U.S. Army, on the other hand, initiated more extensive cryptanalytic reforms shortly after the end of the Arcadia Conference. During much of 1941 a bizarre interservice compromise had prevailed regarding the Magic traffic, with Op-20-G and Army SIS having responsibility on alternate days for the preparation of the Magic decrypts. By early 1942 all parties came to agree that the U.S. Army would henceforth be the sole custodian of the Magic intercepts. On 25 January Cdr. Joseph Redman of Op-20-G and Col. Frank Bullock of SIS made an arrangement whereby the army would do the decryption and Naval Intelligence would receive copies of "all [Magic] messages of interest to the Navy."[47]

On 18 January 1942 Secretary of War Stimson gave the army reform process another forward push by charging a legal acquaintance from New York, Mr. (later Colonel) Alfred McCormack, with the task of carrying through an investigation of the army's procedures for handling cryptanalytic intelligence. McCormack began work immediately, but due to the scale and significance of the intelligence failure that had caused Pearl Harbor, the study required a number of months to complete. In the interim, the army limped along with a provisional arrangement whereby SIS continued to break and translate the Magic messages, while G-2 and the army chief of staff's office bore the responsibility for evaluating the finished texts, as well as circulating them to appropriate "consumers." The G-2 side of this operation was in especially good hands at this moment: Gen. Raymond E. Lee, now acting G-2, brought to the post extensive experience in handling highly secret material which he had acquired during his tenure as American military attaché in London.[48]

While these army reform plans were being developed, few immediate changes could be made in the inefficient and dawdling methods used to collect and process army intelligence, or to lessen the endemic interservice and interdepartmental rivalries. At least as late as January 1942, J. Edgar Hoover still had not delivered on his July 1941 promise to provide the army with Vichy cipher material acquired by the FBI. For its part, even after Pearl Harbor, the army continued to oppose sharing its cryptographic information (the codes and ciphers used by the U.S. Army) with anyone inside or outside the American government. The Signal Corps still maintained that its code-and-cipher system was "at least equally good, if not better, than those used by the British," and it refused to enter into code-making cooperation with the British army or the U.S. Navy, which meant, to say the least, that dubious prospects existed for joint operations.[49]

These American territorial difficulties were compounded by the president's penchant for loose administrative procedures. Franklin Roosevelt was notoriously slow to act in jurisdictional conflicts, and his blithe disregard for orderly administrative methods frequently made matters worse. At the end of December 1941, for example, Roosevelt was compelled to write a general letter to G-2, ONI, the State Department, and other members of his official family, explaining that they should disregard a recent order relating to FBI counterintelligence operations in South America, because he had signed the confidential directive "without examination." The president then ordered his officials to "meet together and straighten out this program" and then advise him on "whatever is necessary by way of an amended order."[50]

Pearl Harbor obviously had not provided a sharp enough knock to clean up all the peacetime inefficiencies of the American intelligence organizations, or the White House, and the cousins across the Atlantic were neither impressed nor amused. The situation at Bletchley and in the British service intelligence departments in the aftermath of Pearl Harbor was, however, also far from ideal. The Park still enjoyed its mastery of the German naval Enigma, although there were worrisome indications throughout December 1941 that the German navy was preparing to go over to a four-rotor Enigma, which would pose formidable problems. There seemed no immediate danger that Red or the German secondary codes and ciphers were about to be altered, but the matter of the naval Enigma was of utmost concern, not only because of its importance to the lifeline, but because no headway had yet been made against the German army ciphers. Bletchley had only sixteen three-wheel bombes at the time, and only twelve of them could be kept on line at any given moment. Its personnel and equipment resources were therefore stretched to the limit, and on top of all these stresses, a more extensive attack on Japanese army, air force, and navy codes and ciphers now had to be made.

The shortages, problems, and frustrations combined in early 1942 to produce a radical alteration of the command structure at Bletchley. In late October 1941, two months after Commander Denniston had returned from the United States, the top technical and scientific men at Bletchley, led by Alan Turing and Gordon Welchman, revolted. Four of them wrote a letter direct to the prime minister on 31 October chronicling the failings of Bletchley's administration in not recruiting sufficient personnel or exploiting the breaches that the scientists and analysts were making in Germany's code-and-cipher system. The thousand-word letter listed three main areas where shortages of personnel were causing dangerous bottlenecks—delay in breaking navy Enigma keys, inability to process Luftwaffe "Light Blue" Enigma from North Africa, and slowdowns in the testing of bombes. All of these problems were caused, the letter asserted, by the unnecessary obstacles being put in the way of the cipher-breaking team by the higher-ups at Bletchley.[51]

The prime minister reacted quickly, ordering General Ismay on the following day to make certain that Bletchley had all the staff and equipment it needed. By 18 November 1941 sufficient reforms had been introduced so that even though not all the changes were as yet complete, "C" could report to the prime minister that Bletchley's requirements were being quickly met.

Yet having the shortcomings of Bletchley's administrators laid before the prime minister reflected badly on everyone supervising Bletchley. Indeed, "C" rebuked Welchman for having written the letter. Once it had been done, however, only a general shake-up could clear the air and allow both the Park and "C" to start again with a cleaner slate. In early 1942, therefore, Commander Denniston, the longtime chief of GC & CS, was removed from his post. Despite the fact that Bletchley had been his child, the British wartime code- and cipher-breaking enterprise had in fact gotten beyond him. Denniston was a mediocre administrator, light years behind the modern world of corporate management. Everything at Bletchley had been arranged on a personal basis through a network of friends and acquaintances, with security considerations always given top priority. Even the billeting officer at Bletchley had been appointed to the post because she was Denniston's neighbor and because he prized her efficiency and discretion.

As a consolation prize for Denniston's achievements and long years of service, he was allowed to direct the diplomatic deciphering section of GC & CS, which was detached from Bletchley and set up at a separate site on Berkeley Street in London. This division of British cryptanalytic work, although not a mortal blow, did lessen the strict centralization that had been one of the most positive features of the Bletchley system. The cover story—that Denniston had left Bletchley to take up his new post because of ill health—also failed to come off without a hitch. For even though he might have appeared outwardly relieved that the great burden of responsibility had been removed from his shoulders, Denniston was inwardly disappointed and embittered. Although he was the only top Bletchley official who had visited the American cryptanalysts, Denniston would never again play an important role in cryptanalytic policy matters, including the vital question of Anglo-American cryptanalytic relations.[52]

This turn of events may have adversely affected the prospects for full Anglo-American cryptanalytic cooperation in early 1942, but before many months had passed, Denniston's successor at Bletchley would show himself equally fond of the United States and highly adept at dealing with American officials. Sir Edward Travis was a professional naval specialist without university training. Although he too was a veteran of Room 40, he was not basically a cryptanalyst, having served the bulk of his career developing codes and ciphers for the Royal Navy. He had only slightly more high-tech orientation than Denniston, but Travis had far more modern managerial experience, having worked with many outside firms, including the post office, while he helped direct the Royal Navy's transition from hand-code books to machine ciphers. As director of Bletchley, Travis was in charge of British code-and-cipher making, as well as breaking, so he still had many colleagues from his code-making days close at hand.[53]

The new director did not immediately quiet all complaints among the cryptanalysts and intelligence specialists, many of whom still felt that Bletchley's management was slow to meet their needs. But nearly everyone at Bletchley considered Travis a managerial improvement, and a rather open and jolly fellow in the bargain. He was unafraid of competent men, even when they outranked him, as was the case with one of his closest assistants, Edward Hastings, who, by the end of the war, was a regular Royal Navy captain. Travis also had a tough streak in his character, which inclined Gordon Welchman to list him among "the Bulldog breed." He was also unpretentious; Welchman reports that on one occasion when a memo had been sent to Travis calling for a drastic increase of equipment and personnel to cope with the explosion of German Enigma traffic, all that came back from the director's office was the first page of the memo with "BALLS" scrawled across it in the brown ink Travis always used.[54] When Travis began to make trips to Washington, beginning in the latter half of 1942, American officials were generally pleased with him, and he too would establish intimate friendships with American cryptanalysts that lasted well beyond the war.

The appointment of Travis as director of Bletchley had an additional important side effect that would directly facilitate closer Anglo-American cryptanalytic cooperation. Since Travis was not a cryptanalyst, it was essential that other high officials with cryptanalytic experience be used to deal at home and abroad with delicate liaison matters regarding code-and-cipher breaking. Travis' administrative deputy, Nigel de Grey, although very efficient, could not play this role. De Grey had been in Room 40 during World War I and in fact had played a part in the breaking of the Zimmermann telegram, which the British government used so deftly to help lever the United States into war in 1917. Perhaps the controversial nature of the Zimmermann transaction, as well as de Grey's unusual appearance—five feet tall, one hundred pounds, and inclined to wear an opera cloak—ruled him out as a suitable candidate for cryptanalytic liaison duties with the United States. The choice therefore fell on the shoulders of Capt. Edward Hastings, one of the few regular naval officers at Bletchley, and a man with long service in "secret matters."

Hastings, efficient and knowledgeable, was given the assignment of serving as Bletchley's representative on the Joint Staff Mission in Washington from late 1941 to late 1943. But only one member of Bletchley's liaison team in 1942–43 was so popular with the Americans that he could be said to have contributed personally to the ultimate creation of the most secret special relationship. Brigadier John Tiltman, who directed naval code-and-cipher breaking at Bletchley, was a cheerful and agreeable man, happily blending a forthcoming personality with a complete devotion to cryptanalysis. On one level he was the epitome of the "back-room" man, for he had done brilliant pioneering work on Japanese and other military codes, receiving an OBE (Order of British Empire) in 1930, and continued to do significant code- and cipher-breaking work throughout World War II as well as perform administrative and liaison duties. An authentic puzzle solver in the Friedman mold, like so many of the British and American cryptanalysts of his generation, Tiltman was neither a theoretical mathematician nor a machine-cipher man. Tall, rangy, equally impressive when attired in his regimental kilts (King's Own Scottish Borderers) or the unconventional mixture of army and civilian dress that he favored when out of the limelight, Tiltman's ability and charm won him universal respect and affection. To the Americans who dealt with him during his frequent journeys to Washington in the years 1942 to 1945, he was the embodiment of British eccentric brilliance, and most of them took him to heart. Tiltman reciprocated their affection and warm feelings. After the war he put his talents at the service of the United States, spending the last fifteen years of his professional life in American employ, retiring to, and dying in, America.[55]

With a new governing team at Bletchley that would soon show itself to be rather philo-American, and with Pearl Harbor not only bringing the United States into the war but making Britain and America partners in adversity in the Far East, one might have expected to see signs in Whitehall of a greater readiness to open up the cryptanalytic doors to the United States. But in fact, during the month of December and into early January 1942, British higher officialdom actually turned in precisely the opposite direction. This time the documentary record is crystal clear regarding both the process by which close Anglo-American cryptanalytic cooperation was rejected by the British government and the identity of the most important Whitehall nay sayers. The opposition to sharing with the Americans did not come from Bletchley Park, where a number of voices seem to have been raised in favor of openhandedness, including, most likely, that of Travis. The Foreign Office also receives a clean bill of health. The individuals who firmly, even vehemently, opposed increasing the flow of Ultra or Ultra-based summaries to the United States were Sir Stewart Menzies, "C," and the service department intelligence heads, especially Admiral Godfrey, the DNI.

A week prior to Pearl Harbor, the American chief of Naval Operations, Admiral Stark, raised the possibility of increased cryptanalytic cooperation with the head of the Joint Staff Mission, Adm. Sir Charles

Little. At approximately the same time, Admiral Noyes, the U.S. Navy's director of communications, raised the same point with Captain Hastings, who relayed the request to "C." The point at issue, in the words of Admiral Little, was that:

> The Navy Department has got it into their heads that we are not playing quite square in regard to the exchange of information regarding Special Intelligence. . . . Their contention is that whereas they have exchanged all the information they have regarding Japanese codes with us, we have not done the same in regard to our cryptographic [cryptanalytic] work in the case of the German codes.

Admiral Little then put the ball in the Admiralty's court by cabling to the First Sea Lord Stark's view that Anglo-American cooperation on naval cryptanalysis should be increased, along with the observation that, although he knew this was "a very difficult matter for you to decide," if the wishes of the American navy could be met, Little believed that it would "probably pay us in other directions."[56]

The first important response in Whitehall to this initiative came from the DNI, Admiral Godfrey, twelve days after the Japanese attack on Pearl Harbor. According to Godfrey, the American chief of Naval Operations was "being given all Special Intelligence which can possibly be of any use or interest to him," by which Godfrey presumably meant the Ultra material wrapped up in OIC reports regarding U-boat deployment in the Atlantic. Godfrey also was not prepared to concede that the Americans had been unfairly treated in the matter of cryptanalytic exchanges. He contended that, as indicated above, when "the American officers were over here" (presumably the Sinkov mission) they had been told "of all our methods and shown our machines." "Our methods are not adaptable to them," Godfrey added, because "they have not got our machines." The DNI then topped off this negative and inaccurate tour de force with the cheerful observation that "the American cryptographers consider that they can achieve the same results by different methods and in order to try this out, they were supplied in October [following Denniston's visit] with information by G.C. & C.S."[57]

All told, the DNI's defense of the status quo and rejection of more complete exchange with the United States were at the very least flawed, if not completely disingenuous. Sinkov and his colleagues had not been shown a bombe or told anything approximating "all" there was to know about Bletchley's cryptanalytic methods. It was true that because full Anglo-American cryptanalytic cooperation had been blocked by the British authorities, the U.S. Navy was preparing to go it alone against the Enigma. It is also likely that some technical information about the Enigma had been sent from Bletchley to Op-20-G by mid-December 1941. But the tone of Godfrey's memorandum is that of a person determined to keep the door firmly closed. The visitor who had surveyed the peacetime United States in the spring of 1941, and returned to London with a dreary picture of the American intelligence system, was apparently not willing to change his view even after Pearl Harbor had brought the United States into the war as a close ally of Great Britain.

Ten days later, when the issue was raised in the Chiefs of Staff Committee, the result was almost precisely the same. The secretary of the British JIC, Cavendish Bentinck, of the Foreign Office (one of only two Foreign Office officials on the Ultra list), asked the Chiefs of Staff for instructions on the straightforward question of the degree to which U.S. service representatives "should be informed of our methods of acquiring intelligence." Brigadier Sir Stewart Menzies, "C," immediately declared "that he was strongly opposed to making any further revelations of our most secret sources of intelligence," adding that "this did not apply to the Far Eastern Theatre where we are working in closest touch with the Americans."

The Chiefs of Staff followed "C" 's lead and decided, as Godfrey too had recommended, that "for the time being our sources of intelligence should not be divulged to the Americans." This decision, coming as it did in the immediate aftermath of Pearl Harbor, might easily have been justified on the grounds that that incident had proved the shortcomings of the American intelligence system. It is also true that there was as yet no clear evidence that Pearl Harbor would bring sharp improvements in American security measures. And in conformity with the need-to-know principle, there was still no urgent operational reason to provide more most secret intelligence to the Americans aside from the wrapped-up Ultra in the Atlantic OIC reports, and the bits of special intelligence passing in and out of the Combined Bureau in Singapore.[58]

In any event, the traditional view, which cautioned that one held onto one's own intelligence information as tightly as possible and shared secret political and military assets only when it paid one to do so, was alive and well in London. Long-held worries about the threat to Britain posed by the rise of the western colossus had been intensified by America's post–Pearl Harbor rush into total mobilization. This combination led, to appropriate Christopher Thorne's phrase, to Britain and the United States becoming merely "allies of a kind." The British Chiefs of Staff therefore put caution, security, and what they saw as self-interest first. Two days before Churchill arrived in Washington for the Arcadia Conference, they passed up the opportunity provided by Pearl Harbor and Arcadia for a fresh start on cryptanalysis.

Another nine months of war, featuring numerous Allied losses and defeats, would pass before the British government would take fate by the throat and offer to provide the Americans with the first piece in a kaleidoscope of partial-sharing agreements that ultimately would combine to form the most secret special relationship.

CHAPTER FIVE
Toward the Navy
Cryptanalytic Agreement

American entry into the war did not bring an immediate reversal of fortune for the armed forces of the Allies any more than it produced a quick union of British and American cryptanalytic activities. On the heels of the Japanese advance in the Pacific came the German counteroffensive in Russia, with Sevastopol falling to the Wehrmacht in July and the Germans seizing huge tracts of southern Russia in the late summer and early autumn of 1942. The war in North Africa continued in stalemate during the first nine months of 1942, and the western powers carried out no offensive operations at all in the European theater.

The only bright spots on the Allied battle maps lay in the south and central Pacific theaters. The first successful action there was the breakeven battle between the Allied (predominantly American) navies and the Japanese fleet in the Coral Sea during May, which effectively stopped the Japanese advance toward Australia. Then, in the June Battle of Midway, the U.S. Navy won a smashing triumph, blocking the Japanese eastward advance across the Pacific and destroying most of her frontline carrier force. Two months later the U.S. Army made its first offensive move, landing on Guadalcanal in the Solomons, thereby taking the initial bloody step on the long "island-hopping" campaign toward Tokyo.

The two naval victories, but especially Midway, owed a considerable debt to cryptanalysis. These triumphs also helped create an atmosphere of renewed confidence in which more inter-Allied naval cryptanalytic cooperation could occur. Although the Japanese navy codes and ciphers were being changed frequently, they also were being relentlessly attacked by the Americans in Washington and Hawaii, while a small combined American and Australian navy cryptanalytic unit worked in Melbourne, utilizing among other things a Magic machine that had been brought from the Philippines. Meanwhile, the British Combined Operational Intelligence Centre did all the cryptanalytic work it could as it moved out of the way of the advancing Japanese by hopping from Singapore to Colombo, then to East Africa, and finally to Delhi.[1]

Obstacles ranging from poor interception facilities to the need to improvise new cryptanalytic organizations in the wake of the early Japanese triumphs seriously impeded the Allied naval code-breaking effort. As late as May 1942, the American naval "Y" units apparently were unable to copy out more than 60 percent of Japanese naval wireless transmissions due to staff and equipment shortages. Only 40 percent of the messages recorded by the Americans could be analyzed, and even then large blanks remained in the texts of the "broken" messages.[2]

In addition, national and interservice rivalries continued to hobble all Allied cryptanalytic endeavors. The U.S. Army and Navy code breakers still worked in watertight compartments in the Pacific theater, sharing little about their methods or results during much of the war. More material did pass back and forth between the Allied navies than had occurred before Pearl Harbor, but in the early days of the Pacific war, shortages of personnel and equipment made code- and cipher-breaking work difficult for all the Allied countries. Even so, a few British decrypts of Japanese naval traffic reached the American authorities in the beginning stage of the war against Japan, and some of these materials got as far as President Roosevelt's files between February and April 1942.[3]

The Allies steadily improved their naval code-breaking operations in the Pacific theater throughout 1942, opening up new interception stations wherever possible—including a highly valuable station near Chungking in September 1942—and increasing the number and expertise of their cryptanalytic personnel. But the Japanese also moved ahead quickly in naval cryptography, making their major naval codes much more complicated in the twelve months following Pearl Harbor, although during the middle and later stages of the war they never put into operation the Enigma machines the Germans had given them.[4]

Only a combination of hard work, skill, intuition, and good fortune made possible the cryptanalytic triumph that was the foundation for the U.S. Navy's dramatic success at Midway. Interestingly, the British had been cut into the information the U.S. Navy had secured on Japanese intentions a full two weeks before this decisive clash. The new chief of Naval Operations, stern and frosty Adm. Ernest J. King, told the British Admiralty delegation in Washington on 22 May that his Magic indicated that Midway would be the target of the main Japanese attack. On 31 May he confirmed that conclusion, despite the facts that the Japanese had made a code change, and that one of their naval formations was already steaming toward the Aleutian Islands on what turned out to be a diversionary mission.[5]

Immediately after Midway, U.S. Navy officers in London received a steady stream of cryptanalytic messages regarding developments in the Pacific war, and it is possible that at least some of this material was also passed on to the Admiralty.[6] In this same period, Admiral King chose to conform to Admiralty security classification procedures and ordered that henceforth all messages based on cryptanalytic sources had to be labeled ULTRA or ZEAL, whether they originated from British or American sources.[7]

Following Midway, Anglo-American naval authorities also linked arms to control the gossip that was running rampant in Washington about the role of cryptanalysis in that battle, and to squelch newspaper stories hinting that the triumph had been caused by the "Magic" secret. Even the U.S. Army joined in this joint cryptanalytic security operation; the new G-2, Major General Strong (the man who had made the original offer of cooperation to the British in August 1940), demanded in July 1942 that American censorship authorities ban all mention of cryptanalysis, even in fiction, for the remainder of the war.[8]

General Strong's sensitivity about preserving cryptanalytic secrets arose in part from the fact that in the South Pacific the U.S. Army had been working closely with Allied countries on the cryptanalytic front. Soon after reaching Australia from the Philippines, Gen. Douglas MacArthur set up an Allied Intelligence Bureau, and a "Central Bureau" to carry on cryptanalysis. The latter group was located initially in Melbourne but moved to Brisbane in September 1942. During the autumn of 1942, American, Australian, and a sprinkling of British personnel, most of the latter escapees from the Singapore disaster, found their way into the Central Bureau. While the organization was still in Melbourne, Washington sent out additional cryptanalysts, including the man who ultimately would lead the Central Bureau, the same Dr. Abraham Sinkov who had taken the Magic machine to Britain in January 1941.[9]

In its early days, including the 1942–43 Guadalcanal campaign, the Central Bureau mainly carried out traffic analysis on low-level Japanese army and air force codes, with little help from other Allied agencies. Its relations with the U.S. Navy cryptanalysts were not just difficult, they were, in Sinkov's words, "non-existent." Some finished intelligence from British decryption sources in Southeast Asia may well have reached MacArthur's intelligence chief, General Charles Willoughby, but it did not bear directly on the Guadalcanal battle, nor was it passed on to the cryptanalysts in the Central Bureau, who received no Allied cryptanalytic material directly from other commands during the entire Pacific war.[10]

But new, and more promising, winds soon began to blow for joint Allied code- and cipher-breaking efforts against Japan. The Japanese Military Attaché Code was broken during the summer of 1942, due to American efforts and those of John Tiltman at Bletchley. Such inviting new possibilities, combined with increasing American successes in Pacific battles, compelled the higher echelons of the American armed services to get their individual houses in order, and then to develop closer high-level collaboration with each other, and with Britain.[11]

The U.S. Army still had a long way to go. The major army "Y" units in the United States, consisting of two companies of the U.S. Third Army, were ordered as late as March 1942 to concentrate their interception work on Axis espionage traffic in the Western Hemisphere, but rather than intercept traffic of German, Italian, or Japanese armed forces, they were told to focus their military efforts on the Mexican army. Nonetheless, by April 1942 the initial phase of War Department cryptanalytic reform had been completed. Colonel Carter Clarke, a tough army regular, was made head of the Special Branch, G-2, and received the exclusive right to deal with the Signal Corps on cryptanalytic matters, as well as the responsibility for evaluation and distribution of information from intercepted messages. Clarke was far from a genius, but he knew how to wheel and deal, and, in the words of Telford Taylor of Special Branch, also knew "where the bodies were buried." He had good "channels" to Gen. George Marshall, and usually struck his associates as a likable fellow. Colonel Alfred McCormack, who remained on Secretary Stimson's staff as an overseer and adviser on cryptanalytic matters (initially without administrative duties), had a sharp mind and good relations with Stimson and Assistant Secretary John J. McCloy, but he was an outsider and had a rather austere personality, with a knack for ruffling feathers among the War Department staff.[12]

McCormack and Clarke attempted to solve the problem of coordination with the Signal Corps by gobbling up its cryptanalytic operations in March 1942, but their effort failed, and the decryption and analysis functions of American army code- and cipher-breaking activity therefore continued to be lodged in two different, and watertight, branches of the War Department. The cryptanalytic operations of the Signal Corps, then entitled the Signals Intelligence Division (SID), did the interception and decryption; Special Branch G-2 was responsible for the intelligence analysis and evaluation. These two organizations actually occupied two different wings on the second floor of the Old Munitions Building in Washington during much of 1942, but no officer of Special Branch was allowed even to enter the portion of the second floor occupied by the cryptanalysts of SID. The only official communication between the army code breakers and the intelligence analysts came via face-to-face meetings between Colonel Clarke and the chief of SID. In late 1942 a cumbersome liaison system was introduced that permitted Special Branch analysts to send specific written questions to an SID liaison officer. But this still left the work of the two units rigidly separated. Their liaison problems were compounded in the autumn of 1942 when Special Branch G-2 was shifted to the new Pentagon building, while the Signal Corps cryptanalysts—recently renamed the Signals Intelligence Service (SIS), commanded by Col. W. Preston Corderman—moved into large new quarters at Arlington Hall in suburban Washington.[13]

The navy's cryptanalytic unit, Op-20-G, did not move to its new quarters, Mount Vernon, a former girls' school on Nebraska Avenue in Washington, until February 1943, but in June 1942 a general shakeup already had occurred in the naval system of processing intercepted radio traffic. In June, ONI lost control over all aspects of cryptanalytic intelligence. The entirety of code-and-cipher intelligence work passed into the hands of the director of Naval Communications, who was immediately under the authority of Admiral King. In the same month, the navy yielded control to the army of all interception and decryption work on enemy diplomatic traffic. Soon after, the army assumed responsibility for providing Magic intercepts to the State Department, while the navy undertook to perform a similar Magic distribution service for the White House. The autumn of 1942 showed further bursts of close cryptanalytic cooperation between the two military services; since Army SIS was making rapid progress against the Japanese shipping code in that period, the navy turned over to SIS large quantities of intercepted Japanese radio traffic enciphered in that code.[14]

These reforms, and the limited moves toward interservice cryptanalytic cooperation that accompanied them, paved the way for the U.S. Army and Navy to go on the offensive against the host of other American organizations operating in the radio intelligence trade. The army fired the first salvo in this campaign during April 1942, calling for an army–navy–FBI monopoly of all radio interception and cryptanalysis. After considerable haggling, a presidential order was issued on 8 July 1942 limiting the American cryptanalytic club to army, navy, and FBI. The Coast Guard was absorbed under the navy rubric for cryptanalytic purposes, and the FBI was added on because Hoover's bureau seemed the most appropriate department to deal with the sensitive matter of clandestine traffic within the United States. The army was then given a monopoly in handling enemy military, air, and diplomatic traffic, and the navy received enemy navy and clandestine traffic outside the Western Hemisphere. The FBI was restricted to clandestine traffic within the Western Hemisphere. The latter section of the agreement soon brought benefits to the armed services: By October 1942 the FBI had prepared a long list of Spanish, French, and Swedish code books and tables which it offered to turn over to the army and navy.[15]

But such generosity on the part of the FBI did not prevent the military services from tightening the screws of their cryptanalytic monopoly. As well as ordering the end of cryptanalytic activity by the FCC, the director of Censorship, and the OSS, a supplemental agreement was issued forbidding the closing down of any clandestine radio station whose broadcasts the army or navy cryptanalytic organizations found useful.[16] The onslaught of the armed forces monopolists, and their FBI fellow traveler, brought howls of dismay from those U.S. government agencies that had been excluded from the cryptanalytic club. The Office of Strategic Services was especially irate at having to shut down its small intercept operation, while suffering the additional indignity of being denied access to the decrypts of certain coded messages that its agents had originally stolen and then turned over to the FBI to be broken.[17]

Six months after the creation of the army–navy–FBI partnership, Gen. William Donovan of OSS was still complaining that the triumvirate was being too rigid in the enforcement of its monopolistic brief. The OSS had good reason to protest, because exclusion meant no access to the intelligence products of cryptanalysis except under rigidly controlled conditions. Most important, from 23 October 1942, OSS personnel were barred from regular JIC meetings because documents that arose from cryptanalysis were discussed there; the army-navy monopolists used this fact as grounds to bar participation in such JIC sessions to all civilians and members of "quasi-military" organizations, such as OSS, who were, by definition, not cleared for Ultra-Magic material.[18]

Not in the least dismayed by General Donovan's lamentations, the army and navy happily attacked all those American agencies whose code-and-cipher transmission practices were suspected of being lax, especially those whose cryptographic failures had been revealed through the reading of enemy radio traffic. OSS received a sharp box on the ears for lax encoding procedures in January 1943, and two months later enemy traffic decoded by the British—rather than a tip from the German resistance, as Allen Dulles would later claim—proved that State Department codes were compromised, as were those used by the American military attachés.[19]

In the long run this matter left much egg on the face of the U.S. Army authorities, especially in their relations with the British, because from the autumn of 1941 until July 1942, the American military attaché in Cairo, Col. Bonner F. Fellers, had been sending to Washington detailed reports about British intentions and operations in North Africa. Due to serious flaws in the American Military Attaché Code, Fellers' messages were read by the Germans and Italians. The Axis cryptanalysts then relayed to Rommel the information regarding British military activities cited by Fellers, and the Afrika Korps made good use of this vital information to block British plans and inflict serious losses on the Eighth Army. The State Department discovered this particular leak when in the summer of 1942 a member of the Italian intelligence service told a friend working in the Vatican that the "Axis had decoded [a] telegram sent [to] Washington by the American Consul in Cairo" describing in some detail the "weaknesses in military equipment of [the] British on the Libyan front." The Italian intelligence man also claimed that receipt of this information had been one of the factors that prompted Rommel "to push on as far as he did [that is, El Alamein]." By 24 July this information on the Fellers affair had reached the American consul in Berne, who immediately alerted Washington.

Once the details of this appalling security failure became fully known, and were shaken down in London later in 1942, they would deepen Whitehall's suspicion of the security of the American army, as well as that of the State Department, and would increase British reluctance to open up the door on the Ultra secret to the U.S. War Department. But in the interim, in order to enhance their prestige with the British government, the American army, navy, and FBI made sure that London knew that they alone enjoyed a cryptanalytic monopoly in the United States. On 27 July 1942 Brig. Vivian Dykes of the Joint Staff Mission was informed of the main terms of the three-way split of American cryptanalysis, with a request that the JSM inform "all agencies of the British Government" concerned with cryptanalytic matters that they should deal only with these three American agencies, and then only in regard to the specializations that the system alloted respectively to the army, navy, and FBI.[20]

The cryptanalytic union of the army, navy, and FBI constituted an important concentration of authority regarding secret matters in Washington. Like the creation of the JCS and the JIC, which had occurred earlier in the year, the union of the army, navy, and FBI would serve as a foundation for the permanent American national security system that arose in Washington soon after V-J Day. Once that system was in place in an era when the United States was one of the world's two superpowers, America's postwar allies would be forced to adjust to that reality and often dance to America's tune. But in 1942, the more even balance of assets and liabilities on the two sides of the Atlantic meant that creation of greater American cryptanalytic centralization was not in itself enough to cause the British to rush forward in search of a special code- and cipher-breaking agreement with Washington.

As of July 1942, the U.S. Army authorities had only two tenuous cryptanalytic connections with the British government. Early in 1942, Col. Palmer Dixon had become the first U.S. Army Air Corps officer stationed in Britain to be taken into the Ultra secret, and only a handful of his Air Corps colleagues had subsequently been added to the most secret list in the course of 1942. Also in early 1942, a Signals Section of the U.S. Army Air Corps in Britain under the command of Lt. R. Doney began to liaise on wireless interception with the British authorities, and Captains Solomon Kullbach and Roy D. Johnson of that office soon had an opportunity to see a limited number of decryption techniques used at Bletchley, as did two Op-20-G officers. Some small Op-20-G and SIS technical missions arrived at Bletchley, including one led by Cdr. Joseph Eachus; such missions continued to come and go, doing specialized work at Bletchley until the end of hostilities. But Op-20-G never had more than two officers together at Bletchley during the entire war, and in 1942 there was no dispatch of Ultra decrypts from Bletchley to the U.S. Army authorities in Washington. Even below the Ultra-Magic level, so little intelligence was being exchanged between the two armies in July 1942 that Col. Rufus Bratton, the chief of G-2's Intelligence Group, called for an overhaul of the entire system of Anglo-American intelligence coordination.[21]

Members of the Joint Staff Mission in Washington, led by Brig. Vivian Dykes, also complained to the cabinet offices in early summer 1942 that the Whitehall ban on American army access to the sources underlying British strategic estimates was seriously impeding the work of the Combined Chiefs of Staff Committees.[22] Not until September 1942 did an American army delegation, led by Col. J. R. Lovell, get to Britain to participate in the first joint meeting on German order of battle (OB). Even then, not all sources of OB information in British possession were revealed to the American delegation, which was given rather feeble excuses to explain the gaps in the source citations used to support British conclusions.

Probably in part to avoid a repetition of such embarrassing incidents, the British persuaded the American army G-2 that henceforth it should concentrate on Japanese OB, while the British army would control the German OB field and continue to monopolize its Ultra sources. Consequently the American army's German "experts" were forced to stumble on as best they could; the first G-2 course on German OB did not begin in Washington until December 1942, just two months before the U.S. Army received its initial bloodying from the Germans at the battle of Kasserine Pass.[23]

The width of the gap that still separated the armies of the two countries on secret matters was indicated by their continued failure to agree on a system of joint field communication. The British had long had difficulties in reaching such an agreement with the Canadian army, and only in May 1942 had Britain and Canada finally settled on a common code-sign system for their ground forces. But the American army still clung adamantly to the view that the British system was basically flawed, and the two countries stumbled toward combined operations in 1942 still lacking an effective means of joint field communication.[24]

Regarding the highest level of intelligence, a few pieces of Ultra did reach the American authorities in 1942—including the U.S. Army staff—through the offices of the Joint Staff Mission in Washington. However, most of this material came to the JSM from the Admiralty and was sent to the head of the Royal Navy delegation in Washington in the form of summaries, code-named "Sunsets," designed to keep him abreast of the information being sent to Washington from Colombo, as well as that information going to American naval officers engaged in the U-boat war. In July 1942 no Ultra information at all was being sent to the army section of the JSM, whereas the flow to the Air Mission was spasmodic and its origin disguised, i.e., "wrapped-up." By October 1942, the small bits of Ultra destined for the Air Mission had ceased altogether, and the navy special intelligence transmissions also had been "considerably diminished."[25]

American army liaison officers in London were equally unsuccessful in acquiring Ultra information. The attaché was still the only U.S. Army officer authorized to receive intelligence information from the British for relay to the United States. Despite some indications that in the pre–Pearl Harbor period the U.S. Army attaché received occasional wrapped-up Ultra, it is abundantly clear that the attaché was acquiring no such material in 1942. That is the conclusion of the American official historian, who has studied the matter in depth using materials that are still closed. His conclusion is confirmed by British records. The deputy director of British Military Intelligence, Brig. J. M. Kirkman, issued a general order on 17 February 1942 setting out the rules for British officers handling requests from the American military attaché. The guidelines were surprisingly restrictive and included a special injunction against passing on anything to the Americans "which emanates from special most secret sources."[26]

Overall, the conclusion is inescapable that throughout much of 1942, aside from cooperation on the spot in the Far East, little intelligence sharing of any kind occurred between the armies of Britain and the United States. Much of the British reluctance to open the door to the U.S. Army on all forms of intelligence relating to Germany arose from the security demands of the "need-to-know" principle, a principle made more convincing by the "Fellers affair" revelations of the early autumn. Until November 1942 no American ground forces were in action in Europe or North Africa; therefore, on the basis of the need-to-know principle, the British were justified in giving them nothing. This produced some awkward moments, and bitter arguments in the CIC, but London seems to have concluded that that was a small price to pay to attain the highest possible level of protection for its most secret sources. But it also must be acknowledged that neither the policymakers nor the intelligence mandarins in Whitehall were saints who abhorred playing politics with intelligence. They could, and did, bend the rules for political advantage when it suited them to do so. As the DNI observed in November 1941, after leaking highly classified information to Lord Chalford to use in a House of Lords debate on Royal Navy policy, "So far as the Official Secrets Act is concerned it will of course be appreciated that the head of any of the Intelligence Services has to take action from time to time which, in a strictly legal sense, involves infraction of this statute." Some of Admiral Godfrey's Admiralty colleagues were troubled by this remark, but the DNI was speaking plain truth when he granted that the circulation of intelligence could be, and often was, a political as well as a military and security matter both at home and abroad.[27]

Seen from this point of view, British tightfistedness regarding the American army in the first two-thirds of 1942 unquestionably contained elements of national and departmental self-interest, which declared that one should not give away a valuable asset unless it was safe and in one's interest to do so. In the same spirit, when the balance of power began to tip decisively in favor of the United States later in the year, it was perfectly understandable that the British position began to shift as well. By the autumn of 1942 American war production was reaching full strength, and U.S. expeditionary forces were being prepared for the Operation Torch landings in northwest Africa. Brigadier Dykes of the JSM quickly grasped the implications of these changes, noting in his diary in mid-October that in the face of America's rapidly expanding power, "we simply hold no cards at all." Dykes attempted to convince the British Chiefs of Staff that they would have to go out of their way to meet American wishes on all matters great and small, because "there are few things which we are in a position to give to the United States; but we are dependent on them for a great many things."[28]

In the latter part of 1942 and on into 1943, the British government did yield to the United States on a number of policy matters, including the sharing first of German navy, and then of German army, intelligence. These initiatives surely had within them large elements of political expediency. On another level, however, it is true that Anglo-American cryptanalytic cooperation developed slowly, because the American army authorities seem to have been unable to grasp the full importance Ultra had for combat operations, and did not act decisively even when the British first indicated they might be willing to open the door.

In February 1942, the prime minister had suggested to the president that there seemed to be a need for more cryptographic cooperation between the two armies, an overture that could have been used by the Americans to raise matters of code breaking as well as of code making. The initiative rapidly descended into the bowels of the U.S. Army chain of command, but it then took G-2 five *months* to frame a reply. When the paper prepared by General Strong did finally appear, it showed no particular eagerness for increased cryptanalytic or cryptographic cooperation with Britain. Strong claimed that "interchange of technical cryptanalytic information between the British and American armies had been in progress for over a year," which presumably referred to the Sinkov mission of 1941 and the dispatch of technical specialists to Bletchley in 1942. The general went on to say that this arrangement "appears to be quite satisfactory on both sides." The U.S. Army G-2 was equally satisfied with the Anglo-American joint encoding efforts, which had "been in progress" for "about three months." No mention was made by General Strong of any U.S. Army desire that Ultra decrypts should come to Washington. General Marshall therefore wrote a reassuring memorandum to the president on 11 July, indicating that the entire matter of cryptographic and cryptanalytic cooperation with Britain was well in hand, and that Field Marshal Dill and General Marshall himself were satisfied with the existing situation. Since that situation—a full seven months after Pearl Harbor—entailed no arrangements for providing Ultra to the American army, and no British assistance to American SIS to help its personnel break into German army and air force Enigma, the British cannot be severely faulted for failing to put their vital general and Ultra intelligence about the German armed forces into the hands of such a blasé American army high command.[29] Until the U.S. commanders faced the problems raised by fast-moving European ground combat, the American army could expect no great intelligence assistance—or an Ultra partnership—from the British.

In 1942, however, the situation was radically different regarding the navies of Britain and America. Joint naval operations in the North Atlantic had gone on for six months by the time America officially entered the war on 9 December 1941. By then the U.S. Navy was accustomed to receiving a steady diet of most secret material wrapped up in the form of OIC reports on German submarine deployment. But immediately following American entry into the war, a series of disasters had befallen the Allied side of the struggle for control of the North Atlantic, which would shake the cooperation between the Royal and U.S. navies to its very foundations.

Anticipating a dilatory American response to full-scale war, Adm. Karl Doenitz hit hard and fast with a series of U-boat attacks in American coastal waters during mid-December 1941. This Operation Drumbeat suddenly struck U.S. coastal shipping from Massachusetts to Florida, including daring assaults inside New York Harbor. The resultant heavy shipping losses were accompanied by civilian panic and highly animated struggles among policymakers in Washington on how best to cope with the U-boat onslaught. For a combination of reasons—including a shortage of escort vessels—Admiral King failed to give coastal convoys a high priority during the first six months of 1942, and as the losses mounted, policy wrangling accelerated both within the navy and between the naval command and the British, the U.S. Congress, political and press representatives on the East Coast of the United States, and an extremely unhappy Franklin Roosevelt. As late as July 1942, the president was firing off memos to Admiral King citing statistics he claimed provided "excellent proof of what I have been talking about for weeks," namely that coastal convoys and more aggressive anti-U-boat measures along the eastern seaboard were urgently required.[30]

The Drumbeat debacle, and the policy struggles that accompanied it, were not caused initially by intelligence or cipher security failures, but code-and-cipher developments quickly made the situation more serious and increasingly difficult to correct. On 1 February, shortly after the first wave of U-boats had turned home from their "happy hunting ground" off the American coast, Doenitz changed the Enigma enciphering system employed by the U-boats. Occasionally during December 1941 and January 1942 individual U-boats seem to have gone over to the full four-rotor Enigma system, but on 1 February, the entire operational U-boat fleet began to use the four-rotor Triton Enigma. Bletchley was instantly silenced, unable to decipher a single word, and except for brief intervals of good fortune due to capture, or German error, including a period of current reading of Triton in June–July 1942, the German Enigma remained virtually immune to British attack until December 1942.

This was a severe blow to Anglo-American antisubmarine cooperation. The submarine positional reports from the OIC, which in this period were sent directly from the Admiralty to the Navy Department in Washington without passing through the U.S. Naval Mission in London, immediately became less frequent and less detailed. One of them, forwarded to the president on 3 March 1942, carried a masterfully understated note declaring that the "sub situation in Atlantic remains obscure." But no one in Britain seems to have thought to take the obvious, if marginally risky, step of informing the U.S. Navy about the cause of the trouble. Admiral King and his colleagues, already shaken and bloodied by Operation Drumbeat, as well as Pearl Harbor, found the intelligence flow from Britain inexplicably stunted just when they needed it most.[31] Suspicion about perfidious Albion bubbled up again. Then in February 1942, to add to the sorrows of the American, British, and Canadian antisubmarine efforts, the German cryptanalytic organization, the B Dienst, scored one of its greatest triumphs of the war, breaking into the British-American-Canadian Naval Cipher Three, which was used by the Allies to control routing and rerouting of the North Atlantic convoys.[32]

The Allies, not knowing that the B Dienst was the cause of their problems, attempted to counter the sharp increase of U-boat successes by conventional means. But lacking large reserves of escort vessels and having as yet no aircraft carriers in the Atlantic, little could be done by such methods except to improve the convoy routing systems. These were, in fact, the subject of British-Canadian-American agreements made on 15 February 1942, and amended on 8 April and 11 July.

But due to the vulnerability of Naval Cipher Three and the lack of U-boat Ultra, as well as the aggressive operations carried out by Doenitz and his captains, Allied losses in the North Atlantic continued to mount. The possibility that the lifeline might be severed tormented London, Washington, and Ottawa throughout 1942.[33]

Since it was the British lifeline that was threatened, and the United Kingdom could least afford the huge losses of cargoes and ships, London took the lead in trying to find a solution. The most important British initiative came in March 1942 with a call for a U.S.–U.K.–Canadian wireless conference, to be held in Washington, emphasizing naval dimensions of the problem. The meeting lasted from 6 to 17 April, with navy, army, and air delegations from Canada and Britain, along with nine U.S. Navy officers, including Commander Safford, Cdr. Joseph Redman (the deputy director of Naval Communications), and the U.S. Navy's top communications and cryptanalytic expert, Cdr. Joseph Wenger. Eight U.S. Army officers were also present, but, fittingly, classified only as "observers" because of the lack of direct cryptanalytic cooperation between the American and British armies.[34]

The British agenda for the meeting called for the first portion of the conference to be devoted to radio interception methods and the second half to methods of obtaining intelligence from intercepted radio traffic, including use of direction-finding equipment. Like most conferences, this one included general presentations, made mostly by senior participants, followed by discussions and the creation of committees to examine specific topics. At the end of the conference, the committees made a series of recommendations, all of which were adopted by the conference after lively discussion and some amendments. Virtually all the recommendations were subsequently accepted and implemented by the British government, and apparently by the American and Canadian governments as well. The most important recommendations concerned technical collaboration to explore new types of radio communication and interception equipment, an understanding about the control of the wireless intercept stations of the three countries, and a detailed agreement covering the distribution of the raw radio traffic that was being intercepted.

Of these three groups of recommendations, it is significant to note that in the first category—technical collaboration—the conference called for the United States to shoulder most of the responsibility and cost for technical investigation and development of new wireless communication and interception devices. This was a natural consequence of the abundance of technical and production assets in the United States, but the carrying out of this recommendation would not only give the Americans a stronger voice regarding such matters during the war, but would help produce the American domination of the fields of radio communications and intelligence technology in the postwar era.

In regard to control of intercept stations, the conference decided that all interception and direction-finding (DF) activities should be controlled from four centers, two Canadian, one British, and one American. All British, Canadian, and "Imperial" DF operations in the western Atlantic would be directed from Halifax; the Esquimalt, British Columbia, station would control all Canadian interception operations in the Pacific. The British center at Cheltenham would receive not only all British home waters and European traffic, but also that collected from the intercept stations on the East Coast of the United States. Finally, the intercept center on Bainbridge Island near Seattle would control all the American intercept stations in the Pacific and act as the reception point for all the data they collected.

The third set of recommendations, concerning the distribution of the raw intercepts, provided a clear picture of the close bonds then being forged between the naval radio intelligence personnel of the three countries, and also contained the most interesting and detailed information on their activities and priorities. All of the intercepted Japanese naval traffic was to be divided between London and Washington, with none going to Ottawa. The Japanese weather traffic intercepted in western Canada would go exclusively to the U.S. center on Bainbridge Island, with no copies sent on to the British. Other Japanese weather traffic, including that of the Japanese (five number) naval fleet cipher, was to be sent only to Washington. The Japanese naval flag officers' messages were to be dispatched to both Washington and London, but only when the British so requested. The Japanese naval and military attaché traffic would be sent to Washington by high-speed transmission methods, but sent to London only by airmail.

Clearly the Americans were to dominate completely the Japanese traffic, especially that useful for immediate operational purposes. The British were determined to do the same for the wireless transmissions of Germany and Italy. German diplomatic traffic was the only portion of this bloc of intercepts that was to be sent to Washington by means of rapid communications systems, but even this was to be done only "when required." Other items, such as German army, air, and weather communications intercepts, as well as Italian military, submarine, and air traffic, were merely to be mailed to Washington by air, while the same items went to London via high-speed transmissions. As might well have been anticipated, "for the present" at least, all German U-boat transmissions were to be sent exclusively to London. The British also took the lion's share of all classes of intercepts from Vichy French sources as well as those from Turkey, Arabia, China, and Portugal. To round out the picture, clandestine radio intercepts would continue to go to the British security coordinator, William Stephenson, "as at present," and the American and British authorities would also continue to handle Latin American traffic independently of each other.

These complex and detailed arrangements moved the three countries—especially Britain and the United States—toward a more systematic and intimate arrangement regarding the distribution of intercepted radio traffic, the most basic aspect of radio intelligence cooperation. The conference was also vitally important in providing a forum in which top American radio intelligence officers could learn once and for all how the British extracted intelligence from intercepted enemy radio traffic and how they put it into a form that could be used in naval operations. Captain H. R. Sandwith, leader of the British delegation, gave the assembled group a short summary presentation on "the British cryptanalytic center," that is, Bletchley Park, which he referred to by its customary cover name as "Station X." Emphasizing that Station X was an interservice organization, including the three armed services and the Foreign Office, Sandwith indicated its size and complexity by noting that its staff at that time consisted of approximately "2,000 men and women," and that it was responsible for code making as well as code breaking. As part of his constantly repeated refrain that interagency cooperation was the key to British success—a message clearly intended for the ears of the American army and navy officers present—Sandwith stressed that no British code or cipher went into service "without consulting the cryptanalysts . . . to tell whether the code is secure." Such explanations probably made the desired impression on his audience—that coordination efforts pay off. Mercifully, none of those present was aware that at that very moment part of their

U-boat problem was caused by the fact that the B Dienst was reading the Allied convoy code.

Sandwith was in a far stronger position when presenting a detailed picture of the organization and operation of the OIC and the Submarine Tracking Room. Although granting that the work of the room had sometimes been characterized as "crystal gazing," the captain felt it was much more scientific than that, even though it did involve "a good deal of guess work." Its data base came from a wide variety of intelligence, including DHF, cryptanalysis, aerial reconnaissance, secret agent reports, and telephone reports from Admiralty plotting centers abroad. These made possible the buildup of a picture of the modus operandi of the German navy, especially that of Doenitz and his U-boat staff, which greatly improved the accuracy of operational forecasts.

To underscore the Admiralty's confidence in the OIC–Submarine Tracking Room system, Sandwith stressed that the Royal Navy had started "a similar organization in Newfoundland," and that Ottawa intended to create a combined center of its own in Halifax in the near future. Although the captain was too polite to say so in the formal sessions of the conference, the message for the Americans was plain. It is likely that in more intimate surroundings Sandwith told the U.S. Navy about Bletchley's problems with the four-rotor naval Enigma, and urged them to jump on the OIC bandwagon by offering the Admiralty assistance in organizing a submarine tracking room in the United States. It is also highly possible that he was the one who, in the words of the official *History of British Intelligence*, "promised" the U.S. Navy a "bombe" in the spring of 1942.

Even as this important conference proceeded, arrangements were being made to bring to Ottawa and Washington the head of the British Submarine Tracking room, Cdr. Roger Winn. Admiral Ghormley appears to have originally made the suggestion to the U.S. Navy that Winn should come to Washington, but he faced uphill work trying to convince the Navy Department of the importance of such a visit. Stressing that even Admiral King "had probably not heard of his [Winn's] name" until Ghormley made the suggestion of a visit, the chief of the U.S. Navy Mission in London told the chief of Naval Operations on 6 April 1942 that Winn's anonymity was due to the fact that "the intimate side of his work here is known to so few," and that "only about twenty-five officers of the British navy are admitted to this [Submarine Tracking] Room."[35]

The combination of Ghormley's recommendations and the ground-breaking work done by Captain Sandwith in the wireless intercept conference was sufficient to bring Winn to Washington and Ottawa on 20 April 1942 for three weeks. Many of the details of what happened during the visit are impossible to ascertain from existing open sources, but Winn definitely sold the American naval authorities on the need to create their own submarine tracking room, and for this achievement he won Admiralty commendation in October 1943. Once that had been accomplished, Winn probably went on to engineer an invitation to Britain for the director of the newly created American submarine tracking room. Commander Kenneth Knowles then journeyed to London in June 1942 and was initiated into both the methods of the Submarine Tracking Room in London and the naval Ultra secret.[36]

These developments came at an especially auspicious moment, because beginning in June 1942, for a two-month period, Bletchley read the current cipher of the Triton four-rotor U-boat, due to a combination of captures and cribs.[37] The scraps of relevant evidence that are now open to researchers indicate that the number and detail of the reports on U-boat locations reaching Washington sharply increased in the summer of 1942. Commander Knowles therefore began his submarine tracking room career holding a handful of aces. The new U.S. Navy submarine tracking room, initially unnamed but under the authority of Op-20, and later called "F 211," scored enough early successes to gain the confidence of Admiral King and his staff, and to block the efforts of local commanders—especially those of the Eastern Sea Frontier, which controlled Atlantic coastal waters—to decentralize all U-boat tracking activities.[38]

Knowles and Op-20 went through a bad period in the autumn and early winter of 1942 when Bletchley lost Triton once again, but from the time the four-rotor U-boat cipher was completely and permanently broken in December 1942, Op-20's position was absolutely secure. To make Commander Knowles' monopoly of U-boat tracking in the United States more efficient, a "secret room," named "F 211," was established in Washington on 27 December 1942. It was located immediately adjacent to Knowles' office and contained wall plots of U-boat positions. When it began to receive Triton Enigma transmissions from the Admiralty in late December 1942, F 211 processed them "from the operational standpoint," altering the wall plots to facilitate Knowles' tracking efforts.[39]

While Winn and Knowles were launching the U.S. Navy onto a more efficient system of submarine tracking, Bletchley and Op-20-G began to move closer to full cryptanalytic partnership in the Battle of the Atlantic. The emerging Winn-Knowles alliance was itself an important spur toward a united attack on Triton. An additional nudge came in the form of developments on joint Anglo-American naval ciphers. An arrangement was concluded in June 1942 whereby the U.S. Navy agreed to produce an adapter to make its electrical cipher machine suitable for joint British-Canadian-American operations at sea. Although the machine, plus adapter, was not operational until November 1943, the conclusion of this understanding, which helped solve the Allied joint cipher problems in the Atlantic, definitely created a more friendly climate in which to secure a naval cryptanalytic agreement.[40]

The continued threat posed by the U-boat also, of course, tended to push the secret activities of the two navies closer together, as did the desire of both navies to appear to be as effective as possible, without endangering their security, image, or bureaucratic prerogatives. But suspicions were still rife. Op-20-G never overcame its jealousy of the Royal Navy or the suspicions that had been aroused by the cryptanalytic "betrayal" of 1940–41. Whitehall remained deeply worried by American lack of centralization, and some British officials were also becoming increasingly nervous about the colossal increases in American power. In his diary, Brigadier Dykes of the Joint Staff Mission repeatedly wrote worried entries about the mounting strength of the United States, the possible appearance of American "military fascism," and the imperialist tendencies he perceived as rising in the United States.[41]

What policies should be followed in regard to security controls also exercised the navies of both countries. Admiral King was highly nervous about lapses of security regarding highly secret matters. The Admiralty, at the very least, shared his concern, and in this period reaffirmed that the U.S. Navy liaison officer in London should be handled gingerly regarding "our sources of intelligence and most secret methods of acquiring it." Other considerations besides those of security obviously contributed to this reserve toward the Americans, but the British government had good reason to be troubled even about its own security practices. The Royal Navy was constantly tormented by the security lapses of the merchant navy, and Whitehall itself was far from completely secure. In late September 1942 highly secret papers for the invasion of northwest Africa were lost in the streets of London, and only fortuitously recovered by a resourceful charwoman. Shortly thereafter, another set of such "Torch" papers was lost when a courier aircraft went down over Spain, having disregarded the most rudimentary precautions regarding transport of vital papers in a war zone.[42]

On the other hand, both the American and Royal naval commands had to cope with pressures to relax the restrictions concerning Ultra. The regulations on access to such material, and the need to make certain that the enemy did not guess that his codes and ciphers were being read, had led to such intensive secrecy regulations that, in the words of Admiral C. M. Forbes of the Royal Navy, they had "been found to militate against the useful employment of this information" in battle. Forbes went on to contend to the DNI in March 1942 that "however secret may be the sources[,] . . . intelligence can never be an end in itself and if it does not lead to action it is valueless."[43] The prime minister, however, was moving in the opposite direction to the views expressed by battle commanders such as Admiral Forbes. Calling for yet tighter Ultra security restrictions, Churchill demanded in the early autumn of 1942 that the Royal Navy reduce the number of officers cleared for Ultra because the Admiralty had three times as many officers "in the secret" as either the army or the Royal Air Force.[44]

With so many interests and desires pulling in different directions on both sides of the Atlantic, a naval cryptanalytic deal was extremely difficult to negotiate. The crucial factor that made it begin to happen in mid-September 1942 was Bletchley's inability to produce a permanent solution to the Triton problem, and its failure to deliver a bombe to the U.S. Navy, as had been promised in June. By August 1942 the senior staff at Bletchley apparently had concluded that a technical attack on a grand scale offered the best hope for a successful assault on Triton. The initial element in such an attack appeared to be acquisition of a large number of high-speed bombes capable of coping with the complex problems that Triton posed. The attractions of the American electrical-electronic industry consequently beamed brightly, and Bletchley took the lead in opening the door to a deal.[45]

The willingness of Bletchley to send a special representative to Washington to woo the American navy in the summer of 1942, and to have chosen a man as personable and authoritative as John Tiltman to do the job, was a major catalyst for success. Neither Bletchley nor

Tiltman underestimated the obstacle, or believed a quick fix was possible. Tiltman was sent by ship with ample technical and personal baggage to provide him with the wherewithal to wage a long campaign if necessary.[46]

Tiltman presumably was the one who first "fully initiated" the U.S. Navy into GC & CS's techniques for breaking the Enigma, explaining finally that the sporadic floods and droughts in the flow of Ultra information in the U-boat war was due solely to the trouble Bletchley was having with Triton. Though impressed by Tiltman and the Bletchley system, some of the top officers of Op-20-G were not completely sold on the necessity of having such a complicated organization as Bletchley Park. These men tended to undervalue the importance of cribs and cillies, and clung to the belief that even Triton could ultimately be broken by high-speed bombes alone if enough electric-electronic power was devoted to the task.[47]

The Op-20-G team had a high overall opinion of Tiltman, and their positive reaction was reinforced by the arrival of another top specialist from Bletchley during August and September 1942. Professor G. C. McVittie flew to Washington for a month-long visit (27 August–27 September 1942) to examine American work on enemy and Soviet weather ciphers and codes. Although not happy with American service rivalries or security measures, the professor was impressed by some of the U.S. Navy's work on meteorological ciphers, noting in a diary his desire "to be able to do something on this when I get back [to Bletchley]."[48] But neither such indications of professional respect nor Tiltman's skill and charm could deter Op-20-G from pushing ahead on its own program of high-speed bombe development.

This project was the brainchild of the U.S. Navy's communications wizard, Cdr. Joseph Wenger. A dedicated, abstemious man, Wenger somehow managed to hold his own among the hard-drinking naval staff despite his sensitive intestinal system and a tendency to worry excessively. Initially cool toward a joint operation with the British, Wenger would have preferred that the U.S. Navy push on alone. On 10 September 1942 the Navy Department followed his lead and approved a plan to manufacture a high-speed bombe, utilizing a system of rotary switches. The developmental cost of the project was $2 million. Wenger estimated that once the first model had been built, five months would be required to reach a production level of one machine per day. The exceptional speed with which the project went forward was due to Admiral

King's success in securing from President Roosevelt highest priority and precedence for navy bombe development. The initial production target was set at 96 bombes and then raised to 112. The first production models were tested in June 1943 and passed with flying colors. Even the British acknowledged that although the American machines were smaller, they had better serviceability than the British versions, at least in late 1943. American production efficiency showed what it could do by turning out these high-speed bombes at a rate of three or four per day in 1943–44.[49]

By the time Edward Travis, the director of Bletchley Park, arrived in Washington in the third week of September to try to conclude a formal arrangement with the U.S. Navy on cipher security and cryptanalysis, the American navy bombe-production contracts had already been approved, and Travis found himself cornered. With thoughts of the "Fellers affair" as well as national interests apparently uppermost in his mind, Travis sought to make an arrangement whereby Op-20-G would join the naval decryption operation at Bletchley, and all Enigma breaking efforts would continue to be centered in Britain. But with Op-20-G already holding its high-speed bombe contract in hand, Travis had to bow to the inevitable and accept some form of division of German navy work between Bletchley and Washington. As for the Americans, once Wenger had been briefed by Tiltman and Travis, he concluded that trying to go it alone entailed greater risks than cooperation with the British. To sweeten the deal the U.S. naval authorities agreed to supply the Admiralty with certain intelligence "from Japanese communications." Accordingly, on 1 October 1942 Wenger and Travis signed the first of the Anglo-American cryptanalytic sharing agreements.[50]

The Wenger-Travis agreement was far from an all-embracing accord. It was limited to naval matters and to the Atlantic area, but it did provide that raw naval Ultra would come to Washington. Beginning in late December, an "Ultra serial" was received "almost daily" from the Admiralty OIC, containing a summary of the latest German wireless traffic, along "with comments and queries by Captain Winn." Shortly thereafter, "replies and comments" were drafted by F 211 "for retransmission to O.I.C." In addition, the 1 October understanding arranged for the pooling of the bombe capacity of the naval cryptanalytic units in the two countries, and included a U.S. Navy promise to limit the production of its bombe to a hundred machines. Bletchley would continue to perform the basic cryptanalytic work against the German naval ciphers, but once a general break-in occurred, the breaking of the daily settings would be divided between Bletchley and Op-20-G.

Not worked out in detail in the Travis-Wenger agreement were how the daily traffic would be divided, and by whom, as well as what the communication system would be between Bletchley and Washington. Therefore, shortly after Travis returned to Bletchley, his naval assistant, a young civilian academic named Dr. Harry Hinsley, was sent to Washington to hammer out the details of the system. Soon after his exhausting transatlantic flight, Hinsley was required to pass the standard U.S. Navy test for outsiders, a late-night gathering with Wenger's staff, intended to measure how long the newcomer could remain above the table. Hinsley, like a Thomas Mann hero, managed to shed his exhaustion and transcend his temperate habits long enough to stay clearheaded and upright throughout this examination. Once that had been successfully accomplished, the young British historian was welcomed aboard, and the detailed Anglo-American follow-up discussions began the next day.

Hinsley first rounded out the account that Travis had given of the problems Bletchley faced with Triton. Wenger and Hinsley, assisted by Wenger's deputy, Commander Wesley Wright, then set about producing a detailed system of dividing up the daily tasks involved in U-boat cryptanalysis. Unlimited interception of North Atlantic U-boat radio traffic was to be carried out by both countries. Then the cryptanalysts at Bletchley would decide each day which portion of the German traffic would be reserved to be worked on at Bletchley. Using secure cables operated by British Security Coordination, the Americans would be informed what Bletchley was doing that day and told what tasks GC & CS thought should be shouldered by the Americans. The cable communication was nearly instantaneous, so it was possible to "discuss" the basic division of labor and try to agree in advance on the most effective plan not only for the present day, but for subsequent days as well. Over time, it became a real partnership, with the Americans suggesting the basic division of labor as frequently as the British. If one side or the other had extra bombe capacity on a given day—as was increasingly the case for the Americans as the war went on—it was used on less pressing German naval traffic, which might contain useful information or provide collateral answers to problems posed by Triton.[51]

The Travis-Wenger deal of 1 October 1942, as refined by Harry Hinsley and his American counterparts, was the first of a pair of Anglo-American wartime cryptanalytic agreements (the other being the BRUSA army agreement to be discussed in the next chapter). This naval agreement bore all the marks that distinguish a pathfinder. It was a cautious, limited arrangement that centered on one problem only, U-boat Triton traffic, and was then expanded to cover other aspects of German Atlantic messages. It ignored other categories of German navy traffic, such as that in the southern Atlantic and the Indian Ocean, as well as the traffic of the Italian and Japanese navies. But once it had been concluded, those responsible for the arrangement were reluctant to change it. Therefore, throughout the remainder of the war, little additional headway was made regarding Anglo-American cryptanalytic cooperation on European naval matters.

The naval agreement had managed, however, to surmount the age-old security fears of the British government and the public speculation about cryptanalysis that had followed the Battle of Midway. Not surprisingly, therefore, Hastings and Wenger on 24 November 1942 formally agreed on a security system covering naval Ultra. But it was the Anglo-American naval agreement itself that was the genuine innovation: It broke with the age-old tradition of caution and suspicion, which admonished even closely allied states not to open their most secret cupboards because today's comrades in arms could well be tomorrow's dangerous opponents.[52]

Wenger and Travis, supplemented by Hinsley and Hastings, had achieved an important, if relatively circumscribed, agreement, whose timing would be nearly as important as its content: The naval pact was concluded just before El Alamein, the Stalingrad encirclement, and the first joint Anglo-American ground offensive of World War II, Operation Torch, which was launched in northwest Africa. Torch would raise broad and deep questions about cryptanalytic cooperation between the armies of Britain and the United States in a most pressing manner. Within six months, building on the basis of the Travis-Wenger naval precedent, the War Office and the War Department would surmount a host of troubles to conclude a cryptanalytic agreement that far exceeded the navy agreement both in the scope of the activities it sanctioned and in the part it played in the creation of a long-term Anglo-American secret relationship.

CHAPTER SIX
BRUSA

**Phase I: Toward the BRUSA Agreement
(November 1942–April 1943)**

In the winter of 1942–43 the Allies launched a series of important military offensives. During October Britain attacked the Japanese position in Burma, and near the end of the month the Eighth Army began its victorious offensive against Rommel and the Afrika Korps. On 8 November, two weeks after Montgomery struck in Egypt, the Anglo-American Operation Torch force, under the command of Gen. Dwight D. Eisenhower, began to disembark on the beaches of Algeria and French Morocco. Ten days after Torch, the Soviets started their autumn offensive, smashing through weak Romanian and Italian formations to begin the encirclement of the German Sixth Army and carry out the relief of Stalingrad.

All of these actions were hard fought and important to ultimate Allied victory, but none of them was a walkover triumph. The British operation in Burma was at best indecisive, if not a disappointment; the two Allied armies in North Africa had to fight until May of 1943 before the German high command surrendered Tunisia. In the east, the Soviets did not force the surrender of the German Sixth Army at Stalingrad until February 1943; that same month, in the Far East, American forces finally cleared Guadalcanal of the Japanese.

Stalingrad, Tunisia, and Guadalcanal were highly significant milestones on the Allied road to victory. By its triumph at Stalingrad, the Red Army decided that there would be no German strategic victory in eastern Europe. The Americans made a comparable decisive move at Guadalcanal, seizing the initiative and relegating the Japanese to the defensive for the remainder of the Pacific war. The end results of El Alamein and Torch were, if not quite as decisive, nonetheless highly important, since they opened up the northern Mediterranean to Allied offensive action and placed Fascist Italy in a highly vulnerable position.

Even if Torch and El Alamein may have been a bit less significant than Guadalcanal or Stalingrad in the overall course of the war, the North African operations were extremely important in the history of Anglo-American intelligence cooperation. Mass movement of enemy forces occasioned by Anglo-American offensive operations produced increased and varied flows of enemy radio traffic, thereby opening up new opportunities for cryptanalytic attack. At the same time, joint Allied ground and air operations, such as Torch, increased the pressure for Anglo-American military cryptanalytic cooperation, just as the joining together of the Royal and U.S. navies in the battles of the North Atlantic had done for naval cooperation.

Furthermore, Ultra played a vital role in the advance of the Eighth Army, as well as in the preparations for Torch, and in the subsequent easterly drive of Eisenhower's armies. The British were convinced by Ultra that the Germans had not accurately judged the target of Eisenhower's invasion—Hitler believing as late as three weeks prior to the North African D day that the Allies were headed for Dakar rather than Oran or Casablanca. Churchill made certain that the president learned that "the secret matter [Ultra]" had proved that Berlin had failed to unravel the mystery of Torch's target.[1]

The British also insisted that Charles de Gaulle and the Free French be kept ignorant of the details of the Torch operation, contending, probably at least in part from Ultra sources, that de Gaulle's headquarters was "leaky." This conclusion was then shared with the Americans, General Marshall relaying the British security concerns to President Roosevelt on 7 August 1942. The initial British move to marginalize the Free French on security grounds was then seconded by the U.S. Navy. Six months later, but still during the North African campaign, Admiral King proposed that all French warships of destroyer class and larger be required to have on board an Anglo-American liaison communications officer with "the entire combined US-British naval signal publication" to guarantee that operational orders based on "highly secret information" would not inadvertently be disclosed to the enemy by the "leaky" French.[2] This proposal was highly offensive to the Free French and soon had to be modified. But even after the French army in North Africa had joined with the Anglo-Americans to fight the Germans in the winter of 1942, the French commanders were not included in the signals intelligence system, which by that time brought Ultra secret intelligence to the higher American, as well as British, commanders in the field. At least one of the French army commanders was told flatly in early 1943 that the British and Americans were benefiting from "a Sigint Service based upon a greatly extended intercept cover[,] directly from the U.K.," but that participation in this system could not be extended to the French.[3]

From the very beginning, therefore, as the British and the Americans drew closer regarding special intelligence, wider gaps were opened up between the countries inside the Ultra-Magic club and those outside it. In the same period when these rebuffs were administered to the French (February 1943), the American JCS also reaffirmed its hardline stand against sharing high-grade intelligence with America's Nationalist Chinese ally. Again this was done on the grounds of poor security. Some of the American doubts about the Chinese quite likely arose from Magic sources. Magic also played a part in providing information for some British security operations in the Far East during this period, such as those aimed at Burmese who collaborated with the Japanese occupation authorities in that territory.[4]

In late 1942, and especially in the early months of 1943, as the British and American offensives gathered steam, a more regular and extensively used system for transmitting Magic intercepts from Churchill to Roosevelt was developed. They now passed through Captain Hastings in the Joint Staff Mission to General Marshall, and from Marshall to the White House. The president thus received his American Magic through U.S. Navy channels and his British Magic through U.S. Army channels.

Nearly all the British information that passed along this route had been extracted from Japanese diplomatic traffic to and from Axis and neutral countries in Europe and the Middle East. Some of the messages did touch on Axis and Japanese intentions, and when combined with other forms of intelligence available to American authorities, in particular their own Magic intercepts, they helped form the basis for important strategic decisions and, on occasion, inadvertently helped to produce inter-Allied cooperation. One Magic decrypt received from the British on 5 August 1942, indicating that Japan would not attack the USSR, so impressed General Marshall that he wanted it passed on to Stalin in order to give the USSR "at least some encouragement" in their current "desperate situation." The Churchill-Roosevelt Magic intercept link also featured such items as the rambling disclosures made by the pro-Axis Duke of Alba to the Japanese ambassador in Madrid (January 1943). Since the Duke of Alba was Spain's ambassador in London, having an ear at the Magic keyhole allowed the British to assess the duke's real views and better gauge the policy and intentions of the Spanish government.[5]

Sharing of information from Magic, and the security considerations arising from joint offensive operations such as Torch, therefore tended to nudge the British and Americans into a closer monopolistic union regarding highly secret intelligence. So too did the command structure used for the northwest African campaign. Shortly after being made supreme commander for the operation, Eisenhower had been taken into the Ultra secret, and through his British G-2 and the Special Liaison Unit (SLU), which accompanied him from the time he moved to Gibraltar shortly before the landings, Ultra intelligence poured into his hands and those of his highest staff. One of the most important consequences of this development was that Eisenhower was soon making decisions on the basis of Ultra information unavailable to his superiors in the War Department in Washington. Such unfathomable independence quickly led to communication and coordination troubles between Eisenhower and all levels of officialdom in the American capital. By early August even the British Joint Staff Mission in Washington was complaining that Eisenhower was being provided with British signals intelligence (SIGINT) material that the JSM was not receiving.[6]

Rising dissatisfaction with this situation prompted fresh initiatives to draw the British and American armies closer together regarding various aspects of both cryptology and cryptanalysis. Two weeks after Torch began, the American Joint Chiefs of Staff finally agreed to establish an Anglo-American committee that would grade the codes and ciphers of the two countries on the basis of their levels of security. In early December 1942 John Tiltman arrived back in Washington to head a three-man British team to help implement this agreement. By mid-December Tiltman and Friedman had expanded the subject of the discussions to include the development of a combined code-and-cipher system to be used in joint operations of the two countries.

The push provided by joint operations may not have been the only factor that inclined the British government to be more sanguine about formal cryptanalytic and cryptologic arrangements with the United States in late 1942 and early 1943. In the seventeen months following June 1941 the British authorities had engaged in various forms of signals intelligence sharing arrangements with the Red Army, Air Force, and Navy. Although the British had initially excluded "E[nigma]" material from their dealings with the Soviets, as the months went by the arrangements between the officials of the two countries edged from simple "Y" interception matters into more sensitive areas, such as low-level German air, army, and navy operational codes, together with forays into joint attacks on German police codes. In September 1942 the top British "Y" representative in Moscow, Edward Crankshaw, attempted to persuade his superiors in Britain, as well as the Soviet liaison officers in Moscow, to make far-reaching "Y" and cryptanalytic arrangements between the two countries in order to move the two governments closer to joint work on German high-level radio traffic. A nervous British government cautiously agreed to explore the possibility of such a deal. The Soviet military authorities provided such a large volume of valuable "Y" and broken low-level German code material for Crankshaw to ship by air to London that the British Military Mission in Moscow believed in November 1942 that a new phase of happy East-West cooperation was about to begin.

Then, on 1 December 1942 the Soviet military command rejected a close Anglo-Soviet cryptanalytic partnership without explanation. Three months later, Stalin told the British ambassador (Clark Kerr) that he would reverse that decision and immediately institute cryptanalytic cooperation between Britain and the USSR, but nothing actually happened; even "Y"-level sharing soon ceased except for that related to naval operations in northern Russia.[7]

Whatever may have caused the Soviets to reject close "Y" and cryptanalytic arrangements with Britain, that decision may well have helped clear the way for a cryptanalytic deal between London and Washington. After December 1942 no danger existed that London might find itself caught in the middle of embarrassing conflicts of cryptanalytic interest between itself and its two major allies. The Soviet decision to pull back on code- and cipher-breaking arrangements may therefore have made London officials believe that in regard to cryptanalytic cooperation their hands were free and they would be able to ease the

Americans into whatever form of Ultra sharing suited British fancy and British interests.

This prospect of a smooth evolution toward harmonious Anglo-American code-and-cipher cooperation on British terms was, however, suddenly threatened from a new, and highly unlikely, quarter in that same first week of December 1942—the arrival in Washington of Alan Turing. The initial assignment of this young, and often otherworldly, British mathematical wizard, whose brilliant theorizing lay at the foundation of much of Bletchley's success against the German Enigma, was to assist the U.S. Navy cryptanalytic team with its part of the Anglo-American Triton-breaking agreement, which had just been arranged by Travis, Wenger, and Hinsley. With the Triton intercepts flooding into Bletchley, and in part being passed on to Op-20-G, coordination and the training of American personnel were necessary to make the agreement work effectively.

If Turing had been allowed to confine his labors to the implementation of the naval agreement, no disruption of Anglo-American secret cooperation would have been likely to result. But the Bletchley emissary had been given a second, highly secret, mission. He had been instructed to visit the Bell Laboratories in New Jersey in order to examine the American progress toward the creation of a scrambler telephone (the "X" system project), which it was hoped would make possible completely secure communication by radiotelephone.[8] Soon after the United States entered the war, President Roosevelt had demanded the development of such a link between London and Washington, regardless of the cost or the formidable technical obstacles that would have to be overcome. By late 1942 Bell Laboratories believed they were close to success. The British authorities were quite naturally interested in the progress that had been made, and ordered Turing to survey the situation before returning to England.[9]

When the Joint Staff Mission made a routine application for Turing to enter the labs, however, it was rejected by U.S. Army authorities. On 2 December 1942 the chief of the British Mission, Field Marshal Sir John Dill, wrote a "Secret and Personal" note to General Marshall explaining the situation and describing Turing as "our leading authority on scrambling devices." While granting that this was "not a big question," Dill nonetheless asked Marshall to "lift the ban on Dr. Turing."

Instead of the polite and helpful response that usually arrived when Dill and Marshall were forced to cope with hiccups in the special relationship, this time the head of the Joint Staff Mission received a reply that gave his organization a sharp jolt and produced a genuine crisis. This conflict, which began just as the battles in southern Russia and the South Pacific moved toward their climaxes, may not have been as bloody as Stalingrad or Guadalcanal, but it was nearly as protracted, and seemed almost as bitter.[10]

In his "Dear Dill" note of 9 December, Marshall apologized for the embarrassment the refusal had caused Turing. But he also emphasized that the clearance the British mathematician had obtained was not valid for the Bell Labs project, and that he would have to reapply directly to G-2. Marshall went on to say that the scrambler phone was classified "Ultra Secret" (an oddly contrived adaptation of the British cryptanalytic security classification), which necessitated that access to it be rigidly restricted. In any event, Marshall added, the British authorities had nothing to complain about, because "I am told that this same policy is being followed by your intelligence people and that there is not interchange on these Ultra secret developments."

On receipt of the Marshall letter, Dill turned immediately for guidance to Bletchley's liaison officer in the Joint Staff Mission, Captain Hastings. Dill received a reassuring response to the effect that as far as Hastings was aware, "British policy is to interchange all information regarding ultra secret developments with the USA." But both Hastings and Dill decided to double-check with Bletchley, and its special emissary in Washington, Brigadier Tiltman, before making a reply to Marshall. On 15 December, having received appropriately comforting responses from these authorities, Dill wrote to the American army chief of staff, noting that he had been "horrified" by Marshall's statement "that we are not giving you all our ultra secret developments in this field." After checking into the matter, Dill had been assured that "we hide nothing from your duly authenticated people," but if the War Department had any doubts about this, Dill added, he earnestly requested Marshall "to let me know."

This letter also failed to do the trick. Instead of a mollifying response from the War Department, another missive came back in which Marshall laid bare the root cause of the U.S. Army's resentment and intransigence. It had nothing to do with Turing, the scrambler phone, or any failure of the British to provide secret information on communications technology. The whole problem arose from the lack of an army Ultra-Magic deal, and General Strong's resentment that he had been cut out of the exchanges of high-level cryptanalytic technology and decrypted Ultra traffic such as that granted to Eisenhower, and to the U.S. Navy, in the previous month. In Marshall's words, the cause of the crisis was the fact that:

> G-2 tells me that we have been unable to get from your people any detailed information on German Army field traffic, or clandestine traffic, although the latter has been promised, or on cryptographic material derived from Slavic nations.* We have also been unable to get complete details of your so-called high speed analyzer [bombe].

The long-delayed moment for a showdown on whether or not the War Department would receive Ultra information had seemingly arrived, and Dill therefore thought it best to use a stalling strategy in replying to Marshall. On the day after Christmas 1942 he merely summarized the system of control over British cryptanalysis exercised by GC & CS** and by "C," and attributed the current troubles to a "mutual misunderstanding of the British and U.S. procedure in making these requests" for Ultra secret information.

Despite this serene veneer, the British Mission in Washington was straining every nerve to beat down the complaints of G-2 regarding Ultra and get approval for Turing's entry into the Bell Labs. Tiltman went to work on both General Strong and the head of Special Branch, Colonel Clarke, challenging them to substantiate the American charge that Bletchley had withheld technical information from the Americans. By early January Strong had accepted Tiltman's word that "nothing was deliberately withheld." This conclusion was substantially confirmed by Colonel Clarke, as well as by the current chief of Army SIS's Arlington Hall cryptanalytic operations, Colonel Bullock. But Tiltman had to agree to additional negotiations between Army SIS and Bletchley regarding Enigma intercepts. He was unsuccessful in his effort to get Turing approved to enter the Bell Labs—General Strong having pleaded that the Tur-

---

*See page 144 for a consideration of this peculiar phrase.
**Recently renamed "Government Communications Headquarters," but the name Government Code and Cipher School (GC & CS) will be used throughout this work.

ing matter "was now out of his hands" and would have "to be decided between the Field Marshal [Dill] and General Marshall."

On the most critical issue of cryptanalytic cooperation, however, the British team seemed to have recovered the high ground, and on 2 January 1943 Tiltman set forth the current position for Field Marshal Dill:

> We make available to any properly accredited representative of the War Department all the processes and results of cryptographic investigation at the Government Code and Cipher School, but in the case of investigation on the higher planes of secrecy [Enigma intercepts] we have discouraged as far as possible the duplication of our work in the U.S.A. or elsewhere.

This statement covered the technical side of the controversy and underscored British opposition to giving the U.S. Army raw Enigma intercepts, but it did not address the question of making finished Ultra messages available to the War Department. Nonetheless, Field Marshal Dill went right back to Marshall on 5 January after Strong had declared that only Marshall now had the power to approve Turing's visit. Emphasizing Tiltman's success in getting General Strong to grant "that nothing was deliberately withheld," Dill asked the U.S. Army chief of staff to open the door of the Bell Labs to Turing.

Marshall was still not prepared to give way on the Turing matter, however. On 6 January he wrote yet another letter to Dill explaining that "other interests" were involved in the "X" project and that even he had not been able to clear the situation "in Turing's favor." The scrambler phone was in fact being developed under the auspices of both the U.S. Army and Navy, and at the midpoint of the conflict over Turing's visit to the Bell Labs, 29 December 1942, Admiral King had decided against permitting any British specialists to see the "X" apparatus.[11]

The U.S. Army chief of staff was therefore temporarily stuck on that side of the problem, but he went out of his way to compensate Dill by trying to meet him on the cryptanalytic matter. Declaring that he understood that General Strong "wanted full [decrypted] information regarding the Germans so that our G-2 could do its own evaluation," Marshall confided to Dill that even Strong had come to agree "that turning this information over to us does actually involve increased hazard."

Therefore the U.S. Army chief of staff had come to the conclusion that Bletchley "should not release to us more detailed data of this kind than they do at present."

This reply, while still leaving Turing outside the laboratory door, pulled the rug out from under those American army officers trying to clinch a code-and-cipher deal with the British. Marshall had all but surrendered the case for U.S. Army decryption work on German Enigma intercepts, as well as any wholesale shipment to Washington of Ultra intelligence, and Dill immediately grasped the opportunity provided by this situation. In a phone call and letter to Marshall, Dill pressed home the case for Turing's entry to the Bell Labs on the basis of "full reciprocity," emphasizing that GC & CS had already permitted "exploitation by the U.S. Navy of one particular type of traffic which we agreed was of vital importance to them." But, Dill stressed, Bletchley would be prepared to go beyond the Wenger-Travis naval deal and share cryptanalytic secrets with the American army only "*in England* [italics added]," not in the United States. If the American army emissaries were prepared to go to Bletchley Park for their enlightenment, Dill wrote, "we are prepared to show your people everything." But no raw German army or Luftwaffe Enigma traffic would be sent to Washington.[12]

Though dressed up in a cheerful wrapper, Dill's 7 January letter amounted to an ultimatum. Should the Americans not open the way for Turing, all aspects of Ultra secret cooperation between Britain and the United States might be at risk. Marshall saw that a solution had to be found quickly. On the following day he ordered General Strong to discuss the Turing affair immediately "with the Sec.[retary] of War." This was presumably done—Stimson then arranging the matter of Turing's access to the Bell Labs with Secretary of the Navy Frank Knox. At the same time General Strong wrote a short paper stressing the U.S. Army's commitment "to complete frankness and reciprocity in all highly secret matters," subject only to the proviso that Britain would not try to "exploit" the information it acquired about American highly secret inventions. Strong's paper concluded with an authorization for Turing to enter the Bell Labs, and on 9 January it was sent to the Joint Staff Mission over the signature of Marshall's deputy, Gen. Joseph McNarney. The Turing affair was thereby officially closed, just a few days before Roosevelt, Churchill, and the Combined Chiefs of

Staff met at Casablanca to discuss the future of Anglo-American joint operations.

The squabble over Turing's visit had opened up important questions not only between the U.S. Army and the British, but also between the American War and Navy departments. Although the U.S. Navy had ultimately yielded and allowed Turing to examine the scrambler phone development, there was unhappiness about this among "lower deck" technical specialists. Once again, as in 1940 when the first abortive cryptanalytic-sharing agreement with Britain had produced the Sinkov mission, the U.S. Navy communications specialists believed that George Marshall and his U.S. Army colleagues had given away navy assets to the British and secured nothing of value in return.[13]

The Turing controversy also compelled the British authorities to give more serious thought and attention to the "X" system scrambler phone and other forms of secure transatlantic communication than they might otherwise have done. By mid-February 1943 Turing reported that although the American scrambler phone was more secure than any previous such device, it was still less safe than one-time pad.* Also, Bletchley complained that, during Turing's visit, he was still not allowed to record certain details and drawings of the "X" system. The British Chiefs of Staff were also not enthusiastic about having such a secret communication system under exclusive American control. Therefore, on 28 April 1943 a Telektron scrambler machine** was attached to the direct teleprint circuit that connected the Admiralty to the Royal Navy Registry in Washington, thereby providing "complete security of communications *including* [italics added] security from the Americans."[14]

In spite of such cautious reservations, the British were forced to use the American technology to tighten security on transatlantic voice communication. The vulnerability of the scrambling equipment employed in the transatlantic telephone circuit utilized by the president and the prime minister compelled the British to allow installation of the "X" system scrambler in London and Washington. It finally went

---

*In one-time pad the equivalences of a code system are changed completely after every single transmission.
**A British electric ciphering machine, much more sophisticated than the German Enigma.

into service in mid-August 1943, just two weeks after the German radio monitors had successfully intercepted a Roosevelt-Churchill conversation that had been made on the old band-split system. The Americans went on to install the "X" scrambler on the Washington-Algiers circuit in November 1943, and later extended it to other overseas locations that the American authorities thought worthy of high-level, direct, and secure telephone communication.[15]

In addition to the role it played in prompting acceptance of the new scrambler machine, the Turing affair gave a note of urgency to the U.S. Army's effort to make a cryptanalytic agreement with Britain. Despite continuously reiterated British rejection of the idea that raw Enigma intercepts should be exploited by the U.S. Army in Washington, London did repeatedly promise "reciprocity" on all "Ultra secret" matters. This gave American Army SIS officials a strong weapon to counter what they saw as British tightfistedness.

Initially, Arlington Hall simply ignored British insistence that no "exploitation" of Enigma should be done by the U.S. Army in Washington, and Friedman himself raised the question with Tiltman in January. Then, after Dill and Marshall agreed on 20 February that all subsequent negotiations on army cryptanalytic cooperation between the two countries would be handled by Captain Hastings and General Strong, the Americans vigorously pushed their claim to carry out independent work against the Enigma. On 23 February the U.S. Army made a formal request that Bletchley send raw Enigma traffic to Arlington Hall, as was then being done for Op-20-G. This proposal was supported by an American army claim that the Signal Corps was well along in developing its own bombe type of equipment, which would give Arlington Hall bright prospects for break-ins to various Enigma ciphers.[16]

On 30 September 1942 the U.S. Army Signal Corps had contracted with the Bell Labs to design a bombe that used relay switching rather than the rotary method employed by the U.S. Navy. The subunit of this machine was a single-frame apparatus similar in operation to the three-wheeled Enigma. By November 1942 the Bell Labs had successfully demonstrated a sample machine, and undertook to produce 144 such frames. So rapid was the development of this rather ungainly bombe, which "looked like metal shelving, with the insides of radio receiver sets" stacked up in an "orderly interconnected arrangement," that on 8 February 1943 Friedman reported to General Corderman that this "E[nigma] solving machine" would be ready for installation by 1 April

1943, and Arlington Hall could then begin an independent attack on the Enigma.[17] Above all, it was the threat posed by the prospect of this separate attack on the Enigma, code-named the "Yellow Project," which forced Britain into yet another round of hard bargaining. Hastings claimed that there was no reason to launch a second attack on the Enigma; Friedman and his colleagues countered with the argument that their new bombe "bore no external nor internal resemblance to the British bombes or associated equipment," and also asserted that it was "capable of solving several other types of cryptographic traffic problems" in addition to the Enigma.[18]

The Achilles' heel of the U.S. Army's bargaining position was the fact that Arlington Hall lacked sufficient Enigma intercept material to carry out a broad-based cipher-breaking operation on its own. There were no American intercept stations in Europe or North Africa, and the stations that did exist on the East Coast of the United States, in Iceland, and in Newfoundland were too few in number, and their reception capabilities too limited, to provide Arlington with enough German army and Luftwaffe traffic to launch a promising independent assault on German ciphers. Only the intercept stations in Britain that serviced Bletchley were capable of producing a large enough volume of German enciphered traffic to make a successful cipher-breaking operation possible. Although the Americans were probably unaware of it, even the British stations were far from omniscient. Throughout the war a substantial portion of German enciphered radio traffic was shielded by weather and distance from the intercept stations in the British Isles and the Middle East.[19]

Whatever the shortcomings of these British "Y" installations, however, the American army authorities believed quite rightly in 1943 that their dreams of an independent attack on the Enigma were dependent on Britain agreeing to share its intercepts. The understanding that had followed the "Y" conference of April 1942 had brought to the United States the Japanese radio traffic intercepted by British "Y" operators in Canada, Australia, and India. By mid-1943 this material constituted about 30 percent of all the Japanese radio messages available to American code-and-cipher breakers. Arlington Hall consequently concluded that if the British could do that well against distant Japanese radio communications, it was surely in a position to turn over vast quantities of German Enigma traffic if it chose to do so.[20]

Arlington Hall also desired British help in securing intercepted radio traffic of one of its allies. In his 23 December 1942 letter to Field Marshal Dill, during the Turing affair, George Marshall had said that Arlington wanted not only German Enigma traffic, but also that "from Slavic nations." When discussing the information that Arlington Hall wished to secure from Britain in early 1943, a postwar NSA study stated that what the U.S. Army wanted were "communications originating in _ _ _ _ _ _ _ [seven letters blacked out by the declassifier] and German dominated countries in Europe." This blacked-out adjectival form of a country's name consisting of seven letters, when applied to the military-political realities of 1943 Europe, could only have referred to Italian- or Russian-dominated areas. Since the document's mention of "German dominated countries" did not prompt a blackening by the declassifier, it is difficult to imagine that the blacked-out word referred to Germany's Italian Fascist partner. So the word was probably *Russian*. When this probability is coupled with General Marshall's "Slavic nations" phrase, it seems clear that Arlington Hall was indeed pressing Bletchley to provide it with Soviet as well as German intercepted traffic. In this regard it should be noted that although the official *History of British Intelligence in the Second World War* declared, in a much-cited remark, "that all work on Russian codes and cyphers stopped on 22 June 1941," Hinsley, Thomas, et al. never declared that the British government ceased to *intercept* Soviet traffic. Certainly the British Y service had ample opportunity to do so, not only from its stations in Iceland, the United Kingdom, India, and the Middle East, but also from a small British wireless intercept station that actually operated in northern Russia throughout much of the war. It is also clear from postwar investigations of the affair of the "Cambridge Spies" that in the late 1940s and early 1950s British and American officials were in possession of some intercepts of secret wartime Soviet radio traffic because Donald Maclean's treachery was finally uncovered by means of a careful study of sloppy enciphering work done by his Soviet minder in 1945.[21]

When Arlington Hall pressed the British to provide intercept traffic to help fuel the buildup of a large and sophisticated American army cryptanalytic operation in Washington during early 1943, the U.S. Army cryptanalysts were apparently focusing not only on the current conflict against the Axis but also on possible future trouble with the USSR. One would have thought that this implied offer of a cryptanalytic partnership stretching beyond the period of World War II would have had genuine appeal for the British government in the spring of 1943. By that time the scale of American technical-productive output, and the size of the U.S. armed forces, had already given notice that America would be a postwar superpower. British nervousness about its own postwar position, plus the possible dangers posed by an expanded and expanding Soviet Union, were also causing concern in some corners of Whitehall. Indeed a body of revisionist historical opinion long contended that even during the midwar period the western powers were already gearing up for a confrontation with the "Soviet threat." But even the possibility of gaining long-range political benefit from a full army cryptanalytic deal with the United States was insufficient to persuade Britain to conclude such an agreement in 1943. Whitehall was not yet prepared to make an incipient cold war code- and cipher-breaking agreement, especially one that involved security risks and entailed relinquishing control of highly valuable British intelligence assets. Therefore, in February 1943, Captain Hastings and his associates issued grave warnings to Colonel Clarke and General Corderman that unless they gave up their attempt to carry out an Enigma decryption operation in Washington, all Anglo-American collaboration on signals intelligence would cease.[22]

The same negative response was made in London when the British Chiefs of Staff were asked to reply to the American proposal that they be authorized to create their own army version of Bletchley—fueled by British "Y" intercept materials—in Washington. Despite the best effort of the U.S. Army mission in London, including those of its chief signal officer, Col. George Bicher, the British Chiefs told the Americans that no form of "exploitation of European traffic performed in the United States" would be accepted. In March 1943 Anglo-American difficulties over cryptanalytic policy led to the abolition of the Combined Enemy Intelligence Communications Committee in Washington.[23]

Having thus run into universal, and immovable, British opposition to their independent decryption plans, Arlington Hall and G-2 finally realized that the effort was doomed. However, this recognition did not mean that Arlington Hall, G-2, or even the British were prepared to abandon the attempt to produce increased Ultra cooperation between the two countries, and negotiations between Captain Hastings and General Strong continued throughout March and April 1943.[24]

Beyond Washington, the progress of the war itself indicated that a close partnership in dealing with the Enigma was necessary. The Tunisian campaign was drawing to a close, and in accordance with the agreements reached at the Casablanca Conference in late January 1943, preparations were already underway for joint Anglo-American attacks against Sicily and mainland Italy. The combined bomber offensive, employing heavy bombers of both the Eighth and ultimately the Fifteenth U.S. Army Air Forces alongside the RAF, was now reaching full stride. Planning had also begun for a large and complex joint invasion of northern France in 1944. All these developments drew the American and British authorities into a closer operational partnership, which increased the number of U.S. Army personnel who had to be drawn into the Ultra secret. The operations, as well as the planning, also occasioned serious high-level policy conflicts in which British officials could only hope to support their views with maximum vigor if the intelligence foundations of their conclusions, including the Ultra components, could be made clear to their American colleagues in Washington as well as those in Algiers and London.

In the same period, the course of the Pacific war was increasing the importance of cryptanalytic activity and intensifying the need for more comprehensive agreements, which would allow the receipt of the full range of decrypted enemy radio traffic by all Allied headquarters in the region. In December 1942, although General MacArthur seems to have been receiving some high-grade decrypts of Japanese traffic from British sources, the U.S. Navy was still reluctant to share with MacArthur's headquarters all the Magic and other Japanese material that it was breaking locally. MacArthur therefore requested authority from Washington to turn the Central Bureau into a complete decryption operation reaching up through Magic. At the end of January 1943 General Marshall complied with that request by sending two Magic machines and their operators to the South Pacific.[25]

Although unwilling to share highly secret intelligence with the U.S. Army, the American navy continued to make important breakthroughs against the Japanese code-and-cipher system. Early in 1943 the "Maru" convoy code was cracked, and three months later the navy increased its success rate by breaking a Japanese navy machine cipher.[26]

In March 1943 the British achieved a significant break-in of their own against Japanese crypto systems. The Wireless Experimental Center in Delhi achieved the first penetration into high-level Japanese army codes during that month. Members of MacArthur's Central Bureau also began to move inside the Japanese army Water Transport Code system during March. The latter code was as significant as its name was awkward, because this was the communication channel used in the transfer of Japanese troops by sea, and it carried highly valuable data on the logistical situation, order of battle, and frequently on the strategic intentions of the Japanese government as well.[27]

Once the Central Bureau team began to make progress on the Water Transport Code, the relevant information was dispatched to Arlington Hall along with the necessary intercept traffic; Frank Lewis made a partial break-in there on 4–5 April 1943. Shortly thereafter two men at Central Bureau made their own partial break-in to the same code. A short delay then ensued while Arlington Hall toyed with the notion of using these break-ins to increase American bargaining leverage in the cryptanalysis-sharing negotiations then going on with the British. But by mid-April the idea of such a crass power-political move had been jettisoned, and the solution of the Water Transport Code was provided to Bletchley and Delhi with no strings attached.[28]

The British authorities therefore had good reason to be pleased both with the code-breaking competence, and the willingness to share, of their American ally in the Pacific war. That in January 1943 the Americans had pushed forward aggressively in one of the shadowy areas of existing agreements—interception and decryption of German weather traffic—may have produced some concern in Whitehall, but in light of the great headway made in sharing SIGINT in the Pacific, as well as the successful operation of the Travis-Wenger agreement on German U-boat traffic, this was a minor irritation.[29]

By early 1943 the U.S. Navy had shown itself fully capable of shouldering the responsibilities laid down by the naval cryptanalytic agreement covering the Atlantic. The Navy Department had even attempted to match the Admiralty's draconian security regulations concerning circulation of Ultra material, and the restrictions it imposed on combat actions based on Ultra information. On 31 March 1943 the commander in chief Atlantic Fleet issued a sweeping order demanding tight restrictions on the distribution of Ultra and requiring guarantees that action based on radio intelligence information could not "be traced [by the enemy] to this source alone." Later in 1943, when the U.S. Navy used two of its carriers for an all-out assault on the

U-boats, many in the Admiralty felt that Admiral King was flaunting his own rules on the importance of shielding Ultra sources, but in the crucial period from February to May 1943, while Hastings and Strong were dueling over the terms of an army cryptanalytic agreement, Admiral King and his staff not only upheld rigid Ultra security in their own operations, they also took a comparably stern line in their SIGINT relations with the U.S. Army. In mid-May the assistant chief of Naval Plans, Rear Adm. C. M. Cooke, rejected any idea of a joint U.S. Army–Navy section "having access to *all* intelligence," in part because, in Cooke's view, Army G-2 continued "to give evidence of lack of appreciation of close security of R[adio] I[ntelligence]." "The important elements of R.I.," Cooke concluded, should therefore "not get out of strictly naval controls."[30] When, in May 1943, General Marshall sought to bend the existing rules to allow a few civilians on a Combined Intelligence subcommittee to participate in a discussion in which information from Ultra might be mentioned, Admiral King flatly refused. "We are getting a great deal of very valuable information from the British," King told Marshall, but this flow was linked to a "definite promise that we would treat it with special secrecy." The chief of Naval Operations was adamant that none of it should be made available to any civilian. King's rigid security stance, which Marshall himself would soon support, could have brought only joy to British hearts. It also, of course, intensified the trend steadily developing in Washington that highly secret matters should be concentrated in fewer and fewer hands, a trend that would smooth the way for the condition of permanent mobilization within the U.S. government, which would characterize America in the postwar era.[31]

While high-level British and American cooperation was increasing on such top-secret matters as Ultra security and the war in the Pacific, the movement toward completion of an army Ultra agreement was also nudged forward by the progress that had occurred regarding conventional military intelligence and security cooperation. In March 1943, following a meeting in London between the ubiquitous General Strong and the Director of Military Intelligence (DMI), Gen. F. H. N. Davidson, the British and American armies finally reached a comprehensive understanding in respect to German order-of-battle intelligence, as well as intelligence on German treatment of Allied POWs and intelligence secured from German POWs in Allied hands. During the final stage of the North African campaign, a daily interchange of information regarding German order of battle began between the OB specialists from the two armies; at the same time preparations were begun to achieve the same close relationship between the OB specialists of the RAF and the U.S. Army Air Corps. Regarding the various aspects of secret prisoner-of-war intelligence—much of which originated from informers and the bugging of holding cells—all indirect methods of British-American exchange were abolished by the end of March 1943. Thereafter, British POW intelligence reports (that is, those from MI 9, MI 19, and MI 19a), as well as the comparable reports produced by American authorities (MIS-X and interrogation reports), were exchanged directly by the POW Branch of the U.S. Army Military Intelligence Service (G-2) and the DDMI/PW section of the War Office, without having to go up and down the chains of command of the two armies.[32]

A comparable, and equally significant, understanding had been reached in December 1942 between British MI 6 and the American OSS in respect to counterintelligence information; this agreement specifically created a limited form of cryptanalytic cooperation. By March 1943 OSS counterintelligence (X-2) personnel had joined hands with Section V of MI 6, and were allowed access to the "ISOS" intercepts of German Abwehr agent radio traffic at the British center at St. Albans. This arrangement, formally approved by the American Joint Chiefs of Staff in February 1943, was comparable to what had been arranged between the Admiralty and Op-20-G regarding Triton Enigma traffic, with the notable difference that under the OSS X-2 arrangement with MI 6, American personnel were integrated into a British operation that studied raw decrypted traffic in England. The OSS men were not taken into Bletchley Park, but their partnership at St. Albans was the closest possible arrangement short of full American participation in Bletchley's hut system of intelligence analysis.

The OSS–MI 6 arrangement may well have prompted the weary negotiators in Washington, led by Strong and Hastings, to believe that the best way to cut the Gordian knot tying up army cryptanalytic cooperation might be to send a high-level American Special Branch and Arlington Hall delegation to Bletchley. American examination of Bletchley's operations might well suggest ways in which the United States' need for German Enigma information could be met without threatening the success of the other Anglo-American intelligence cooperation arrangements that were now being spread worldwide.[33] The War Department seems to have concluded by the early part of April 1943 that a mission to Bletchley was necessary, because on 8 April the chief signal officer was given direct authorization to carry out a series of (unspecified) exchanges with the British. A high-level mission destined for Bletchley was formed shortly thereafter, consisting of William Friedman (Arlington Hall) and Col. Alfred McCormack and Lt. Col. Telford Taylor, from Special Branch.[34]

The composition of the mission was not without its hiccups and fortuitous elements. Whereas Friedman was the most seasoned American army cryptanalyst, McCormack (a civilian lawyer pressed into military service) had very little direct experience with cryptanalytic intelligence, and Taylor had only arrived in Special Branch five months earlier. Although Taylor was a highly able young lawyer and had been briefly attached to Arlington Hall for initiation into the cryptanalytic mysteries, he was a decidedly junior member of Special Branch. He had come to the attention of Colonel Clarke only because, as a bachelor, he had been chosen for many of the unpopular watch officer assignments, such as those on weekends and holidays; Clarke grasped Taylor's ability and included him in the London team.[35] On the other end of the experience scale, the senior member of the mission, William Friedman, was perhaps a bit past his prime, and was saddled with the burden of having lost and won too many bruising battles in the deadly world of Washington rivalry over military cryptanalysis. G-2 actually insisted on imposing a series of "restrictions"—the specifics of which have been withheld by NSA—on Friedman's "technical and social contacts with the British" while the mission was in England.[36]

Despite these tensions and troubles, once the mission reached London on 25 April 1943 nearly everything turned up roses. For professional cryptanalysts who had spent a lifetime cut off from their peers in other countries, this release from secrecy and anonymity must have been like escape from a pleasant but confining prison. At last these men were able to deal with foreign colleagues and enjoy the delights of intellectual interaction with people who were their equals in experience and skill yet brought different perspectives to code- and cipher-breaking problems. Friedman was received as a bosom colleague by Denniston and the other senior British code breakers. Well into the late 1950s

Friedman's personal correspondence reflected the close bonds he had formed with British cryptanalysts during this visit. Like Friedman, many of the professional and academic code breakers at Bletchley, such as Tiltman and E. R. Vincent, relished tackling medieval and renaissance code-and-cipher puzzles, and while America's senior code breaker was in England, many happy social evenings were spent discussing literary codes from Bacon to Shakespeare.[37]

Friedman, McCormack, and Taylor began the business side of their mission with official courtesy calls. All the important bases were touched by the American trio, ranging from the offices of the G-2 and the senior signal officer of the American forces in England (ETOUSA), to Denniston at Berkeley Street, Travis at Bletchley Park, and the titular head of GC & CS, Sir Stewart Menzies ("C"). The American trio was given an unprecedented authorization to explore nearly every aspect of signal interception and cryptanalysis in the British Isles. The visitors observed Y operations ranging from the most modern British stations to an American army signal company in training at the British intercept station at Tidworth.[38] But their primary responsibility was to examine British cryptanalytic operations at Bletchley Park and Denniston's London diplomatic-commercial operation on Berkeley Street. The three Americans realized very soon that the American intelligence and cryptanalytic officers in Washington were languishing in an "inadequate understanding of the complexities of the British effort." Two years of cautious liaison arrangements between Bletchley and Arlington Hall/ G-2 had failed to provide senior American officials with the wide-ranging yet detailed survey that would have been necessary for them to grasp Bletchley's modus operandi and the scale of its achievements.[39]

Although it must be emphasized that the American mission was shown Bletchley's bombe operations only *after* the signing of the Strong-Hastings "BRUSA" agreement on 17 May 1943, Friedman, McCormack, and Taylor were able to survey immediately every other step in the British signals intelligence process, from the original interceptions to the circulation of finished intelligence to military commands. The scale of the British operation—Bletchley then had a personnel roster exceeding 5,000—and the variety and complexity of its activities truly stunned the Americans. "It's not good. It's superb" was McCormack's judgment on Bletchley. This high-powered lawyer, dressed up as an American army colonel, was especially impressed by how much the British had accomplished by eschewing rigid military formalities and getting "the best man for the job."[40]

The complex arrangements embodied in the hut system for annotation and elucidation of decrypted messages made the greatest impact on the G-2 members of the team—McCormack and Taylor; Friedman seems to have been nearly as impressed by the wide range of cryptanalytic approaches used at Bletchley, and by the British success in using high-technology methods in their attacks on the many variations of the German Enigma. McCormack was convinced that the Americans lagged far behind the British. He cabled Colonel Clarke: "If Corderman [of Arlington Hall] wants his people to learn what makes this operation tick[,] he had better send them over to learn it because they never on God's green earth will learn it from anything Arlington will be able to do in any foreseeable future."[41]

The U.S. visitors bombarded their superiors at home with favorable impressions of British methods and organization, as well as recommendations on how the U.S. Army cryptanalytic and intelligence system might benefit by close cooperation with the United Kingdom. These dispatches seem to have been received, both in G-2 and Arlington Hall, with a mixture of skepticism and jealousy. But the steady flow of eyewitness observations could not help but nudge the U.S. Army toward some compromise arrangement with Britain. The American visitors had three fundamental points they repeated over and over. The U.S Army had nothing to lose and much to gain by an agreement. The Pentagon would acquire much information on cryptanalytic technology and the use of secure methods of distributing Ultra-type material, while gaining a large volume of high-grade intelligence. All the War Department had to do was face reality, abandon its foolish dream of attacking the Enigma on its own, and sign a compromise agreement. Then, the door to "cryptanalytic paradise" would be opened unto them.

Finally, on 17 May 1943, four weeks before McCormack and Friedman returned to the United States, word reached Bletchley that Arlington Hall and G-2 had agreed to a deal. A compromise had been found; Captain Hastings and General Strong had come to terms and the BRUSA agreement had been signed. By that act a new era embracing the most intimate intelligence cooperation ever enjoyed by two sovereign states was, at last, about to begin.

Phase II: The Agreement and After

The BRUSA agreement, formalized in 1943, was the written constitution upon which arose the Anglo-American cryptanalytic partnership that flourished during the final two-and-a-half years of World War II and, in modified forms, has continued until the present. Compared with the Anglo-American naval Enigma-breaking agreement of November 1942, BRUSA was a much more complex and wide-ranging pact between London and Washington. Consequently even the form and method of ratification of this understanding had its own short, but important, history.

In spring 1943, the British and American negotiators representing U.S. Army G-2 and Bletchley Park had wrestled to a draw over the American attempt to create an independent Enigma-breaking operation in Washington. This struggle was so tense and unpleasant that an NSA historian has characterized it as "G-2 and the British authorities walking around and eyeing each other like two mongrels who had just met."[42] As the cautious circling continued, Whitehall became increasingly uneasy about the danger it posed to broader Anglo-American cooperation. The British Chiefs of Staff finally addressed the problem by drafting a compromise proposal, subsequently named BRUSA (Britain and the USA), which was then sent along to the American army chief of staff, General Marshall, by Field Marshal Dill in the late spring. Marshall found the British proposal a possible foundation for an understanding, and he, in turn, approved using it as the basis for more detailed negotiations between General Strong and Captain Hastings. By mid-May these two men had turned the British Chiefs of Staff paper into a compromise agreement, which Sir Edward Travis for Bletchley and Gen. W. P. Corderman for the U.S. Army Signal Corps then signed on 17 May.[43]

As with all undertakings that entail obligations similar to those exacted by a written constitution, the first set of signatures merely called forth more; soon after Travis and Corderman had put their names to the document, General Strong ratified it for G-2, as did the supreme authorities in Whitehall and the War Department, Henry Stimson adding the final signature for the United States on 15 June 1943.[44]

The agreement was quite short—sixteen brief paragraphs in the body of the text, with eight additional paragraphs contained in an appendix.

A number of copies of the document exist in open records, but all of them have been heavily "blackened" by the declassifiers; except for one short sentence introducing the broad provisions of the agreement, the censors have been unusually consistent in wielding their felt-tip pens.[45]

From the open portions of the document, however, a number of significant points emerge. First, BRUSA dealt primarily with the sharing of finished intelligence that had originally been acquired from enemy radio traffic. No provision was included regarding the exchange of raw intercepts, the British having successfully blocked the creation of an American version of Bletchley to attack the Enigma in the United States. The agreement did bind the two countries to distinguish between three types of intelligence obtainable from enemy radio traffic, ranging upward both in importance and in the need for tight security controls. At the bottom level was simple traffic analysis, which had the lowest priority and security grading, and was designated "TA" by the Americans and "Y Inference" by the British. Then came low-grade enemy field SIGINT ("Special Intelligence B" to the Americans and "Y Intelligence" to the British), and finally, high-grade enemy codes and ciphers (such as Ultra and Magic), which the Americans referred to generically as "Special Intelligence A," and the British merely called "Special Intelligence."

After underscoring the security concerns of both governments in the handling of all types of signals intelligence, BRUSA limited the range of the cooperative agreement to information acquired from specific categories of the high-level radio traffic of particular foreign countries. Britain and the United States bound themselves "to exchange completely all information concerning the detection, identification and interception of signals from, and the solution of codes and ciphers used by, the Military and Air Forces of the Axis powers, including secret services (Abwehr)," but no reference was made to enemy navies. The U.S. Army assumed "as a main responsibility, the reading of Japanese Military and Air codes and ciphers," while Britain continued to take on the parallel responsibility regarding "the crypto systems of Germany and Italy."

Unfortunately, the point where the security screeners first became busy with their felt-tip pens was a general provision regarding what intercepted traffic would not be covered by the agreement. However, an application under the Freedom of Information Act plus two subsequent appeals—all focused on General Strong's transmittal letter, which accompanied the agreement on its initial journey to General Marshall on 10 June 1943—finally revealed a sentence stating that BRUSA did "*not* [italics added] cover traffic from non-service enemy or neutral sources."[46]

This provision is both curious and highly interesting. Curious because Britain and the United States had exchanged, and would continue to exchange, "non-service enemy" traffic, the most obvious instance of such cooperation being Japanese "Magic" diplomatic messages. Furthermore, even before the BRUSA agreement had been signed, Commander Denniston offered to admit American participant observers to his diplomatic decryption operation on Berkeley Street. In June 1943 the first venue in which American personnel were actually allowed to screen traffic decrypted by the British was Denniston's diplomatic and commercial cryptanalytic center.[47]

The second interesting aspect of the sentence liberated from General Strong's transmittal letter is that it does not exclude from the agreement either the military traffic of neutrals or any form of the radio traffic from the *allies* of Britain and the United States. Obviously one must be careful about building sand castles over omissions or obliterations produced by security screeners (especially in highly secret documents), but it should at least be noted that since 1945 the declassifiers of both countries have been extremely vigilant in stopping the release of any information regarding Anglo-American intelligence operations in neutral countries in World War II. As has been noted above, the American authorities have remained equally sensitive about any hint that they sought British assistance in securing Soviet radio traffic during the war, although enough evidence has now slipped through to show that they seem to have done just that in early 1943.[48]

In summary, one may conclude that although the focus of BRUSA certainly fell on the sharing of German, Japanese, and Italian military signals intelligence, as well as technical information regarding the "detection, identification, and interpretation" of the signals used by these three powers, it is within the realm of the possible that BRUSA's provisions also embraced neutral, and even Allied, military SIGINT (signals intelligence.)

In its follow-up provisions, the BRUSA agreement bound both signatories to establish special security regulations for signals intelligence, and to make certain that extreme care was taken in the transmission of such intelligence material. Special liaison officers were to be utilized by both Britain and the United States for Ultra briefing of high-level field commanders of the two countries, and Ultra distribution was to be limited by a rigid application of the need-to-know principle. The special control regulations affecting Ultra information heretofore applicable to British commanders in the field would henceforth be utilized by both countries. The number of field officers allowed in on the Ultra secret was also to be strictly limited, and no Ultra items were to be mixed in with general intelligence data unless the whole of the resulting material was then treated as "Top [or Most] Secret Ultra."

Regarding the procedures to be used in carrying out actual exchange of special intelligence, the BRUSA agreement provided for the stationing of special liaison officers from each country within the code- and cipher-breaking centers of its partner. Such British liaison officers would henceforth be stationed at Arlington Hall and G-2, while equivalent American teams would settle in at Bletchley and the War Office. Each of these groups of liaison officers would be authorized to screen the flow of decrypts produced by the host country and to select from them the items they thought would be of value to their superiors. The selected items then would be sent by the liaison officers to the appropriate authorities in Washington and London (the chief of staff G-2 or the DMI), thereby guaranteeing full mutual access to all cryptanalytic intelligence that was important for the successful prosecution of the war.

A special "Appendix (A)" covering Enigma specified that "all [information] desired from this source will be made available to the War Department in Washington." Enigma decrypts selected by the American liaison officers at Bletchley and the War Office that related to order of battle were to be sent through the existing channels established by the March 1943 Order of Battle Agreement, that is, via the U.S. Army liaison officers in the War Office and the Air Ministry. Other Enigma material destined for transmittal to Washington could be sent via "existing British channels," which meant that the original intention was to send at least some of it via the high-security cable routes already being used by BSC New York to carry the German U-boat Enigma intercepts and decrypts back and forth between the Admiralty and the U.S. Navy's "secret room," F 21 and Op-20-G.

BRUSA was a model of good sense and a spirit of compromise. Ultra's security was protected by the agreement, while Bletchley's Enigma decryption monopoly was not disturbed. The U.S. Army not only had its needs for Special Intelligence satisfied, but its long-term interests were safeguarded because through BRUSA the Americans would, in the words of General Strong, "gain the experience required for achieving independence in this field." Even American future high-grade cryptanalytic development was protected, since the British had accepted that "research into new technical methods of attack on German Enigma communications would continue to be conducted in Washington" as well as at Bletchley. By July 1943, Enigma decryption problems were in fact being routinely sent from Bletchley to Arlington Hall and Op-20-G, because American high-speed bombes were faster and more reliable than those developed in Britain, as the enormous American potential for high-level technological development began to be revealed. Along with the U.S. Navy's high-speed bombe equipment, the U.S. Army's Yellow Project was reborn, employing its ungainly "RAM" bombes against the German Enigma within a close partnership supervised by Bletchley Park.[49]

BRUSA was a unique innovation that transformed the secret informational aspects of relations between modern states. Never before had two countries agreed to share the most profound secrets they possessed about their enemies. Even more significant, no governments previously had obligated themselves to carry out an exchange of personnel within such sensitive and secret operations as those committed to cryptanalysis. Here was a true revolution in interstate relations that would, almost without significant reinforcement from any other factor, guarantee a postwar continuation of the special relationship, because once the two countries so completely opened up their cryptanalytic secrets to each other, there was no way to terminate the arrangement without seriously lessening the intelligence-gathering capability of both partners. In addition, once the highly complex processes of secret-information gathering used by Britain and the United States had been shared between them, their secrecy could be maintained only if the partnership was maintained. The partners would learn too much about each other through BRUSA to go their separate ways in peacetime because, in gangland parlance, unless they "stayed bought," they would be capable of doing grievous harm to each other.

It is very probable that the high officials of Britain and the United States did not fully comprehend the long-term consequences of what they were doing when they signed the BRUSA agreement in the summer of 1943. However, within the high command structure of the U.S. Army, the immediate multisided advantages that could be gained from BRUSA were grasped very quickly by both Special Branch and Arlington Hall, and the leaders of these two organizations anticipated a welcome upswing in their bureaucratic fortunes. Three days prior to the formal signing of BRUSA, G-2 was ordered by the office of the army chief of staff to send in estimates for an increase in the number of personnel "which would be required to interpret and evaluate enemy intercepts in the way G-2 thought it should be done to obtain optimum results." General Marshall and his colleagues clearly foresaw the bright prospects that would be opened up by a flood of high-level intelligence from Bletchley, and within two days Special Branch was authorized to increase its strength by 45 officers and 118 civilians.[50]

In July a new section of Special Branch, labeled "C" and nicknamed "Bunker Hill," was established to handle Enigma messages. Section "C" 's initial strength was only three officers with two civilian assistants, because in the first phase of BRUSA, before all the kinks were worked out at the Bletchley end, all that came to Section "C" were copies of the condensed and often cryptic "Sunset" notes that the British Joint Staff Mission received from London. But Section "C" did manage to produce its own "Military and Naval Supplement to the Magic Summary" almost immediately.[51]

The heroic early innovations of the embryonic "C" section could not solve all the personnel problems of the Special Branch, which in July was given the additional assignment of acting as a clearinghouse for providing the British and Australian armies, as well as that of the United States, with information on Japanese army order of battle and related subjects. This entailed preparing filing cards on the 46,000 officers of the Japanese army as well as correlating the available information on Japanese troop movements (drawn principally from the Water Transport Code) with the current data on Japanese merchant shipping. These problems relating to the Japanese army had recently led to the creation of a large "B" section of Special Branch, which was to be concerned exclusively with Japanese army technical and personnel matters. The old "A" section was left with the now traditional activity of working with the intelligence drawn from Magic and from Axis "subversive" messages.[52]

Regular U.S. Army order-of-battle specialists were assigned to Special Branch for the first time in October 1943 to help its badly understaffed "B" section to cope with Japanese army problems, and its "C" section to deal with the Enigma intelligence that began pouring in from Bletchley in November 1943. But even such infusions of new blood, and the numerous administrative reforms made in the aftermath of BRUSA, were insufficient to provide easy sailing for Special Branch. Some of the reform efforts themselves unearthed skeletons in G-2's closets that seriously complicated Special Branch's attempt to improve its signals intelligence activities. In August 1943, a member of the branch, while casually extracting routine documents from G-2 records, discovered to his horror that "some papers of the highest security classification" involving cryptanalytic activities "had found their way" into low-level files; to make matters worse, these top-secret papers "had been elaborately cross-indexed." Upon further checking it was found that a "substantial amount of work" was required to repair the damage, because although most of this cryptanalytic material was of recent origin, some of it dated from as early as 1938![53]

Since G-2 was supposed to be the heart of the U.S. Army's intelligence system, such incidents indicating low efficiency and shockingly slipshod security did little for its reputation within the War Department. As early as the first week of June 1943, G-2 had begun tightening up its security procedures for cryptanalytic material, but as General Marshall confided to his deputy in November, Secretary of War Stimson was still "not favorably inclined to G-2." General Strong's organization therefore needed every success that Special Branch could muster in implementing the BRUSA agreement to help polish up its dingy image.[54]

During the summer of 1943, the code- and cipher-breaking section of the U.S. Army Signal Corps was more successful than G-2 in improving its position and appearance in the post-BRUSA era. Arlington Hall managed to avoid any security scandals, and also acquired additional personnel to help cope with its expanding cryptanalytic activities. In addition, it dressed itself up with a new name, becoming the Signal Security Agency. This new title both avoided confusion with the British Secret Intelligence Service (SIS), at a time when the two countries were moving closer together in their secret partnership, and provided Arlington Hall with a measure of heightened dignity commensurate with its new duty as one of the principal guardians of the Ultra, as well as the Magic, secret.[55]

While at home in Washington the point men in the various branches of the War Department struggled forward with varying degrees of success, Taylor, McCormack, and Friedman continued their work at Bletchley.

After the 17 May signing, these three Americans expanded the range of their studies to include Bletchley's bombe operations, and began to lay the foundations for the implementation of the agreement in England. Friedman and McCormack returned to the United States just three days before Secretary Stimson gave his formal approval to BRUSA (12 June 1943); from then on, Telford Taylor assumed full responsibility for American cryptanalytic liaison activities in Britain.[56]

Before leaping headlong into the task of building up an Ultra selection unit in the great maze of Bletchley Park, Taylor prudently decided that it would be best to get his feet firmly on the ground of British cryptanalytic practice at the smaller, and more easily understandable, diplomatic and commercial operation directed against neutral and enemy code traffic by Commander Denniston on Berkeley Street in London. Denniston welcomed this decision as part of his broader proposal for a close Anglo-American partnership in the breaking of diplomatic and commercial traffic. The director of Berkeley Street wanted his organization and Arlington Hall to exchange everything, from intercepted radio traffic to captured code books. The first step toward such a close partnership, in Denniston's view, was to have Taylor assigned to Berkeley Street. The diplomatic and commercial section would then make available to him "such telegrams as they considered of interest and value to [American] G-2," precisely as they did for the British service departments. Taylor was allowed to select and send "certain telegrams" to Washington on the cable transmission system "used by Bletchley Park," that is, the BSC system. He was also to serve as the conduit through which the British sent "certain" special messages to the State Department and other branches of the American government.

These latter items may well have been British taps of international cable traffic. When hostilities began in 1939 the British severed 130 miles of an Atlantic cable serving northern Germany and the United States (the Horta-Emden cable), and after the fall of France other cable sections had been severed or rerouted. But some links had been allowed to remain as long as they began, passed through, or ended in areas under British control. Not until 21 December 1943 did the U.S. government secure use of a transatlantic cable that could not be tapped in the British Isles, but the newly laid cable section connecting New York with Algiers via the Azores passed through Gibraltar and therefore could still be tapped by the British authorities.

London may or may not have tried to break into American coded messages carried by these cables, but it is certain that they did break some of the secret cable traffic of other countries. By October 1943, as a result of BRUSA, the American army Special Branch was definitely receiving copies from the British of "almost all the diplomatic traffic that goes over cables other than the cables passing through the United States." Little wonder that five months after BRUSA was implemented, Colonel Clarke concluded that it "had increased by 50% the amount of intelligence available to the United States Government from diplomatic sources," which was no small accomplishment for an agreement that had not been intended to cover diplomatic traffic at all![57]

While Taylor was at Berkeley Street, most of the technical aspects of the Anglo-American cryptanalytic partnership continued to be handled directly between Arlington Hall and Berkeley Street, but the American colonel was occasionally required "to clear up [technical] questions hard to solve by letter or telegram," even as he performed his main intelligence-sharing duties. After a six-week stay, Taylor left Berkeley Street to assume direct responsibility for Special Branch activities at Bletchley. Taylor's post in Denniston's establishment was first taken by a civilian, Roger Randolph, a Special Branch expert on diplomatic intelligence who remained at Berkeley Street until replaced by Capt. Bancroft Littlefield in December 1943. Littlefield was in turn succeeded by Capt. W. J. Fried early in 1944, with Capt. Lewis T. Stone holding the post from the end of 1944 until the conclusion of World War II.[58]

At Bletchley, Taylor, soon promoted to full colonel, was assigned to Hut 3, where interpretation or "emendation" work was done on the German army and air force Enigma traffic that had been decrypted in Hut 6. By the summer of 1943, Huts 3 and 6, as well as the navy cryptanalysis hut (number 8), had been moved into new quarters in a large brick building; the old hut numbers—3, 6, and 8—were retained to identify the differing functions of the three sections. In Hut 3, assisted by Maj. Samuel McKee, Taylor set up an American subsection labeled "3-US," which studied the methods of the British Hut 3 intelligence analysts and began to screen output for items that should be sent back to Washington. The British authorities agreed early on that a series of Enigma intercepts designated as "C," which were routinely sent to the British Service Intelligence directors, would also henceforth be sent to Marshall, Clarke, McCormack, and the G-2's office in Washington.

The American group at Bletchley increased steadily in size over the summer of 1943, and by all accounts the inclusion of the "cousins" in Bletchley's inner sanctum went off smoothly. A few old Bletchley hands later grumbled that the Americans were a bit clannish, but Peter Calvocoressi spoke for the vast majority of British Bletchley veterans when he wrote glowingly after the war of the warm British-American personal bonds that were formed. The influx of these new personnel, from a foreign country, had "occurred so smoothly that we hardly noticed it," wrote Calvocoressi, and that opinion was the highest possible tribute to the effectiveness of BRUSA.[59]

Even at the time, Commander Denniston exuded genuine satisfaction regarding the arrival of the American intelligence and cryptanalytic men at his operation on Berkeley Street. In October 1943 he wrote a personal letter to William Friedman about a recent visit by General Corderman to Berkeley Street. "He is a grand type to cooperate with," Denniston enthused, and went on to add:

> I must say that A[rlington Hall] and Special Branch have set a very high standard in senior officers who have visited us this autumn and having met you and got to know you personally I feel our joint ship should sail briskly along with a fair breeze until even the Pacific has been sailed in triumph.[60]

BRUSA had brought British and American cryptanalysts and intelligence specialists together in every sense of the word. They had gained mutual respect and found they could work together. Because they had been accustomed to practicing their trade in isolation, and were inclined to a high degree of secrecy and suspicion toward every variety of outsider, the growth of this sense of camaraderie, and a genuine pleasure in each other's company, gave the secret special relationship a basis of hard fact. In this atmosphere of genuine good cheer and best wishes, 3-US became operational at Bletchley during the fourth week of August 1943; on 27 August the first Enigma intercept processed by the American team at Bletchley was dispatched to Washington. But no sooner had the BRUSA system for sharing Enigma intelligence begun to operate than it was stopped abruptly.

In early September General Strong visited Britain to study the new situation and evaluate the arrangements that had been made to implement BRUSA. Apparently members of the old establishment at Bletchley, led by one of Travis' deputies, Nigel de Grey, seized on the opportunity offered by Strong's appearance to try to close the door once again on the sharing of Enigma decrypts with the Americans. Strong was temporarily persuaded by the Bletchley old guard that the sending to Washington of finished Ultra messsages—code-named "CS/MSS" by the Americans—was unnecessary for the successful conduct of the war and constituted a serious threat to security.

If the leaders of Bletchley had known of the grave security lapses made by G-2, which have been described above, it is probable that they would have pushed even more determinedly for a stop order. In any event, Taylor's selection and transmission of CS/MSS to the War Department was halted by General Strong, and much of the ground that had been covered preceding BRUSA in the battle over the specifics of Anglo-American cryptanalytic cooperation had to be fought over once again. After intense argument, Taylor and his colleagues convinced Strong that his stop order had been an error; before returning to Washington in late September, the American G-2 reversed himself once again and let the Enigma decrypts roll westward.[61]

On 25 September 1943 a supplemental understanding was agreed to, stipulating the future duties of Taylor and his 3-US team. Henceforth, four U.S. Army officers would alternate on duty in the "Watch Room" of Hut 3, where German army and air force Enigma material came in from the cryptanalysts of Hut 6. There it was "emendated, translated and [then] disseminated" to the British service ministries by teletype (or in memoranda for less urgent matters), with some material sent in the form of informational messages to commanders abroad. Taylor and his men were to select from this flow of intelligence material the German army and air force Enigma items they wished to send to Washington, merely informing the War Office or Air Ministry which documents they had chosen. An additional American liaison officer henceforth sat in the War Office at the point where Ultra came in from Bletchley, so he could advise U.S. liaison officers at the Park which additional, or explanatory, material should be sent to the Pentagon.[62]

Between September and December 1943, with the ground now finally and firmly cleared for selection and transmission, Taylor worked out the details of his own organization and transmission system. The most urgent materials were to go by cable, with the remainder sent pouched via steamship, until June 1944, when the latter category of documents was delivered by air three times per week. This system delivered so much material to Washington that as early as November 1943 shipments were made two or three times every day to "C" section of Special Branch in the Pentagon.[63]

By the early winter 1943–44 the BRUSA system of sharing Enigma intelligence information with the War Department had finally become fully operational. But it had taken five to six months from the signing of the agreement before a substantial flow of such material actually reached Washington. In the interim, Sicily had been invaded and conquered by the Anglo-American armies, Mussolini had fallen from power, General Bernard Montgomery had crossed the Straits of Messina, the Italian Fascist government had capitulated, and landings had occurred at Salerno on the Italian mainland. All of the military operations that had been planned and executed during this period had taken place without the War Department being in possession of large quantities of Ultra material.

One should therefore be cautious about leaping to conclusions regarding the degree to which BRUSA helped make possible the Anglo-American advance in the Mediterranean theater in the second half of 1943. During that period, American commanders in Sicily and southern Italy continued to benefit from the system whereby special liaison officers provided Ultra to them just as had occurred during the campaign in northwest Africa. But the strategic decisions regarding Italy made by the War Department up to the end of 1943 were made without assistance from the Ultra specifics upon which British planners built their case for the invasions of Sicily and Italy.

In the autumn and winter of 1943, while the battles in Sicily and Italy, as well as that in Bletchley, roared on, the other aspects of the BRUSA agreement were being gradually implemented. The American security regulations concerning the handling of signals intelligence, which had been mandated by the agreement, were finally issued in October 1943. Efforts were then made to recruit American Ultra liaison officers, renamed "special security officers," who would be trained at Bletchley by Special Branch in order to provide the Ultra briefings to U.S. field commanders, an activity previously performed by the British. In a parallel development, new procedures went into effect authorizing the American watch officers in Hut 3 to insist that specific Ultra items should be sent to American subordinate commanders (such as Mark Clark serving under Montgomery) if the watch officer believed that any particular item would be of importance.[64]

The development of a system to create, and use, American special security officers was enthusiastically promoted by Colonel Clarke of Special Branch when he was in England during the latter part of 1943 and early 1944. Telford Taylor worked diligently, and ultimately successfully, to convince General Eisenhower's headquarters that henceforth American special security officers, selected and trained by Special Branch, should be attached to the G-2 sections of U.S. Army staffs in the field in order to provide a special channel of Ultra information to American officers on the Ultra list.[65]

Special Branch also managed to extend its hand into the cryptanalytic side of the counterintelligence exchange that OSS had pioneered with British MI 6. Major W. L. Caffee of Special Branch was sent to Britain to work on counterintelligence in the summer of 1943. Fifteen months later, Captain Littlefield moved over from Berkeley Street to assist Caffee on the special intelligence side of Anglo-American counterintelligence activities. In February 1944 Colonel McCormack successfully demanded that G-2 as well as OSS should have a say in who actually received information from the counterintelligence decrypts.[66]

The regular American army formations in England at the time of the BRUSA agreement found that some of their activities were significantly affected by the new Anglo-American cryptanalytic understanding. On 23 July 1943 the chief of the American army Signal Security Agency detachment in the European theater, Col. George A. Bicher, received his BRUSA implementation orders from Arlington Hall. He was told that the primary duty of the agency's personnel in England would be to continue "to learn how to produce S[ignals] I[ntelligence]." The resulting operation, apparently code-named "Beechnut," saw three detachments (6811th, 6812th, and 6813th) sent from Arlington Hall to Britain beginning in 1943. These units consisted of intercept operators, machine processors, and cryptanalysts, respectively. Major (later Lieutenant Colonel) Roy Johnson exercised broad authority over the three companies, with Capt. (later Major) William Bundy directing the cryptanalysts of the 6811th Company.

Johnson arranged for the dispersal of the detachments to locations suitable for the study and practice of their respective crafts. The intercept unit went to a site on the heath near Bexley in Kent, where an intercept station was created, code-named "Santa Fe." By D day "Santa Fe" had managed to train fully 100 proficient intercept operators, and in the process decisively broke the former British monopoly on the interception of German army Enigma. The machine-processing detachment, with its working station in the GC & CS bombe unit at Eastcote and its living quarters seven miles away at Harrow on Hill, had harder going and made slower progress. But the analytic group under Bundy's direction took shape quickly despite the slow arrival of some G-2 clearances. By mid-December the 6813th was quartered at Little Brick Hill, four miles north of Bletchley on the Great North Road. Bundy's analysts were rapidly taken into Bletchley, where they were assigned to Hut 6 to begin their training on German army and air force traffic. Whenever one of the novice American cryptanalysts made substantial progress with the Enigma, he was taken on as a regular member of the British cipher-breaking team. In this way, a group of American cipher breakers, ultimately reaching a total of forty-five, was gradually created, each of whom was fully proficient in British high-grade cipher-breaking techniques.[67]

This did not always mean there was complete and many-sided "integration" at Bletchley Park. Although American and British personnel cooperated fully within each hut, contacts between huts were rare. The cryptanalysts in Hut 6 never visited the intelligence specialists in Hut 3 or talked shop outside duty hours. The wall between the army and air huts, 6 and 3, and the navy huts, 8 and 4, was even higher. During his two years at Bletchley, William Bundy knew virtually none of the British personnel in the navy huts and had no official contact with the U.S. Navy's cryptanalytic liaison officer at Bletchley, Cdr. Joseph Eachus.

The on-the-job training, and subsequent integration of American personnel into the British teams, not only created the basis for the production of important intelligence, it also shredded the total secrecy that had enshrouded Bletchley Park. Henceforth, there would be no overall Ultra secret separating Britain and the United States, because some American would be privy to every detail of the British cryptanalytic system. Across the Atlantic the same would be true of the detailed knowledge acquired by British personnel working in G-2 and Arlington, although, in sharp contrast to the popular belief that the British government is always more secretive than the American, we know far less about the inner workings of Arlington than we do about Bletchley Park.[68]

How deeply the BRUSA agreement and the process of joint cryptanalytic-intelligence operations changed things may be seen in the determination of the British and American authorities to link arms immediately to punish those who threatened the security of their joint signals intelligence activities. The test case organization, which felt the combined wrath of the new cryptanalytic partners, was, as usual, the American OSS. With incredibly bad, though unconscious, timing, Donovan's organization chose a date just three days after the secret signing of the BRUSA agreement to ask the chief signal officer of the U.S. Army whether an intelligence paper prepared by OSS-Lisbon, based on information acquired from Japanese cipher materials, would be of value "to our cryptanalysts."[69] Brigadier General Frank Stoner, the chief signal officer, quickly replied to the deputy director of OSS, Brig. Gen. John Magruder, that although the material forwarded was "useful to us, we do not believe it is of sufficient importance to warrant the risk involved on the part of your agent." This reply seemed to end the affair on a calm and polite basis. But, in the meantime, the original OSS report had come to the attention of Special Branch, and on 11 June 1943 Colonel Clarke reported the incident to General Strong. Clarke noted that OSS was apparently not violating regulations by carrying out cryptanalytic activities, but its acquisition of the Japanese material—by whatever means—as well as the circulation of it in a low-security classification involved "a great element of risk." Never one to miss an opportunity to ring the alarm bells regarding the activities of OSS, General Strong immediately carried out his own investigation, including an interrogation of OSS Deputy Director Magruder. On 6, 7, and 8 July 1943, Strong sent long, impassioned reports to General Marshall and to Sir Stewart Menzies in London, detailing the transgressions of OSS-Lisbon.

Donovan's agents in the Portuguese capital apparently had gained access to decrypted Japanese messages either by direct break-in operations at the Japanese consulate, or by purchase from a consulate insider. The Japanese messages had been encoded in the Japanese Military Attaché Code, a code that General Strong characterized as "one of the most difficult to solve," and one that finally had been broken only by joint British-American efforts "extending over a long period and involving some of the best cryptanalytic talent available to the United Nations."

Stressing that the Japanese Military Attaché Code was "one of the most important sources of Japanese military intelligence at the present time," and that recently decrypted Italian traffic suggested that the Japanese had become suspicious that something was wrong with the security of their encoding operations in Lisbon, Strong charged that "it appears obvious that the ill-advised and amateurish efforts of OSS representatives in Lisbon [had] so alarmed the Japanese that it is an even money bet that the codes employed by the Japanese are in imminent danger of being changed." If that happened, Strong continued, "we will face a blank wall, with the possibility of catastrophic results as far as the activities of the State, War, and Navy Departments are concerned." That would be a "tragic price to pay," the American G-2 mused, all because of what he saw as "the folly of letting loose a group of amateur spies in neutral countries."

Sir Stewart Menzies ("C") was not quite as exercised nor as colorful of expression as General Strong, but he did "agree that the incident is highly disturbing and may possibly result in our losing J.M.A. [the Japanese Military Attaché Code]." Menzies also emphasized the "moral" that "no agency should attempt penetration of neutral Embassies and Legations without authority from the highest quarter as any success which might ultimately be attained would, if discovered, alarm [the] occupants regarding cipher security." Any "uncontrolled negotiations for purchase of ciphers or 'en clair' texts" should also be forbidden for the same reasons.[70]

Menzies' solution to the problem posed by the OSS-Lisbon affair was to suggest that the rules governing OSS operations be tightened and that U.S. clandestine agencies operating in neutral countries should "seek the advice of my local [MI 6] representative before becoming involved" in operations that might adversely affect Anglo-American cryptanalytic activities. This proposal raised the question of just how far British and American intelligence amalgamation should be allowed to go, for having any of its secret operations appear to be controlled by the British was a very sensitive matter for American operational independence and American pride. Not even an old OSS hater such as General Strong could accept such a solution, and the punishment meted out to OSS was therefore probably moderated because Menzies had overplayed his hand. The American G-2 recommended that a purely American investigation be made of the "reckless operation of OSS in Spain and Portugal," which would clip Donovan's wings in the name of Anglo-American cryptanalytic security without turning over to the British supervision of American secret-agent intelligence operations.[71]

Strong got his way, and the resulting inquiry, which lasted into the autumn of 1943, resulted in OSS units in the Iberian peninsula being placed under the supervision of the United States ambassadors in Spain and Portugal. The ambassadors immediately declared operations against cryptanalytic targets off limits. The Lisbon affair thereby made it absolutely clear that Anglo-American code- and cipher-breaking cooperation under BRUSA would be the preeminent intelligence activity of the western powers, and that no "reckless" political or secret-agent activity would be permitted to endanger it.[72]

The drawing of this hard line did little or nothing, however, to smooth out the perennial differences between the two American service branches. No sooner was BRUSA agreed upon than the U.S. Army and Navy launched into a new round of quarreling over code- and cipher-breaking activities.

General Strong did attempt a measure of damage control by writing directly to the director of Naval Intelligence immediately after BRUSA was signed, setting out the general terms of the agreement and adding that under its provisions Special Branch would henceforth be obligated to guarantee that strict control would be exercised over the dissemination of the material from Bletchley. "Under no circumstances," Strong emphasized, could "such information be passed to any other agency of the United States" except the War and Navy departments. The U.S. Army and Navy thereby widened the gap between themselves and those U.S. government agencies and departments outside the Ultra-Magic club. But not even joint club membership was enough for all the higher officers of the U.S. Navy.[73]

Receiving admonitions about the need for tight security from the War Department, which many in the navy had always felt was itself leaky, probably caused some of the trouble. In addition, the U.S. Navy's unhappiness with BRUSA was surely prompted by what, from its point of view, was the unfortunate timing of the agreement between Bletchley and the U.S. Army. After a great deal of planning and negotiation, the navy had just managed to develop a highly secret system for revealing some of the results of its partnership with the British to a select group outside the Navy Department. By 30 March 1943 the complete daily U-boat plot—much of which came from British sources—was being circulated not only to the U.S. Army Antisubmarine Command

and the Intelligence Section of the U.S. Army Air Corps, but also to General Strong and to the White House. But the intelligence triumph that made this impressive daily plot possible—the naval cryptanalytic agreement with Bletchley—would be dramatically upstaged by the U.S. Army once the flood of German army and air force Enigma decrypts from Bletchley began to pour into Washington.[74]

A limited peace agreement was nonetheless arranged between Op-20-G and G-2 on 14 June 1943; it provided that if an item of special intelligence was to be disseminated to "outside agencies," the service that had "originated" it should be consulted in advance. Since under the terms of BRUSA the Special Branch of the U.S. Army was about to receive a far wider and deeper range of SIGINT material from the British than would the U.S. Navy, the army would be able to claim it had "originated" more material within the American system, and therefore could control access to a greater volume of cryptanalytic property.[75]

The blow to the status of Op-20-G posed by BRUSA was not lost on the navy cryptanalysts. In late June 1943 E. E. Stone of Op-20-G sent a detailed, and highly critical, evaluation of BRUSA to the U.S. Navy's Signal Office. This paper has been heavily "sanitized" by the declassifiers, but the portions that are readable criticized the Anglo-American army cryptanalytic accord for being too broad, and enthusiastically charged that it clashed in a few minor details with the current American division of the cryptanalytic spoils that had been agreed upon by the U.S. Army, Navy, and the FBI.[76]

Admiral King was nevertheless advised by his staff not to make a fuss over BRUSA because there was at this moment "no duplication between [the] Army and [the] Navy in R[adio] I[ntelligence] work." However, in laying out the details of how enemy weather traffic was being handled, the staff report to King unintentionally illuminated the seriousness of the rivalry between the cryptanalytic agencies of the two services. The report explained to the chief of Naval Operations that although "the Navy furnished the Army Weather Central [office] with a weather map based on the intercepted Jap weather reports," it refused "to give them the raw material on which the map is based for security reasons"—even though both the army and the navy were by this time providing volumes of cryptanalytic information to the British![77]

The army's Special Branch seems initially to have been prepared to overlook such foolish inequities. During the summer and autumn of 1943 it continued to provide the navy with the daily Magic summary, and after the first "Sunsets" arrived from the British, these were included in the "Supplement" sent to the Navy Department. By late 1943, however, Colonel Clarke had become embittered by the navy's failure to loosen up its distribution restrictions and provide more "in return" for the army's increased cryptanalytic offerings. The prime bone of contention was the refusal by the navy to supply "collateral information" from decrypted Japanese naval traffic that might help the army code breakers who were trying to crack the main Japanese army cryptosystems. What made this an especially bitter pill to swallow was the U.S. Army's discovery that the American navy was giving to the British the very information it refused to supply to Arlington Hall![78]

In the army's view, this was the last straw. When, near the end of 1943, Arlington made a full break-in to important sections of Japanese army traffic, Special Branch restricted the flow of the resulting decrypts to what G-2 decided would be the navy's "operational needs." The resulting struggle between the cryptanalytic branches of the two American services came so close to all-out war that General Marshall and Admiral King were compelled to intervene.[79]

On 4 February 1944 the army chief of staff and the chief of Naval Operations signed a pact covering the exchange of communications intelligence regarding Japan; the pact was supposed to establish inter-service peace and fair play regarding this important matter. To offer any hope of achieving understanding and cooperation, even this measure had to be restricted to the Washington area; both service chiefs acknowledged that in the Pacific theater of war, the rivalries between Nimitz and MacArthur would make any such general agreement impossible to enforce.[80] The Marshall-King agreement provided for the exchange of liaison officers between the communications intelligence sections of the two services in Washington, and authorized the officers in charge to examine the Japanese communications intelligence materials held by the other service. Marshall and King must have thought that such a simple and clear-cut measure would solve the problem. But the resulting interservice tranquility in Washington endured for less than a month. On 4 March 1944 Colonel Clarke wrote to General Clayton Bissell (who had replaced General Strong as G-2) that the navy was imposing such rigorous restrictions on the army liaison officer assigned to Op-20-G that the "peace treaty" between the special intelligence sections of the two services was virtually null and void. Clarke went on to threaten that if the navy was unwilling to accept "the interpretation of the Agreement which we consider reasonable . . . it is believed that all cooperation with the Navy in the radio intelligence field should be suspended,"[81] and yet another compromise had to be patched up between the two American services.

The bitter army-navy wrangling over special intelligence proved beyond a doubt that BRUSA and the Anglo-American naval cryptanalytic agreement had not solved all the cryptanalytic problems that troubled the two nations. Miscreant outsiders such as the OSS had been dispatched with comparative ease, but interservice, as well as national, political rivalries remained, especially in the Pacific, where these "Allies of a Kind" had very different interests and visions of the future. The cryptanalytic bonding that had occurred was definitely not the result of a midwar increase of warm feelings between the populations of Britain and the United States. The year 1943 had seen no decrease in British resentment regarding the three American "overs" (overpaid, oversexed, and over here), while in the United States the population had, by 1943, begun to levitate in the surety of its own power, and to complain that the old and worn-out colonialists in the kingdom by the sea were no longer pulling their own weight.

The new British and American cryptanalytic partners therefore had to continue smoothing out rough places and quieting conflicts in their relationship, while the march toward victory produced stresses and strains between London and Washington, and ever greater contrasts between the power, prosperity, and prospects of the two countries. By going forward as partners in their vital secret enterprise, without regard for the bumps or fluctuations of government or public opinion, the British and American cryptanalysts therefore made a highly important contribution to Allied victory, and also helped lay the groundwork for the continuation of the secret special relationship in the postwar era.

CHAPTER SEVEN
Highways and Byways in SIGINT Cooperation

Purloining usually begets apprehension, and the booty-sharing arrangements made in 1942–43 regarding the codes and ciphers of Germany, Italy, and Japan inevitably raised British and American uneasiness about the safety of their own code-and-cipher systems. Anglo-American secret communications always had needed to be secure to ensure the secrecy of Allied operations and intentions, but in the latter half of the war Tokyo and Berlin also had to be kept ignorant of the fact that the western powers were directing a massive joint cryptanalytic attack on their radio communications. In addition, the 1942–43 cryptanalytic agreements between Britain and the United States may well have caused special security worries in London and Washington because of latent nervousness that one of the partners might begin snooping into the codes and ciphers of the other.

Luck was on the Allied side in regard to both Italy and Japan; neither of these countries seems to have launched successful assaults on the radio traffic of Britain or the United States. The German B Dienst was another matter, however, for it continued to score important successes in the naval war throughout 1943 and, to a lesser degree, in 1944. Despite their security worries, British and American authorities consistently underestimated the scale of B Dienst achievements in the Battle of the Atlantic, even though they had a huge bureaucracy concerned with such matters and were well aware that during the middle phase of the war Germany was operating one of the largest radio intercept stations in the world in the Netherlands. During a British-American-Canadian convoy operations conference, held in Washington in March 1943, improvements in the speed and security of convoy-related communications were deemed "essential," but little of importance was actually done. The B Dienst was allowed to pick away at the Allied merchant navy codes for another eighteen months; even though steps were taken to replace the British naval cipher with a joint cipher machine, its first use did not occur until November 1943.[1]

In May 1943 the Admiralty finally had distinguished clearly between responsibility for the establishment of cipher policy within the Royal Navy and its implementation, but it was not until January 1944 that the new DNI, Capt. E. G. N. Rushbrooke, reported to the First Sea Lord that he, along with other high Admiralty officers, plus "C" and the secretary of the War Cabinet (Sir Edward Bridges), believed that immediate measures were required to improve British code-and-cipher security. As a result of this initiative, the British Cipher Policy Board was created, along with a new section of the Government Code and Cipher School charged with developing new British ciphers and working out the best means to protect their security.[2]

No sooner had the British begun to clean up their own house than they insisted the Americans do the same. In February 1944 a large cipher-security conference was held in Washington. The main business of the conference was to produce Anglo-American agreement on security classifications, especially those that would apply to intelligence acquired from cryptanalytic sources, although the security of the codes and ciphers used by Britain and the United States was also given high priority. Characteristically, although the U.S. Army and Navy were happy to take increased care that their codes and ciphers were secure, and to discuss with the British the measures they would undertake to this end, the American services would not discuss their enciphering methods with each other.[3]

Despite conferences, consultation, and worry, evidence of security problems regarding American codes and ciphers continued to appear well into the spring of 1944. In early May, just four weeks before D day, President Roosevelt ordered the Joint Chiefs of Staff to carry out a study of the cryptanalogic systems of all American departments and agencies. Even this was insufficient to produce a completely satisfactory reform of the merchant navy code, and the B Dienst continued on its merry and successful way against State Department codes. Only in July 1945, two months after V-E Day, did the U.S. government finally realize just how successful the B Dienst had been. On 22 July, "entirely by chance," a U.S. Army team discovered a large chest on the bottom of the Schliersee near Munich "containing deciphered messages of diplomatic traffic involving most of the world's states" from the period between 1942 and September 1944. Among these documents were a thousand American diplomatic messages that had been cracked by the B Dienst, including dispatches from "most of the Embassies" the State Department maintained around Europe, including those in Stockholm, Berne, Moscow, Ankara, Madrid, and Helsinki.[4]

The Germans had been unable to break any of the British or American high-grade machine ciphers, however; nor were these systems vulnerable to attack by other powers. The ultimate communications secrets of both London and Washington therefore remained inviolate from each other as well as from their joint enemies. The American army SIGABA machine, introduced in the summer of 1942, and its more rapid successor, the M-228 or SIGUM, which went into service in 1943, were a generation ahead of the Enigma, and were not penetrated by anyone during World War II. The British army TYPEX machine was also much more sophisticated and complex than the Enigma, and was as secure as the American high-security machines. In 1943–44 each of the partners in the Atlantic union took additional measures to secure their highest level communications, with the Americans introducing their advanced machine and the British replying in July 1944 with the equally sophisticated ROCKEX II. To obtain absolute protection for their secrets, the British even developed a special security classification in late 1943, called "Nonesuch" or "Guard," to indicate information that was *not* to be revealed to the Americans.[5]

While chronicling the western powers' technical successes regarding communication systems, cryptanalysis, and security, it is important to note that not every such effort was successful. Britain and the United States tried in vain to push forward independent projects to improve the scrambler phone, whose development, and the security precautions surrounding it, had been one of the formative factors prompting the BRUSA negotiations. The deficiencies of the Bell Labs' apparatus frustrated officials of both countries—those trying to use it sounded like two "very old men with quivering and uncertain voice." Yet despite their best efforts, neither Britain nor the United States could get beyond the Bell machine by war's end.[6]

Sometimes the efforts to ensure message security edged closer to the realm of the ridiculous than the sublime. In August 1943 the prime minister became obsessed with the need to find suitable code words for Anglo-American operations; he lectured all and sundry on the importance of avoiding "boastful" words, such as "triumphant," or words suggesting despondency, such as "flimsy, pathetic, or jaundice." In the prime minister's view, code words should not be "ordinary" words, such as "smooth" or "sudden," and certainly not disparaging or undignified words, such as "bunnyhug." During the first Quebec Conference the prime minister turned his code-word enthusiasms toward General Marshall, having "quite a talk" with the American army chief of staff about the inappropriateness of code words such as "Soapsuds" for potentially high casualty operations, such as the costly air raids on Ploesti. The prime minister's espousal of this relatively low-level code-security matter soon had the British and American staffs working overtime to find suitable code words. Marshall was thrown so completely on the defensive that in September 1943 he pleaded with his G-2 and his assistant chief of operations to come up with alternative and acceptable words quickly "because he [the prime minister] will probably bring it up to me while he is here [in Washington] on the present visit."[7]

Such were the security policy burdens that had to be shouldered by the higher officers who served Churchill and Roosevelt. Nor were the controversies over code words the only occasions when communications security policy threatened to turn into slapstick comedy. On 7–8 October 1943 a supposedly secret, and scrambled, transatlantic telephone conversation between the president and the prime minister was inadvertently transmitted on an ordinary commercial, lightly scrambled circuit, instead of on the high-security Bell scrambler phone. The information in the conversation was easily picked up by the Germans, and anyone else who cared to listen, including monitors of the U.S. Censorship Board, who easily unscrambled the conversation and then sent a full transcript of it to the White House as an instance of poor security practice![8]

Even this embarrassing snafu did not win the grand sweepstakes for comic security measures. On 2 February 1944 J. Edgar Hoover soberly, and seriously, reported to the president that a confidential FBI informant had reported to the director that a colonel and two captains "of the German General Staff," dressed up in Soviet uniforms and speaking Russian "without any trace of an accent," had been present at the elbows of the Big Three during the most secret Roosevelt-Churchill-Stalin conversations held at Teheran! The president did not even turn a hair at such tomfoolery, and on 5 February he asked General Marshall if the report should be sent on to Stalin, of all people. The general managed to persuade Roosevelt not to trouble, or perhaps baffle, the Soviet leaders with such absurdities, and the FBI's fantasies about Teheran and the German General Staff were ultimately returned to the files.[9]

It should not be imagined that all the high-level security embarrassments that arose during the latter part of the war were candidates for the vaudeville stage, or that they all occurred on the western side of the Atlantic. Even the land of the Secret Intelligence Service and the Wizard War had its share of secrecy shockers in 1944 and 1945, along with the as-yet-undiscovered Cambridge spies. The Official Secrets Act itself seemed to wobble for a moment in late 1944 when a Royal Navy officer outside the charmed circle of senior Admiralty officers took a leaf from the confidential book of his superiors and leaked a classified document to a member of Parliament. The Admiralty staff immediately exploded into a chorus of righteous indignation, denouncing the deed and calling for the offender's head. But the culprit claimed that he had leaked the document because he believed he was conforming to the dictates of a higher law. To give support to his case he had the temerity to point to a paragraph of the Official Secrets Act itself. Section 2 of the 1911 act seemed to say that it was an officer's duty to communicate information outside the chain of command if "it is in the interest of the State" to do so. The Admiralty staff, including the DNI—who in the past had routinely slipped information to outsiders when they thought it was in the interest of the nation, the navy, or themselves to do so—brushed aside this argument and called for stern measures to be taken against the offending officer. When a senior member of the Admiralty staff asked the director of Public Prosecutions for an opinion on the merits of the case, however, the shocking reply was that the culprit might well be right—"in certain circumstances it might be held that it would be a person's duty, in the interest of the State, to communicate information to a Member of Parliament even though he was not authorized to do so."[10] With that, the matter was quickly and quietly dropped, amid staff muttering that "it might have unfortunate consequences if that view were upheld by the courts."

Even though official silence, rather than official secrecy, was maintained in this case as well as many others, and even though Britain and the United States beat all the odds by keeping Ultra, Magic, their cryptanalytic partnership, and their high-level communications immune from enemy attack throughout the whole war, it would be inappropriate to conclude that this success was due to the perfection of British and American security measures. These measures were comparatively good, and certainly much better in the latter stages of the war than at the beginning. On balance it is also true that British security was better than American. But it is nonetheless the case that serious security blunders did occur, and Anglo-American security success was due at least as much to Axis and Japanese intelligence failures as it was to the brilliance of London and Washington. The secret agent activities of Germany, Italy, and Japan, which prompted the "Fifth Column panic" and might in theory have revealed the Ultra-Magic secret as well as that of the atomic bomb and a host of other vital matters, were in actuality hopelessly incompetent and relatively easily controlled by the Allied security services. Not only did enemy agents fail to discover what went on at Bletchley Park, they never uncovered the *existence* of this enormous institution, even when the number of its staff soared into five or six figures during the latter stages of the war.

The Axis and Japanese espionage efforts not only failed to uncover Anglo-American cryptanalytic activity, but their own code-and-cipher security was so poor that this contributed to their undoing. When, for example, the Germans put an Enigma machine into service in November 1943 on the circuit that connected their agents in Argentina with Germany, they began by sending parallel messages on a lower-security Kryha machine for a number of months. This act of abysmal enciphering practice, comparable to what the Japanese had done with the Red and Purple machines in 1940, provided Op-20-G with ample opportunity to work into the Enigma settings; this traffic therefore became an open book to the Allies up through V-E Day.

In addition to their troubles in the field, intelligence and security officials in Tokyo and Berlin vied with each other in spinning snug cocoons of myth for themselves and their superiors, none of whom wished to believe that the Axis and Japan were vulnerable to crypt-analytic attack, or that the blundering and decadent Anglo-Americans were capable of launching a sustained, high-tech, secret, and well-coordinated assault against their codes and ciphers. The closed societies of which Hitler, Mussolini, and the Japanese leaders were so proud failed decisively in their secret battle with the West. One should be cautious, however, in attributing this to the flaws inherent in totalitarian regimes, for one of the most prominent closed societies of the wartime era, the USSR of Joseph Stalin, was at least as successful in the security aspects of wartime intelligence as its Anglo-American partners.

On balance, Anglo-American security met the crucial tests it faced, despite all the difficulties and against the apparent odds. That success was decisive in allowing BRUSA and the other cryptanalytic agreements to be implemented on the broad scale, which yielded maximum benefit to the Allied cause. A great stream of undetected Americans journeyed to Britain between 1943 and 1945 to work alongside British intelligence and cryptanalytic personnel, while many additional American high-level special emissaries to the United Kingdom were briefed there on the modus operandi of Britain's most secret operations at Bletchley Park and other locations at home and abroad.

Large numbers of British cryptanalytic and intelligence officials, led by Travis and Welchman, also traveled back and forth between London and Washington in these years; many junior British officers were assigned directly to Arlington Hall, where they joined American personnel toiling on Japanese codes and ciphers. The secret special relationship worked out so well at Arlington that in August 1944 Travis offered to begin transferring to Washington "the whole of our present effort on Japanese Army-Air codes and ciphers" to make the transition easier when, following Germany's defeat, Britain could commit most of its cryptanalytic "resources to the struggle against Japan."[11]

Impressive and transcendentally significant though this mutual cooperation was, all was not always smooth sailing either at Bletchley or Arlington. British and American cryptanalytic and intelligence personnel still faced formidable challenges in the European theater of operations during 1944–45. The Germans made frequent changes in their cipher systems during this period. These required the development of new cryptanalytic methods, including use of the only pure computer employed during World War II ("Colossus"), which went into service at

Bletchley in early 1944. Changes also were made in the roles Britain and the United States played in handling different categories of German radio traffic. By 1944, for example, Op-20-G had developed its capabilities to a point where it was "bearing the major share of the Signal[s] Intelligence load in the Atlantic," and the British authorities acknowledged that the U.S. Navy handled this responsibility very well.[12]

The broad and rapid expansion of Allied offensive military operations also called for large increases in intelligence information, and the development and extension of secure methods for transmitting such information to field commands. The need for good intelligence extended far beyond information drawn from cryptanalysis, and 1944 saw Anglo-American intelligence cooperation broadened to include such mundane but important matters as "factual intelligence," which covered technical information, OB, and even the serial numbers and manufacturers' markings on enemy equipment. Some consumers of combat intelligence considered such technical and descriptive data, as well as that secured from enemy prisoners of war, to be of more value than cryptanalysis. A confidential postwar study made by 12th Army Group in Europe, for example, ranked cryptanalysis third in importance as a combat intelligence source, behind POW interrogation and tactical photoreconnaissance. But cryptanalysis was almost always held to be a highly important element in the intelligence mix of combat units, and at the strategic level of planning and decision making it nearly always reigned supreme.[13]

The Ultra processing and distribution system for Europe continued to be fine tuned and expanded throughout 1944 and 1945, despite the fact that as late as March 1944, the U.S. Navy still refused to share its European Enigma decrypts with the U.S. Army, or allow Bletchley to do so. Combat units, such as the U.S. Eighth Air Force, which had received only wrapped-up Ultra during 1942 and the first half of 1943, were put fully into the Ultra picture in the second half of the latter year. The code-name systems—for example, "Magic" or "Dexter"—used by various British and American agencies to disguise the source of cryptanalytic-based intelligence were also systematized, and in May 1944 the armies of both countries agreed that the word *Ultra* would always be employed in designations for high-grade cryptanalytic intelligence.[14]

None of these coordination and standardization efforts was completely successful. Bits of paraphrased "special material" were now and then slipped to unauthorized recipients. Even high officials were prepared on occasion to allow extra copies of highly secret materials, such as the daily Magic Summary, to be given to the British Joint Staff Mission on a temporary basis. But the main stream of development regarding Anglo-American signals intelligence was the achievement of very tight security and the commitment of large numbers of personnel to the tasks of producing and protecting Ultra. By 1945 the number of British service personnel assigned to work on "strategic" cryptanalysis and intelligence at Bletchley had risen above 6,000 (1,371 army, 1,590 RAF, and 2,703 Royal Navy). (These numbers included civilians assigned to work for the various services.) Large numbers of British military personnel stationed in London were also "in the Ultra picture," including 929 Royal Navy officers in November 1944. The intelligence community in Washington also grew enormously during the latter stages of the war. At the end of 1944, 1,275 U.S. Navy officers and enlisted personnel were assigned to intelligence duties in the American capital, of whom 275 officers were on one of a series of "Ultra lists."[15]

In the European combat theaters similar large rosters were developed listing those involved in Ultra activities or cleared to receive Ultra intelligence. A Supreme Headquarters Allied Expeditionary Force (SHAEF) list of such British, American, and Canadian army and air force personnel, prepared on 25 March 1945, covered close to twenty typed pages and listed more than 500 names, ranging from Ultra liaison officers for combat units to Bomber Command officers, and Colonel Taylor's organization in the U.S. embassy in London. Even this lengthy list did not take into account British and American navy personnel who were cleared for Ultra, nor those in the Mediterranean theater, nor most of those assigned to the Air Ministry or the War Office in London.[16]

The large groups of British and American personnel involved with Ultra during the last stage of the European war were paralleled by formidable cadres of officers and enlisted personnel "in the secret" who carried on the final phase of the war against Japan. Although the American armed forces in Asia and the Pacific were larger than those of Britain, and this war zone had a higher priority in Washington than in London, the Anglo-American cryptanalytic cooperation in the struggle against Japan was expanded and intensified during 1944–45.

Quite naturally it was Ultra-Magic cooperation between the two western armies, rather than between the two navies, which led the way in this region, because BRUSA specifically mandated Pacific-Asian cryptanalytic cooperation by the Anglo-American armies, whereas the 1942 naval agreement did not. Two high-level conferences held in Washington on Japanese army and air force order-of-battle intelligence, one occurring in September–October 1943 and the other in July 1944, were the forums in which the cryptanalytic intelligence acquired by the two western great powers (and the Dominions) was combined with other types of intelligence to create a single overarching picture of the Japanese ground and air forces. In March 1944 a comparable high-level joint meeting at Arlington Hall produced an agreement on the division of cryptanalytic responsibilities between the two countries, as well as Australia and New Zealand, for the breaking and interpreting of Japanese army and air force codes and ciphers. The March meeting came on the heels of the first large inflow of decrypts of Japanese air force traffic, and coincided with the initial break into the Japanese army administrative code (the latter, unfortunately, being lost again in the spring of 1944).[17]

British authorities were eager to push on to full cooperation in all aspects of the work against Japanese codes and ciphers; in the spring of 1944 Bletchley and Op-20-G worked closely together in breaking the Japanese naval attaché cipher used in Berlin (Coral), and during September "C" ordered a substantial increase in the number of British cryptanalysis personnel assigned to Japanese targets. The rising importance of Japanese matters to British intelligence planning during 1944, when coupled with the good relations Bletchley enjoyed with both the U.S. Army and Navy organizations working on Japanese codes and ciphers, prompted Whitehall to believe that the time was ripe for an overall Anglo-American agreement on Japanese army, navy, and diplomatic intelligence. But in May 1944 when the British appealed to the Americans for a collective deal on Japan, the overture was rebuffed; in October 1944 when the DMI (Gen. J. A. Sinclair) again proposed such an arrangement, the Americans rejected it out of hand. Washington would not even permit a combined meeting of the joint intelligence committees of the two countries to discuss Japanese issues, although, as usually occurred in Anglo-American matters, each of the American service intelligence chiefs was happy to meet with his British counterpart separately. American interservice rivalries were still too intense to make possible an all-service "BRUSA" agreement in the Pacific, even though the Allies were then only ten months away from V-J Day.[18]

Striking headway was made, however, regarding such intelligence on the Japanese army as order of battle, captured documents and military equipment, as well as POW interrogation. On 5 October 1944 General Bissell (the G-2) and the DMI (then General Sinclair) agreed that henceforth all "coordination of factual intelligence pertaining to the Japanese ground forces will be centralized in the War Department, Washington." In this same period (October–November 1944) all parties, including the U.S. Army and Bletchley, also agreed that the U.S. Navy would be responsible for attacking the Japanese shipping code ("Maru") and that other British and American cryptanalytic organizations whose work touched on Maru would assist Op-20-G whenever possible. In November Admiral King finally created the U.S. Navy Strategic Intelligence Section in Washington, which promised to "closely coordinate" with the cryptanalytic and intelligence authorities of the British and the American armies. Soon afterwards, when Admiralty officials began preparations for the deployment of a large British battle fleet in the Pacific (in addition to the fleet in the Indian Ocean), the Royal Navy received substantial intelligence assistance from the U.S. Navy. By March 1945 the naval section of the Joint Staff Mission in Washington was finally cleared to receive a regular flow of Pacific war cryptanalytic material directly from Op-20-G without it having to pass back and forth to London.

Yet even this picture of increasingly warm Anglo-American naval cryptanalytic cooperation in the war against Japan had a major shortcoming, for bonhomie was still possible only in Washington. Out in the real world of the China-Burma-India (CBI) theater, the Southeast Asia command, and the Southwest and South Pacific commands, matters were far more complicated, because although resources and manpower were limited, service and national rivalries were intensified by the egos of Douglas MacArthur, Chester Nimitz, Albert Wedemeyer, James Somerville, and Lord Louis Mountbatten.

In MacArthur's area of command, the Central Bureau had developed a large and highly efficient system for intercepting Japanese radio traffic and feeding it to Arlington Hall, as well as carrying out code- and cipher-breaking operations on the spot. The interception and cryptanalytic operations of Central Bureau included Australian as well as American personnel, and by December 1944 these men and women (there was a large contingent of both Australian and American women soldiers in Central Bureau) were intercepting tens of thousands of Japanese messages per day. Shortage of communications facilities meant that only about half of these messages could be sent on to Washington, but all of them were available for Central Bureau's own attacks on Japanese codes and ciphers.[19]

During late 1943 and early 1944 uniform U.S. Army regulations had been established for handling Ultra material at MacArthur's headquarters; soon after a trip to the area was made by Colonel Clarke, special security officers, comparable to the special liaison officers in Europe, took over distribution of the high-grade cryptanalytic intelligence, originated by Washington, to U.S. Army commands in the Pacific theaters and CBI. Also in early 1944 Royal Navy and U.S. Navy intelligence liaison officers were exchanged in the South and central Pacific headquarters, as well as in Colombo. But whereas in Washington the U.S. Army and Navy managed to carry out some degree of cooperation on high-grade intelligence matters, very little occurred in the field either in Asia or the Pacific.

On occasion one of the service headquarters in Washington would pass cryptanalytic intelligence to the other service, which then relayed it on to its combat units in the Pacific. In June 1944 Admiral Nimitz did allow the U.S. Army Air Corps to station tactical intercept and cryptanalytic units on one spot of "forward" navy turf in the Pacific. But no navy material reached MacArthur's Central Bureau, nor was any of the British cryptanalytic intelligence that did reach MacArthur's staff ever shown to the Central Bureau's cryptanalysts. In Delhi and Colombo, although British intelligence relations with each American service were usually very close, the American army and navy cryptanalytic activities in CBI were sealed off from each other so tightly that British officials frequently had to act as unofficial, and secret, middlemen, maneuvering intelligence information from one American military service to the other.[20]

When anyone attempted to alter the convoluted and inefficient intelligence arrangements prevailing in Southeast Asia and the Pacific, they were usually slapped down hard. In June 1944 the U.S. Army Air Corps indicated that it planned to engage in "separate" cryptanalytic intelligence operations in the Pacific area, but Admiral King immediately cried foul. The Army Air Corps was quickly ordered to stop any independent or "uncoordinated" activities in the region. In the same month, when the Royal Naval command in Colombo proposed to sidestep Bletchley and carry out direct cryptanalytic liaison with Op-20-G by dispatching Malcolm Saunders to Washington, the DNI, Capt. E. G. N. Rushbrooke, dismissed the idea out of hand. Casting doubts on Saunders' suitability for dealing with Americans, and emphasizing the dangers inherent in upsetting the existing labyrinthian arrangements in Southeast Asia, the DNI clinched his case by asserting that "it is surely undesirable for Anderson [the Royal Navy headquarters in Colombo] to become a complete subsidiary of Washington."[21]

So organizational and national self-interests continued to prevail, and the complex and often inefficient cryptanalytic liaison arrangements in Asia and the Pacific remained frozen in place until the end of the war. Despite their shortcomings, the liaison systems did provide vital intelligence to the western armed forces facing Japan. Just as in the European war, cryptanalysis in the Pacific not only supported combat operations, it also to some degree reshaped them. On 15 December 1944, for example, the director of American Naval Intelligence, Rear Adm. Hewlett Thebaud, complained to the Joint Chiefs of Staff that during the advance across the Pacific, "radio stations had been singled out for early destruction" during preliminary bombardments; Japanese "communications centers have also been attacked *prematurely* [italics added]," prompting the Japanese to change the patterns and coding of their radio communications. Admiral Thebaud, heavily reinforced by Admiral King, therefore called upon all American Army Air Corps and navy commanders in the Pacific to eschew aggressive exuberance, and henceforth yield first priority to the needs of radio intelligence.[22]

Seen from the perspective of the long-term development of Anglo-American cryptanalytic cooperation, however, even such transformations in the relative importance of intelligence collection and the wishes of combat commanders may have been less important than a series of reforms undertaken during 1943–44 in that mazelike and disordered setting for code- and cipher-breaking matters, the headquarters of the U.S. Army in Washington. Until the U.S. Army cleaned up its house, no extensive or effective form of permanent cooperation was possible even with the U.S. Navy, and until the U.S. Army and Navy came to terms, no comprehensive and lasting cryptanalytic bond with Britain could be made.

Only in the middle years of the war (1943–44) did General Marshall and his staff begin a serious overhaul of the confusion and chaos, which

ranged from the Magic distribution system to the cannibalistic relations between Arlington Hall and Special Branch. Until February 1944
the president and other top officials of the U.S. government were supposed
to receive Magic in various summaries and "Brown Books," with
additional spot items arriving in the White House from many sources,
such as the British Joint Staff Mission and the prime minister. The army
chief of staff then believed that the president was seeing these Magic
intelligence summaries every day. But on 12 February Marshall discovered that an officer on the White House staff actually screened the
material before it was sent to the president's office, marking "a very
few portions for Admiral [William] Leahy's attention." Leahy, in turn,
had "very seldom" sent any of the material in to the president. To bring
some order to this muddle, Marshall ordered that a daily series of bound
"Black Book" pamphlets should be prepared to highlight the most
important Magic material for his own use and that of other top U.S.
officials. Once the new Black Book system was created, Marshall immediately explained its importance to the president and the White House
staff. In late February Roosevelt began receiving a daily ration of Magic
highlights, as did the other top officials in Washington, including Field
Marshal Dill of the British Joint Staff Mission (the latter distribution
beginning in late June 1944).[23]

Paralleling these attempts to improve and rationalize the Magic
distribution system came a series of reforms to the troubled relations
between G-2 and the cryptanalytic section of the U.S. Army Signal
Corps. The appointment of General Corderman as chief of Arlington
Hall was a principal catalyst for reform, because the general fully grasped
the importance of the liaison difficulties and took vigorous steps to
resolve them. In early 1943 a G-2 liaison officer had been, for the first
time, permanently assigned to Arlington Hall and "given free access"
to nearly all of the translation and code- and cipher-breaking sections
of SIS. A series of exchange visits between G-2 and SIS specialists
soon followed, and these produced a sharp increase in the volume of
valuable intelligence going to G-2.[24]

By June 1944 the greatly expanded flow of secret information, both
cryptanalytic and conventional, reaching G-2 from British and American
sources, coupled with the increasing need for more and better intelligence by U.S. Army units embarking on the decisive phases of combat
in both Europe and the Pacific, produced a major shake-up in the army's

intelligence organization. Special Branch was reorganized, Colonel Clarke was given more authority, and, for the first time, arrangements were made to combine cryptanalytic intelligence with the other types of information the G-2 used when preparing specialized appraisals of enemy intentions, weaponry, and order of battle.[25]

As a result of these changes, G-2 successfully initiated closer and more comprehensive intelligence liaison with the State Department and even with the U.S. Navy. During the spring and summer of 1944 committees of the two U.S. armed services met regularly to coordinate their cryptanalytic attack on Japan. The navy cautiously suggested that some venue be arranged where discussions could be carried on by the two services in the hope of improving cryptanalytic cooperation. The resulting Army-Navy Communications Intelligence Coordinating Committee (ANCICC) was informal, consultative, and largely exploratory, but it constituted an important step toward bringing the bitter American service rivalries over cryptanalysis under control, and in so doing nudged the U.S. cryptanalysts toward the kind of interservice cooperation that was indispensable for any form of postwar national security system, as well as for a continuation of the cryptanalytic bond linking London and Washington.[26]

By October 1944 the navy began daily deliveries to Special Branch of all the signals intelligence the naval cryptanalysts in Washington produced about Japan. Unfortunately, this spirit of cooperation still did not extend into the combat theaters of the Pacific or Southeast Asia. Nor was there much navy openhandedness regarding the cryptanalytic side of the European war, despite the fact that formal army-navy liaison arrangements were made in November 1944 to deal with this matter.[27]

Nonetheless, American reform and coordination had made great strides in 1944. By December the U.S. Army's intelligence and cryptanalytic housecleaning had progressed to a point where only one serious bottleneck remained—the fact that code-and-cipher breaking was still in one branch of the War Department, whereas intelligence processing and evaluation was centered in a completely different branch. On 10 December 1944 General Marshall was finally persuaded by G-2 that this anomaly too must end, and, effective 15 December, all of Arlington Hall's interception and cryptanalytic activities were put under the control of G-2. Even though the Signal Corps retained some administrative rights in Arlington Hall, which kept territorial squabbling alive for another year, Marshall's 10 December order at last gave the U.S. Army a unified cryptanalytic intelligence service, integrally connected to the War Department branch responsible for army intelligence.[28]

The cryptanalytic reforms made by the U.S. Army during 1943–44, along with the improvements in Magic distribution, sharply increased the volume of high-grade intelligence reaching American authorities at home and abroad. The reforms also provided more such material to the British, who, under the terms of BRUSA, were entitled to share in all the cryptanalytic achievements the American army chalked up against the Japanese. These mutual benefits, when added to those provided by the joint labors of the cryptanalysts of the two countries at Bletchley and Arlington, plus the successes in developing joint secure, and highly secret, Ultra distribution systems, gradually strengthened and tightened the secret bonds that had been formed by the naval and military cryptanalytic agreements of 1942–43.

This increasingly intimate union undoubtedly showered intelligence benefits on the Allied cause, but as the secret links between the great Atlantic powers grew stronger, one inevitable consequence was the widening of the gap between those Allied countries within the most secret special relationship and those outside it. This side effect would have many long-term negative consequences. Within three months of the conclusion of the BRUSA agreement (September 1943), Colonel McCormack began routinely declaring that no "special information" from British sources should be passed on to other governments without the approval of London. Then, in early 1944 crises arising from the Anglo-American policy of rigid control over information related to cipher security and radio intelligence brought sharp clashes between the Ultra-Magic authorities and some of their closest colleagues in the Grand Alliance, starting with the Nationalist Chinese and the Free French.[29]

The main issue between the Anglo-Americans and the Chinese arose from the western conviction that Chiang Kai-shek's officials were trying to arrange broad intelligence liaison with Britain and the United States mainly to try to tap into their secret sources of intelligence. Since at this time both Bletchley and Arlington were intercepting and reading much of Chungking's radio traffic, the two governments probably had solid grounds for this belief; they also had no illusions about the security of Chinese codes and ciphers. In February 1944, therefore, the Combined Chiefs restricted the information that might be given to Chinese authorities "to that required for immediate prosecution of the war against Japan." During the summer of 1944 some British officials in China momentarily considered going it alone on intelligence relations with the Chinese, because, in the words of one British official in Chungking, the "Americans have many organizations here which are if possible even less coordinated than ours and certainly display greater internecine jealousies." By August, however, London had pulled back from any idea of solitary intelligence adventures in China, because it too was convinced that the primary goal of the Chinese was to get the "radio intelligence material."

By 1945 the leaders of the two western armies were so sensitive about poor "security conditions in China" and the Chinese authorities' "skillful maneuvering" to gain intelligence information from the West that the British and American attachés in Chungking restricted themselves to a weekly presentation to Nationalist Chinese liaison officers of a "complete Order of Battle Bulletin" on Japanese armed forces, while refusing to provide any additional information, especially any items from cryptanalytic sources. Op-20-G insisted, in the same period, that British authorities cease providing the Chinese with Ministry of Economic Warfare summaries or "any other publications known to contain Ultra information." In March 1945 the British military attaché in Chungking telegraphed MI 2 in London asking that no "material based on ULTRA" be sent even for his own use, because security in China was so poor.

To confirm their suspicions of the Chinese, by at least the spring of 1945 both London and Washington possessed clear proof from intercepts of Japanese coded material that the codes and ciphers used by the Chinese military attachés were hopelessly compromised, and "that a great deal of useful intelligence is leaking to the Japanese as a result." But because Britain and the United States could have documented this Chinese cipher insecurity only by revealing the scale of their own successes against Japanese codes and ciphers, the two countries were compelled to give no explanation for their action to Chinese officials, even as they erected ever higher and thicker walls to prevent the flow of high-grade western military intelligence to China.

It is not possible to document the reaction of Chiang Kai-shek and his staff to this policy of exclusion, but it seems highly probable that increased suspicion and Nationalist Chinese resentment against the West was the result. Since at this time (spring 1945) the United Nations Charter was being prepared, and that document would feature Nationalist China as one of the "Big Five" on the Security Council, preparatory to acting as one of the regional "policemen" in Asia, the intelligence freeze-out certainly conflicted with what the western powers saw as one of their important long-term interests in Asia.[30]

The significant political overtones that accompanied the barring of China from the Ultra-Magic secret in 1944–45 were also manifest in the case of the Free French, who suffered a similar exclusion. On 17 February 1944 the British Chiefs of Staff cabled the Joint Staff Mission in Washington that "definite evidence has recently shown [that the] enemy interception and cryptologic organization facilities in Greece are reading with ease [the] bulk of French Naval, Army, Air Force and political W/T [wireless] traffic emanating from [the] Levant." The British authorities concluded that the Germans had not broken into "the high grade cipher used [by the French for communication] between Syria and Algiers," but the German cryptanalysts had cracked the other French code-and-cipher systems used in Syria "by pure cryptanalytic means" and "without using [captured] documents or other assistance" such as secret agents.

Soon after receipt of this message, and due to the obvious need for maximum cipher security prior to the Normandy invasion, the Combined Chiefs of Staff began to wrestle with the problem of how to control the "leaky" French without giving away the Ultra secret, alerting the Germans by wholesale code changes, or allowing the French to enter the Ultra-Magic club. Despite previous confrontations with the French over poor security, the Americans seemed inclined to the "soft" solution of inviting all the "allied governments [that is, the Free French and the governments-in-exile in London] urgently to investigate the security of their ciphers and codes." But the British, led as usual by "C," and then supported by the Chiefs of Staff, opted for a "hard" solution, prohibiting "Allied" governments the use of "cyphers which we regard as insecure." The British authorities were not prepared to give the French, or anyone else, any "more information than is absolutely necessary to insure that their cyphers are [made] secure. . . . We can base our arguments on our wealth of experience in these matters and need not disclose in any way the source of our doubts regarding their present insecurity."

On 10 May 1944 the Combined Chiefs of Staff declared that henceforth every "Allied" government "would be required to communicate all military information in British or American ciphers," while the security of their code-and-cipher systems was checked by the Anglo-Americans. This order brought no joy to General de Gaulle or the Free French, but London and Washington were in no mood to compromise. Even after the successful invasion of Normandy, and an investigation by the CCS, which finally concluded that French military ciphers had been made secure in late September, the Anglo-Americans still banned the use of some French diplomatic ciphers that General de Gaulle—quite understandably—had refused to turn over to the British and Americans for security examination because of his desire to assert French right of sovereignty.

These unpleasant incidents still did not prevent the Anglo-Americans from accepting cryptanalytic intelligence from the Free French when they thought it paid them to do so. In August 1944 Op-20-G learned that the U.S. Navy's forces on the "Moroccan Sea Frontier" were regularly receiving decrypts of the radio traffic of Franco's Spanish armed forces from the French cryptanalytic service, "Prano." Although Op-20-G desired the French to continue supplying this information, the U.S. Navy high command did not want to involve itself directly in the exchanges, since "we do not desire to associate with the French in this field." The Spanish decrypts therefore continued to be quietly accepted by the U.S. Navy authorities in the western Mediterranean, and Washington took no official notice of French generosity in providing this material.[31]

The French code-and-cipher crisis, which dragged on for ten months in 1944, clearly intensified the sharp divisions that separated Gaullist France from the "Anglo-Saxons." As in the case of China, the exclusion of France from the Ultra-Magic club meant that another member of the future United Nations inner circle had been snubbed due to what seemed to be Anglo-American clannishness and arrogance. Since, in the postwar era, France would be a vital component of the hope of every American, and especially every Briton, that a counterweight to both Germany and the USSR could be created in Europe, Paris ultimately would have many more opportunities than Chungking to get back at the Atlantic powers for wartime slights such as those that occurred in 1944 over codes and ciphers.

French officials would long carry resentment regarding the rough treatment they received from London and Washington. One should not conclude, however, that the BRUSA partners followed restrictive policies toward the French in 1944–45 because of some special animus against the France of Charles de Gaulle. Other allied and "friendly" governments in addition to China and France had equally good reason to feel aggrieved by the treatment regarding signal security that they received from London and Washington in this period. Both the Greek and Norwegian governments-in-exile were barred from use of some secret methods of communication, at least in part because of Anglo-American doubts about the security of their codes and ciphers. In these cases, too, the offending countries were never told why London and Washington acted the way they did.[32]

Therefore, in 1944–45 the march toward victory was certainly accelerated by the intelligence information garnered by the Ultra-Magic partnership. That partnership also acted as a magnet, drawing the governments in London and Washington into a closer union, just as it helped force the American army and navy into closer cooperation on cryptanalytic matters. But it is also true that, beyond London and Washington, resentment against the cryptanalytic policies of the Atlantic powers was increasing in Paris, Chungking, and elsewhere—resentment that would continue to boil and bubble long after the war was over and the original Ultra-Magic agreements had passed into history.

CHAPTER EIGHT

The Last Phase of the War and Continuation of Cryptanalytic Cooperation

The final year of World War II seems in retrospect to have pivoted both on huge showdown battles in Europe and Asia, and on a series of developments that pushed the postwar era into a superpower cold war. The western powers' ability to quickly shake off the effects of the Battle of the Bulge, cross the Rhine, and strike into the heart of central Germany and Austria, while the Soviets encircled Berlin and Vienna and then smashed westward, guaranteed that the European continent would definitely be divided between east and west. In the Pacific, on the other hand, the decisive moves in the defeat of Japan were made overwhelmingly by American forces. Japanese naval and air power were destroyed by the U.S. Navy as it struck northwest, conquering Saipan in mid-1944, Iwo Jima in February–March, and Okinawa (thanks to the U.S. Army) in April 1945. Beginning in the late winter and early spring of 1945, Japan was devastated by the most concentrated strategic bombing campaign of the war, as American B-29s incinerated Japanese cities through conventional bombing and then, in August, dropped atomic bombs on Hiroshima and Nagasaki.

Although British forces fought a successful campaign against the Japanese in Burma during the second half of 1944 and on into 1945, while the Soviets overran Japanese units in Manchuria during late August 1945, and Chinese and American forces drove the Japanese back in southern China during the summer of 1945, American naval and bomber offensives in the Pacific were the decisive blows that broke Japan. These massive attacks destroyed resistance on the high seas and in the home islands while putting on a dazzling display of American firepower and the greatest concentration of high-tech destructive force the world had ever seen. Therefore, although the war ended in a joint victory of the Allied powers—the Soviets taking possession of vast tracts of territory and the British still maintaining large forces in the field—the form of the final battles seemed to proclaim that the United States was indeed a high-tech colossus. Just as Henry Luce had predicted in the previous year, the American century had seemingly dawned.

The speed and totality of the final Allied triumph also played important roles in the history of Anglo-American cryptanalytic relations during the final year of the war. So did the great increase of American power, the comparative weakening of Britain, and the increasing significance of Soviet strength in eastern Europe and the northern portions of the Asian continent. In addition, although Churchill's replacement as British prime minister by Clement Attlee seems to have exerted only a minimal influence on Anglo-American public and secret relations, it appears at least possible that the death of Franklin Roosevelt in April 1945, and the succession of Harry S. Truman to the presidency, made a contribution to the postwar continuation of the British and American secret special relationship.

Well before Truman became president, both British and American officials had begun to consider how to adapt the wartime intelligence machinery to the new conditions that would exist in the postwar world. During the winter of 1945 the density of the jungle of intelligence boards, committees, and information-collection agencies in Washington had finally compelled President Roosevelt to recognize that something would have to be done. On 17 January 1945 Roosevelt ordered Acting Secretary of State Edward Stettinius to take the lead on intelligence reform because, in the president's words, "at the end of this war there simply must be a consolidation of Foreign Intelligence between State and War and Navy." But Stettinius failed to address the situation, and the president, burdened by overwork and declining health, let intelligence matters drift. Roosevelt did not even interfere in early 1945 when a plan for creation of a postwar central intelligence agency, put forward by OSS director William Donovan, was sabotaged by a strident press campaign, which had quite likely been orchestrated by Donovan's opponents in Army G-2.[1]

The Army and Navy departments were compelled to try reforming the cryptanalytic portion of the Washington intelligence muddle on their own. One important feature of their early effort was a campaign to prepare, and have passed by Congress, a law authorizing them to intercept and decrypt radio traffic in peacetime. So convinced were the military authorities that such a law was necessary that an officer in Op-20-G with the lowly rank of lieutenant, junior grade, declared to all who would listen in July 1944 that "the fundamental principles of American life, freedom of speech and freedom of the press, will have to be modified somewhat in the future, if the work of cryptanalytic agencies of the United States is to be unimpeded." Military and naval cryptanalysts continued to pursue the possibility of passing such a law well into 1946, until the issue was subsumed in the process that finally created a cryptanalytic control board in 1946 and the National Security Agency in 1952.[2]

During the last months of the Roosevelt administration, the senior officers of the U.S. Army and Navy tried to establish at least some form of coordination between the cryptanalytic branches of the military services. General Marshall approached the matter cautiously, because he did not want overall supervision of army-navy cryptanalysis to occur within the Joint Chiefs of Staff organization. There were too many civilians on the various JCS committees for Marshall's taste; he also did not want to grant the U.S. Army Air Corps equality with the army and navy on cryptanalytic matters. If broad authority over cryptanalysis had been lodged in the JCS, the Army Air Corps chief of staff, Gen. Henry "Hap" Arnold, would then have had a voice and vote as powerful as that of Marshall or King; this status recognition could have become an important step in turning the Air Corps into a separate air force.

In a rare display of cooperative spirit, therefore, Admiral King (fully briefed by the director of Naval Communications, Admiral Redman) recommended to Marshall on 14 February 1945 that the Army-Navy Communications Coordination Committee, which had been formed in May 1944 as a purely advisory body, should be converted into the Army-Navy Communications Intelligence Board (ANCIB) to oversee the cryptanalytic activities of the two military services. Marshall immediately agreed to this proposal and on 10 March 1945 the ANCIB was created as a special joint army-navy organization responsible only to King and Marshall, and not answerable to the JCS.

Although Admiral King would not allow the ANCIB to go as far as full army-navy cryptanalytic integration, the new board immediately began resolving outstanding issues between the two services, such as coordination in the development of cryptographic and cryptanalytic equipment. It also made possible the formation of an army-navy united front for dealing with any other U.S. government agency that tried to intrude into the field of cryptanalysis, thereby raising the possibility that interdepartmental order might soon be brought to the rivalry and compartmentalizing still prevailing throughout American code-and-cipher breaking.[3]

On 12 April 1945, five weeks after the creation of the new Army-Navy Communications Board, President Roosevelt died; five days later the existing system for providing the White House with Ultra-Magic was reconfirmed. On 17 April General Marshall sent President Truman two Ultra summaries together with a general explanation of the Ultra secret. Marshall told the new president that Ultra information came from "a purely British source, which incidentally involves some 30,000 people, and we have bound ourselves to confine its circulation to a specific and very limited number of people. Therefore I request that this be 'For Your Eyes Only.' "[4]

These two short sentences were far from a comprehensive explanation of most secret Anglo-American cooperation, especially when one considers that although Truman had been vice president since the November 1944 election, he had not been informed of such fundamental secrets as the development of the atomic bomb or of Ultra. But Harry Truman was tough, determined, and ready to learn, and he quickly showed that, though inexperienced, especially in foreign affairs, he was quick, thorough, and a believer in tight and efficient organization. Henry Stimson's diary entries for April and May 1945 testify to the secretary of war's delight in the crisp manner the new president used to handle cabinet meetings, insisting that an agenda be followed and that members perform their duties by the book.

Within three weeks of taking the presidential oath, Truman brought his brisk approach into the American intelligence thicket, ordering a study of the FBI's activities in South America. On this occasion the new president confided to the director of the Budget Bureau (Harold Smith) that he was worried by the use of unvouchered funds by intelligence organizations and that he opposed the buildup, or retention, of any secret organization that threatened to create an American "Gestapo," by which he apparently meant any organizations using secret funds and secret agents. Five weeks later Truman told two members of his staff (Frederick Vinson and Samuel Rosenman) that although he wanted an arrangement made to provide "adequate intelligence . . . to keep him informed in international affairs," the president was fearful that overcentralization might create the "possibility of a Gestapo in this Country."[5]

Truman's reluctance to have large, amorphous, and potentially dangerous intelligence organizations continue into the postwar world was thwarted by pressures from a number of quarters. Although Germany surrendered on 8 May 1945, the war with Japan continued for three additional months. As long as hostilities lasted, the armed forces easily blocked any effort to limit their intelligence activities, even as the first preparations were being made for a transition of American government institutions into the postwar era. Admiral King was adamant that nothing should be done at any government level that might affect the collection, distribution, or use of secret Ultra intelligence related to the Pacific war as long as Japan continued to resist the American onslaught.

In addition to the obvious importance of not tampering with Ultra during the Pacific campaign, pressure was rising within the American military-naval establishment to guarantee that the U.S. armed forces would have a strong postwar cryptanalytic capability. In mid-June 1945 General Bissell reported to General Marshall that a recently conducted army study showed that at least 5,000 personnel would be required to meet the army's essential intercept and cryptanalytic needs after V-J Day, but the postwar planning that had been done up to that date had not reflected the need "for the continuation of signal intelligence activities."[6]

The pressure to guarantee the postwar position of American cryptanalysis was intensified by general worry in Washington that the United States might face serious security threats in the postwar world. Aside from the difficulties that would inevitably arise for Washington because of its vastly increased military and economic power, there were areas of the world such as Southeast Asia whose postwar instability might well pose a threat to world order. In addition, the USSR might make an overt challenge to general stability; American military intelligence authorities were quick to take note of the expanding power of the USSR well before victory had been achieved against Japan.

It should be emphasized, however, that during the war, overt intelligence activities directed at the USSR by Britain and the United States developed slowly and erratically, despite the fact that in 1943

Arlington Hall and G-2 had wanted the British government to supply them with intercepted Soviet secret radio traffic during the dickering that preceded the BRUSA agreement. When, on 30 August 1944, the former DMI and current head of the British Military Mission in Washington, Gen. F. H. N. Davidson, took the opportunity provided by a dinner at the home of John Franklin Carter, one of President Roosevelt's confidential information gatherers, to ask whether the United States could be counted on to march with Britain in the "next war" against Russia, he received no joy from Carter, who disapprovingly reported this probe to the White House.[7]

Among the U.S military intelligence people, matters were more complex. A series of microsteps were taken beginning in early 1944, which ultimately caused a partial Anglo-American intelligence partnership aimed at the USSR to be in place well before V-J Day. This sequence of events began in February 1944 when a team of U.S. Army order-of-battle (OB) specialists met in London with their British counterparts to study the order of battle of the Red Army. This was ostensibly done because Moscow had been tightfisted with information about its own forces, and also about the German formations stationed on the eastern front; therefore western planners were uncertain how successful the Soviets would be in tying down German units during the D day invasion. In actuality, Moscow provided substantially more information to the West regarding the eastern front forces of the Nazis during the days preceding D day than London and Washington have ever admitted. Regular Soviet meetings with American and British specialists on Axis order of battle occurred in Moscow throughout most of 1943 and the first two months of 1944. In this period the Soviet authorities were also more generous about supplying information regarding their own forces than they had been in the past, or would be again until the disarmament discussions of the late 1980s and the collapse of the Soviet system in the early 1990s.[8]

Nonetheless, between 4 and 15 February 1944 British and American order-of-battle specialists met in London to hammer together a joint OB picture of the Red Army and Air Force. The American team was led by Col. J. R. Lovell, and featured two former military attachés in Moscow, Colonels J. A. Michela and Richard Park, as well as two of the War Department's top specialists on the Russian military, Maj. D. B. Shimkin and Lt. Randolph Zander. The British delegation, headed by

Col. F. Thornton, contained at least one high-level Soviet order-of-battle expert, Major N. Ignatieff. Most of the men in both teams had long specialized in various aspects of intelligence on the USSR, and at least in the case of Michela, Park, and Thornton, they harbored engrained hostility to the Soviet Union and deep suspicion of Stalin's future intentions.[9]

At some point during the fifteen months following this conference, an arrangement was made between the War Office and the War Department to exchange regularly Soviet order-of-battle information (the Ignatieff-Zander agreement). This understanding was, in itself, an undertaking to share at least indirect cryptanalytic intelligence on the USSR between London and Washington, because much of the important information the War Office and the Air Ministry possessed about the Soviet armed forces had been gained from Ultra sources. The Germans obtained copious amounts of data regarding the Red Army and Air Force in the course of their military operations on the eastern front; the British, in turn, were able to gain possession of a large percentage of the German reports by means of Ultra breaks into the Luftwaffe and related circuits being used for communication between the eastern front and Germany. To draw on this material, as well as to make use of direct interrogations of captured German experts on Soviet military and air intelligence, a U.S. Army intelligence team, led by Col. (later Supreme Court Justice) Lewis F. Powell, performed liaison functions on Soviet air matters at the Air Ministry in London in mid-1945.[10]

While these British and American intelligence officers were moving ever closer in their cooperation regarding information on the USSR, an incident occurred four weeks prior to the end of the European war which showed that at the very top of the U.S Army command there was no certainty that a postwar conflict between the USSR and the United States was inevitable. On a number of occasions during the spring of 1945, thinly wrapped-up Ultra and Magic messages were sent to the Soviet authorities in Moscow in General Marshall's name. One of these, dispatched on 20 February 1945, concerned Hitler's intention to transfer an SS Panzerkorps to the east and commit it against the center of the advancing Soviet line. The Americans thought this was solid information because its source was a Magic intercept of a report to Tokyo by Japanese Ambassador Oshima in Berlin soon after he'd concluded a long conference with Hitler. Unfortunately, the information contained in the message turned out to be false. After the meeting with Oshima, Hitler had changed his mind and ordered the SS Korps to be moved to Hungary. The matter rested there until April 1945 when, during a shouting match with the Soviets over American efforts to arrange a German surrender in northern Italy (Operation Sunrise), Stalin accused Washington of having sent him false information in the past, and cited in support of his accusation this message indicating the wrong attack point for the SS Panzerkorps.

On 10 April 1945, to defend himself and help clear the air, Marshall sent to the Soviet General Staff a complete account of the development of his SS Panzerkorps message of 20 February. The heart of Marshall's explanation was that his statement regarding Hitler's intentions had been based on an excellent source. He went on to tell the Soviet leaders that it had come from an "interception from the Japanese sources in Berlin" of "information given by the Germans to Japanese Ambassador Oshima."[11]

Marshall thereby revealed the Magic secret to the Soviets. Intelligence from Oshima's message could have originated only from cryptanalysis or from an agent at the very top of the German or Japanese governments. Since the Soviets had previously received fistfuls of such top secret and most reliable messages regarding high-level German and Japanese intentions from the British and the Americans, they already must have doubted that an agent, no matter how well placed, could have acquired and rapidly transmitted so much high-grade material. In any event, on 10 April Marshall frankly told Moscow that the information had come from an "interception" of Oshima's communications, and the Soviets therefore knew for certain that the western secrets were the product of cryptanalysis, whatever else they may have heard about such matters from spies such as Kim Philby, Donald MacLean, and John Cairncross.

Marshall's revelation of the Magic secret to Moscow was certainly a grave breach of the rules that he himself had instituted to protect the security of cryptanalytic intelligence. But the chief of staff's move also proves that at the time he sent his clarification to Moscow, Marshall still put a high value on Red Army operations against Germany, and that he did not then consider the USSR to be an inevitable future threat to the United States. Marshall was imprudent when he made his explanation to Moscow, but it was the act of a man who seems to have envisioned more cooperation than conflict with the Soviet Union. If at that time, a month prior to V-E Day, the higher reaches of the American armed services had already burned their bridges and had mentally committed themselves to the belief that an all-out intelligence attack on the USSR was necessary, then Marshall's action over the Magic message would have been an act of true madness rather than one of simple folly.

Nor does the documentary evidence now available show that in the spring of 1945 the directors of the British intelligence system had reversed course and had ceased to provide high-grade intelligence to the USSR. Ever since June–July 1941 the British government had supplied the Red Army high command with intelligence, including some Ultra items. The latter material was usually transmitted to the Soviet authorities by the British Military Mission in Moscow, and was wrapped up by claiming that it had been provided to the British by an unidentified "Most Reliable Occasional Source."

Although even now Whitehall remains extremely circumspect about the details of its wartime intelligence transmissions to the USSR, it can be firmly established that the British continued to provide the Soviets with wrapped-up Ultra throughout the late winter of 1944 and well into the spring of 1945. Copies of British intelligence transmissions to the Soviets were frequently sent to the U.S. Military Mission in Moscow; copies of three of the Ultra transmissions, dated 22 February, 4 March, and 11 April 1945, have now been opened to public examination through the Freedom of Information Act. Although none of the specific intelligence information they contained was earthshaking—that of 4 March reported details on the position of the Third Panzer Army and the defensive position around Stettin—the existence of these documents proves that as late as four weeks prior to V-E Day, the British continued to share high-grade intelligence with the USSR as if it was an ally, not an enemy.

Therefore, a high-level, top-priority, Anglo-American intelligence alliance aimed at the USSR does not seem to have existed in April 1945. But soon after V-E Day (8 May 1945) the Pentagon's attitude quickly moved toward serious worry regarding future Soviet intentions, and that change immediately manifested itself in intelligence targeting. In late May and on into early June 1945 the U.S. Army and Navy made a number of informal agreements pledging to work together in formulating future intelligence arrangements with the British, and in collecting intelligence data regarding the USSR. On 25 May a message from the Naval Research Staff to Captain Wenger of Op-20-G set forth a plan for the U.S. Navy to jump aboard an American army plan to carry out an "Ultra" study in occupied Germany. As early as September 1944 the navy had begun to consider projects to study German radio intelligence after victory was won in Europe, but by late May 1945 many of the subjects that the U.S. Navy thought were of special interest directly concerned such Soviet matters as U-boats "on the Murmansk route" and "German Naval support of land operations in [the] Eastern Baltic." By 4 June 1945 the commander of U.S. Naval Forces Europe reported openly to Washington that his staff was interviewing captured German naval officers to secure "information on Japan and Russia."[12]

By 5–6 June 1945 General Marshall and Admiral King had agreed to cooperate with the British on cryptanalytic work, including "intercept material, recoveries, collateral aids and results," directed against a country they designated by the code name "Rattan." The matter was obviously one of great sensitivity, because after speaking with Admiral Ernest King regarding the matter, General Marshall instructed Gen. A. J. McFarland to make the presentation of the formal Rattan proposals to the navy orally and then "burn this paper." Since Germany was already defeated, and the British and American authorities had in place cryptanalytic-sharing agreements regarding Japan, the only countries that might, even in theory, have been hidden under the code name Rattan were China, the Soviet Union, and France. The British and Americans were already breaking Chinese codes with ease, so there was no pressing need to create a hush-hush project simply to share decrypted information acquired about the government of Chiang Kai-shek. Despite the fact that British and American relations were strained with de Gaulle's government in Europe, and serious trouble was brewing between France and the United States over Indochina during the summer of 1945, neither Washington nor London took France seriously enough to prompt development of such important and sensitive clandestine plans that they could not be committed to paper even within the innermost recesses of the Pentagon. The Soviet Union was ipso facto the most likely target for a top secret intelligence campaign because of its power, assertiveness, and the fact that it was already showing less than warmhearted cooperation with the western powers regarding access to central and eastern Europe. Furthermore, in June 1945, Moscow still had not set a date when it would join in the war against Japan.[13]

Therefore Rattan—which incidentally bore a striking resemblance to "Russia" both in the number and positioning of its component letters—was in all likelihood aimed against the USSR. Any doubts that might linger about whether the intelligence chiefs of Britain and the United States were prepared to take such measures in gathering secret intelligence about the Soviet Union in mid-summer 1945 are eliminated by the survival of a frank exchange of views between Colonel McCormack of G-2 and the British deputy director of Military Intelligence, Brigadier Brian P. O'Brien, which took place on 21 July 1945. McCormack felt that lower-level officials were being overly cautious in actually exchanging information on Soviet order-of-battle intelligence, including that derived from Ultra sources. The American chief of the U.S. Army's Military Intelligence Service consequently wrote a blunt note to O'Brien in which he emphasized that:

> The important thing is that full cooperation be attained. My personal opinion is that there is no field of intelligence in which it is so essential that [the] British and ourselves work closely together, because when a nation begins to throw its weight around here, there and everywhere, it is a good idea to have an accurate idea of how much weight is involved. Furthermore, I do not worry much about the "dynamite" aspects of the subject. The Russians themselves go after intelligence by any means and from any source that may be available. If I had the responsibility for talking to a Russian G-2, I would not hesitate to tell him that information about his country, army, air forces, etc. are important to the rest of the world and that we intend to work on it as hard as possible. Nor would I have any hesitation in saying that we would get as much help from other countries as they were willing to give us.[14]

The opportunity that this message opened up for extending intelligence cooperation with the Americans into the postwar world was not lost on O'Brien. Britain found herself heavily dependent on the United States in the summer of 1945 not only in financial and supply matters, but also in the intelligence field. Under the terms of BRUSA, as

well as a series of agreements covering "factual" intelligence concluded since mid-1943, Britain had been given the dominant voice in
respect to Germany and the U.S. Army had been granted the dominant voice in all intelligence matters concerning Japan. Once the Third
Reich had been defeated, however, Britain lost much of its intelligence
bargaining power, while remaining dependent for many categories of Japanese intelligence on the openhandedness of the American authorities.
Memories are short, and quid pro quo is king in intelligence exchanges.
In the late summer of 1945 the Joint Staff Mission was even compelled
to plead with the Pentagon for intelligence information covering some
of the responsibilities that would fall to Britain as the senior postwar
occupying power throughout much of Southeast Asia.

During the spring and summer of 1945 the Americans were tightening up on various forms of Anglo-American cooperation outside the
intelligence field. In March 1945 the JCS had issued orders banning
the provision of information on high-tech military projects to foreign
governments. When Admiral Stark inquired of the Navy Department
whether this restriction applied to the British government, he was told
that it most definitely did. The Americans also began closing down
the hatches on the combined communications systems with the British that had existed since 1942. Because of this American resistance
to a continuation of high-level communications cooperation, in the postwar
period Britain was forced into the unwelcome and expensive task of
developing a new generation of secret communication devices.[15]

Understandably then, Brigadier O'Brien immediately agreed that an
exchange of factual intelligence on the Soviet Union, carried out both
in Washington and in London, should begin forthwith. The British DDMI
tried to sound as blunt as his American counterpart, noting that
McCormack's vision of the need to pursue self-interest by all available means "is exactly the way it looks to me." O'Brien went on to
observe that "we need men with nuts in intelligence" who could emulate
what on "the Russian end is [simply] realism."[16]

In this mood of macho realpolitik the American and British military leaders pushed on through the final stage of the Pacific war. On
5 August the atomic bomb was dropped on Hiroshima; three days later
the Soviet government displayed its own brand of realism by tearing
up the nonaggression pact with Tokyo and attacking the Japanese forces
in Manchuria and Korea. The Americans came back with another atomic

bomb on 9 August, this one on Nagasaki. Faced with no prospect of successfully continuing the war, the Japanese emperor then directed his government to endure the unendurable by immediately making peace with the Allies. The Tokyo government accepted Allied surrender terms on 14 August, and on the following day, V-J Day, World War II was truly over, and the British Chiefs of Staff signaled their American counterparts that they had finally come to "journey's end."

On 27 August 1945 American occupation forces began to land in Japan. Included among them were code-and-cipher specialists, who were quickly able to establish that the Ultra-Magic secret had been completely maintained throughout the war with the Japanese. After V-J Day, Japanese officials remained blissfully ignorant of the fact that many of their codes and ciphers had been stripped clean by Anglo-American cryptanalysts; the Allies did nothing to enlighten the Japanese about Magic, in hope that they could continue to eavesdrop on the radio traffic of Japanese units that were still sprinkled across the Pacific and the mainland of Asia.

Study of captured Japanese records also demonstrated how effectively the Anglo-American cryptanalysts had done their job, especially during the last phase of the conflict. When the staff of the Strategic Bombing Survey carried out on-site inspections, they discovered that in the latter part of the war, information amassed by the U.S. Navy cryptanalysts about "the size and location of the Japanese merchant fleet on V-J Day had been more exact than the records of the Japanese Ministry of Merchant Marine."[17]

The totality of the American triumph in the last phase of the Pacific war, and the significant part that Ultra-Magic had played in that achievement, increased the status and importance of the western allied cryptanalysts, especially those of the United States. The men who had directed the Ultra-Magic effort therefore moved on to exploit their successes by tidying up their organizational systems and using their wartime triumphs to guarantee that they would be well funded in the postwar era, and that some form of transatlantic "most secret special relationship" would continue after the war.

An especially important concern for Britain was that the secrecy that had blanketed the joint cryptanalytic effort during the long struggle should be maintained after 1945. Whitehall had a long history of secret activities both in peace and war, and in the weakened condition in which Britain found herself in 1945, she urgently needed to maintain enough assets to carry on shadow operations in peacetime. Many of the British emergency organizations, such as the Special Operations Executive (to carry out clandestine operations), the Political Warfare Executive, and the Ministry of Economic Warfare, were quickly abolished, just as OSS, the Office of War Information, and the Board of Economic Warfare were immediately eliminated by the United States. But Britain retained its Joint Intelligence Committee and Chiefs of Staff organization, and of course maintained the Security Service and the Secret Service as well; a somewhat shrunken Bletchley simply carried on under the overall direction of "C." Because the traditional secret organizations continued into the postwar era, it was easy for the British government to salvage useful elements from the wartime secret units due to be abolished, and transfer them to MI 6 or MI 5. Some of the "clandestine" specialties of SOE were taken into MI 6, and it is reasonable to assume that some of the reforms of MI 5, which Eden and others had demanded since late 1944, included the absorption into the Security Service of some activities and skills that had been harbored in special emergency organizations during the war.[18]

None of these reforms and remodelings of the British secret world could have been fully effective unless they were carried through in complete secrecy, and for that to occur, the most sensitive World War II matters would have to remain secret as well. The Achilles' heel in the whole British secrecy effort—if one chooses to ignore Philby and company—was the link with the United States, a country essential for Britain's postwar recovery but so overpowering and self-centered that a weakened Britain might well be smothered in her embrace. America was also still inclined to leakiness and lacked a tradition of peacetime secret operations or tight security.

The British authorities therefore launched a campaign even before hostilities ended to keep a lid on the most delicate joint wartime secrets. This entailed not only preventing release to the public of information on sources of intelligence and the secret cooperation with the Americans, but also prevention of anything appearing in print that might, in the official phrase, cause political difficulty or embarrassment. On the day before the A-bomb was dropped on Hiroshima, the British Chiefs proposed that the Combined Chiefs of Staff immediately direct that special intelligence should be kept out of the hands of all official historians.

Britain wanted no mention of Ultra or Magic to be made in any official history, and desired that official historians be instructed "not to
probe too deeply into the reasons for apparently unaccountable operational
orders being given." The British Chiefs also recommended that only
"important battles" should be written up, and only by "personnel already
indoctrinated," who could be trusted to keep Ultra-Magic secret.

The Americans were not keen to restrict matters quite so tightly;
presumably, with Pearl Harbor investigations already underway, it was
obvious that not all American cryptanalytic activities could be kept
under the rug. On 7 September 1945 the Joint Chiefs of Staff concluded
that every sliver of special intelligence could not be kept out of the
hands of American official historians, but secrecy should be maintained
regarding the "degree of success attained, the techniques and procedures employed and the special intelligence produced." The British
therefore did not succeed in imposing every one of their draconian security
procedures on the Joint Chiefs of Staff, and through them onto the
American official histories. In December 1945, however, Admiral Chester
Nimitz, Admiral King's successor as chief of Naval Operations, did
order American official naval historians to be "substantially guided by
the security rules set forth by the British," thus taking the U.S. government much farther down the "official secrets" road than it had ever
gone before.[19]

The American army and navy were also ready, in the immediate
aftermath of the Japanese surrender, to rationalize their cryptanalytic
systems and to begin effecting a merger of some intercept and cryptanalytic operations of the army Signal Security Agency with those of
Op-20-G. On 18 August 1945 General Marshall directed a memo to
Admiral King suggesting that, although the army would be able to keep
supplying the White House and other authorities with diplomatic decrypts, in light of the end of hostilities and the need to review cryptanalytic relations with the British, the time had come to consider "the
advisability of combining army and navy intercept and cryptanalytic
activities under appropriate joint direction or, if this should be impossible
for any reason, to recommend procedures to insure complete integration." At any previous moment in the history of American army-
navy relations, this idea would never have been broached by one
American military service, or accepted by the other. However, just three
days after Marshall sent his letter to Admiral King, the chairman of

the Army-Navy Communications Intelligence Board, Adm. Hewlett Thebaud, reported to both Marshall and King that it was "advisable to combine Army and Navy intercept, cryptographic and cryptanalytic activities under appropriate joint direction." Thebaud went on to state that the cryptanalytic needs of the customs and immigration services could be met by the new joint agency, while all other departments of the U.S. government would be barred from cryptanalytic work except the FBI, which would be allowed to carry on cryptanalytic activity only in regard to "criminal activities in the U.S. and its possessions."[20]

A week later, President Truman put the icing on the cake, issuing an executive order to the Joint Chiefs of Staff and other departments of the U.S. government prohibiting anyone from releasing to the public "except with the specific approval of the President in each case," any "information regarding the past or present status, technique or procedure, degree of success attained, or specific results[,] of any cryptanalytic unit acting under the authority of the U.S. Government or any Department thereof."[21] With the issuance of that order, and the decision to move toward a blending of army-navy cryptanalytic activity, the U.S. government moved much closer to the realm of the Official Secrets Act, and in so doing left its cryptanalytic childhood behind and began to take on the security procedures and organizational arrangements appropriate for a superpower. The leaders of the U.S. Army immediately grasped the significance and increasing tempo of these changes, and on 4 September 1945 the secretary of war ordered all cryptanalytic and communications activities of the U.S. Army to be combined in a new Army Security Agency, thereby finally ending the age-old conflicts between G-2 and the Signal Security Agency (formerly Army SIS).[22]

That this group of important innovations all appeared just as the war came to a close was both fitting and understandable. At that moment such arrangements could be carried through secretly under the president's war powers; if they had been delayed, and the glow of victory had been allowed to pale, Congress might well have become inquisitive and meddlesome. That would, at the very least, have undermined the effectiveness of the reforms, for cryptanalysis thrives on secrecy and cannot long survive either open congressional hearings or cloakroom chatter.

Opportunities and dangers on the world scene also played their part in forcing the pace of intelligence reform in August and September 1945. While arrangements were being made for the merger of army and navy cryptanalytic activities, both General Marshall and Admiral Thebaud emphasized that one of the reasons to push forward on cryptanalysis reform was to take "the fullest advantage . . . of the presence of U.S. occupational forces in Europe and the Far East to establish and maintain any further world intercept coverage considered necessary."

The absence of bases from which German and Soviet radio traffic could have been acquired had been one of the major factors that forced the U.S. Army to settle for the BRUSA agreement in 1943. By the end of the hostilities, American forces were stationed close to those of the Soviets in Germany, Austria, Korea, Japan, and China, just as the political climate between East and West was becoming even chillier. The American government therefore had an opportunity both to track the activities of the USSR through its radio traffic and to fulfill long-held dreams of creating a large and efficient cryptanalytic service.[23]

The very destructiveness of the power the Americans had unleashed against Japan, especially its use of the atomic bomb, also, paradoxically, intensified the security worries of the U.S. authorities. Nuclear weapons instantly revolutionized warfare, sharply increasing the dangers of surprise attack, and effectively negating traditional defensive shields, like the two oceans, which had long been fundamental to American feelings of security. Although in August 1945 American leaders were certain that they had a substantial lead on the USSR and every other possible competitor in atomic research, worries that Moscow might rapidly close the nuclear gap were already manifesting themselves. In late August, during a discussion of the need for overall intelligence reform, a Joint Chiefs of Staff committee gave voice to the long-term torment produced by the existence of atomic and other forms of new weapons technology. The committee declared that "recent developments in the field of new weapons have advanced the question of an efficient intelligence service to a position of importance vital to the security of the nation in a degree never attained and never contemplated in the past. It is now entirely possible that failure to provide such a system might bring national disaster."[24]

These considerations still were not sufficient to make possible the full integration of U.S. Army and Navy intelligence. Nor were they strong enough to produce acceptance of William Donovan's plan to create a postwar central intelligence agency pivoting around a large network of secret agents. Secret agents were always a sensitive issue for American public opinion, and this worry was intensified in 1945 by residency in the White House of a president who was troubled about the possibility of creating an American "Gestapo." In addition, establishment of a formal central intelligence agency would have cost a great deal of money, and parsimony was the fashion in late 1945. Such a proposal inevitably would have entailed an acrimonious public battle in Congress over the effort to secure the charter and the money to run such an organization. To compound matters, the OSS director had tried to win his case by leaking information to the press, and by sending masses of unsolicited intelligence reports to the White House, rather than employing discreet lobbying and a campaign to jockey his proposals upward through the chain of command.

President Truman wanted things done by the book, and the impetuous Donovan was incapable of following a staid and orderly routine, or playing by the rules. A mutual antipathy seems to have developed between the two men, and since Truman had the ultimate power, Donovan was bound to lose in the end. Throughout August and the first week and a half of September, the president held his fire on Donovan's proposal to create a CIA. In part this hesitation may well have been caused by the fact that during this period another plan for developing a long-term intelligence shield for the United States was also moving toward its moment of decision.[25]

General Marshall had noted on 19 August that the Ultra-Magic arrangements with the British would "require re-examination and readjustment in the light of the post-hostilities situation." At that time American personnel were still assigned to Bletchley Park and Berkeley Street, and their British counterparts continued to fulfill duties at Arlington Hall. William Friedman had just completed a survey trip to Europe, spending considerable time with his British and American colleagues at Bletchley. During his stay discussions on the question of a continuation agreement would have been difficult to avoid. Certainly, by the late summer of 1945 British officials showed themselves fully primed to make another deal. Sir Edward Travis and Dr. Harry Hinsley made a survey of British cryptanalytic operations in the Pacific during that period, spending so much time at the American naval headquarters at Pearl Harbor that Travis had to arrange through the Foreign Office for a cash advance to keep him solvent. Then, after a stop in San Francisco to examine the communications system being operated in the Pacific area by British Security Coordination, Hinsley and Travis traveled on to Washington, where they began to discuss with American officials the ins and outs of continuing cryptanalytic cooperation between the two countries.

On the basic question of whether such cooperation was desirable, the British emissaries quickly discovered that they were talking to the converted. United States intelligence and cryptanalytic personnel were just as eager to carry on the partnership because the Americans fully understood the mutual benefits involved, and apparently also grasped the enormous difficulties, and possible dangers, that would be entailed in trying to separate the two halves of the Ultra-Magic system. In the higher echelons of the American government the British also found a warm and understanding welcome. Not only were both American service chiefs prepared to support an extension of cryptanalytic cooperation with Britain, Army G-2 was so eager to continue sharing "factual" intelligence with the British that American army intelligence officials even offered to create a Combined Executive Organization to carry out exchanges in that most difficult of all places for Britons to enter, General MacArthur's headquarters in occupied Japan.[26]

By the second week of September the question of continuing a cryptanalytic linkup with London had reached the level of the American cabinet. On 12 September 1945 Secretary of War Henry Stimson was joined by Secretary of the Navy James Forrestal (who had replaced the late Frank Knox) and Dean Acheson (who was serving as acting secretary of state) in submitting to the president a formal recommendation that such a continuation arrangement should be agreed upon. The resulting Three Secretaries memorandum began by surveying for President Truman the "outstanding contributions to the success of the Allied forces in defeating Germany and Japan which have been made by the cryptanalytic units" of the U.S. Army and Navy. "Not only were many military and naval victories of the Allies made possible by learning the plans and intentions of the enemy," the Three Secretaries stressed, but this kind of intelligence work also would have special value in dealing with the kind of problems that would be posed in the postwar world, since the Ultrac-Magic process had shown that "much important diplomatic and economic information, otherwise unobtainable," could be produced by cryptanalytic cooperation with Britain. Truman was also reminded that "during the German and Japanese wars, the United States

Army and Navy and the British Government Code and Cipher School collaborated closely in regard to cryptanalytic techniques and procedures[,] and exchanged in full the intelligence derived from cryptanalysis." The latter portion of this statement, especially as it was applicable to the sharing of naval cryptanalysis, overstated the degree of cooperation, but the Three Secretaries were certainly correct when they went on to declare that "the results of this collaboration were very profitable."

After two lines enumerating specific benefits gained by the Ultra-Magic partnership—lines that have been blacked out by NSA—the Three Secretaries went on to declare that "in view of the disturbed conditions of the world and the necessity of keeping informed of the technical developments and possible hostile intentions of foreign nations [here again, NSA blacked out a line, which, if it did not include a reference to the USSR, and perhaps the atomic bomb, would be quite surprising], it is recommended that you authorize continuation of collaboration between the United States and the United Kingdom in the field of communication intelligence."[27]

The president thereupon signed a one-sentence top secret memorandum on 12 September 1945, which read:

> The Secretary of War and the Secretary of the Navy are hereby authorized to direct the Chief of Staff, U.S. Army, and the Commander in Chief, U.S. Fleet, and Chief of Naval Operations, to continue collaboration in the field of communication intelligence between the United States Army and Navy and the British, and to extend, modify or discontinue this collaboration, as determined in the best interests of the United States.

The president signed only one copy of the memorandum, and that copy was given to the secretary of state, perhaps because he could act as an honest broker in any dispute between the army and the navy over the terms and qualifications of the continuation authorization. Additional, unsigned, copies of the order were provided to the War and Navy departments, and the president also retained one copy in the White House Naval Aide's files. By 17 September the U.S. Navy's copy of the presidential order had already made the rounds through the offices of Admiral

King, the ONI, the director of Naval Communications, and the navy member of the Army-Navy Communications Intelligence Board.[28] Also on 17 September the Combined Chiefs of Staff issued general instructions for all Ultra recipients, ordering them "to continue to maintain the secrecy of Ultra in peace as closely as it has been maintained in war." The Combined Chiefs warned that there should be no lessening of security, because,

> to disclose now or hereafter the measure of our success on techniques or procedures[,] or any of the specific results[,] would be most hazardous because (A) Ultra will be required for knowledge of the activities of the Germans and the Japanese and for controlling underground movements among them. It is essential that their suspicions be not aroused if knowledge is to continue. (B) Other threats to world security may arise in the future[,] and knowledge of what has been achieved by Ultra in this war could only serve to put our future enemies on their guard thereby rendering similar success far more difficult if not impossible.

Consequently, although "in the years to come there may be leaks and partial disclosures," the Combined Chiefs insisted that it was "most important that these be given no official confirmation or [be] reinforced by additional statements by those who were also in the know." Ultra-Magic veterans must resist "all temptation to divulge the Ultra Secret," because "the present and future best interests of our countries demand that it be maintained."[29]

The basis for nearly fifty years of total official secrecy regarding Ultra-Magic cooperation, as well as the selective, still-continuing secrecy policies of the two countries, was thereby laid. The presidential authorization order clearly had made the British and American military authorities extremely anxious about security, because they wished to guard and protect their continuing Ultra-Magic partnership. The 12 September 1945 order may also have decided Truman on what should be done with OSS, and Donovan's expensive and controversial proposal for a large postwar central intelligence agency. On the day following his authorization of continued cryptanalytic cooperation with Britain, the president directed his budget director, Harold Smith, to prepare an order abolishing OSS, "even if Donovan didn't like it." A week later, the president signed the OSS dissolution order "without comment."[30]

On 20 September 1945 Harold Smith's Budget Bureau staff finally completed its proposal for the organizational arrangement of postwar American intelligence. Amid much vague theorizing, the plan actually confirmed the traditional independent collection prerogatives of a series of federal government departments and bureaus ranging from State, through War and Navy, to the FBI. Some small concessions were made to the principle of coordination and liaison, but the budget specialists left intact most of America's failed system of fragmented intelligence collection and processing. In regard to only one aspect of postwar American intelligence collection, aside from the purchase of maps, did the Budget Bureau assert that "the case for central direction [was] particularly strong," and that was, of course, cryptanalysis.[31]

Thus, for the most hardheaded of doubting realists—the director of the Budget Bureau—cryptanalysis may well have taken on the characteristics of something close to a wonder weapon in September 1945. It had a proven track record, was inexpensive compared with the central intelligence plans of the spendthrift Donovan, and could be kept totally secret. The latter point was especially important, because a strong consensus had not yet formed in the United States for an assertive postwar foreign policy, and not even the White House seemed at this moment to have a clear idea of what the future held regarding America's relations with the rest of the world. If the staff of the Budget Bureau had been privy to either the wartime Ultra-Magic sharing agreements or the continuation authorization just approved by Truman, they most likely would have been even more enthusiastic about cryptanalysis, since the arrangements with the British offered the prospect of further lessening American intelligence costs by securing free access to Britain's worldwide radio and cable interception nets, as well as to a substantial portion of its code- and cipher-breaking capability.

Such crass budgetary considerations may seem in dubious taste when applied to as pathbreaking and significant a matter as the September 1945 Anglo-American decision to continue the cryptanalytic partnership into the postwar era. That decision created a secret special relationship that would evolve into the longest-lasting confidential partnership in the history of the world. But there are no indications in the patchy open records now available that Bletchley, any more than the American military services, supported continuation of the wartime arrangements because of any farsighted vision of the future. Nor is there any compelling reason to conclude that an unusually broad viewpoint then dictated the perspective of Clement Attlee, any more than it did of Harry Truman. Both leaders were conscientious and hardworking, but hardly inclined to seek out distant realities beyond the horizon.

The cryptanalysts and the intelligence specialists in the two countries wanted the partnership to continue because it worked well for them, and if it were broken off each side would know too much about the cryptanalytic methods of the other to let either Whitehall or the Pentagon rest in peace. Furthermore, Britain was even more desperate to cut its costs than was Washington in September 1945. Whitehall faced a crushing burden of foreign and domestic debts, the Empire was clamoring for reform and independence, the public at home demanded an expensive welfare state, and postwar occupation and military expenses promised to impose additional burdens on the Exchequer. Britain had to seize hold of anything that could lessen its financial troubles and permit it to gain benefits from the special wartime relationship it had enjoyed with the now seemingly all-powerful United States.

Continuation of Anglo-American cryptanalytic cooperation was therefore a natural. The overarching interests of the tax men and the wishes of the intelligence and code-breaking professionals were united at a time when parsimony and worried suspicion in international affairs were the orders of the day. The situation prevailing in the immediate postwar world cried out for an arrangement that might assist in the West's pursuit of stability. The world was devastated, with international trade reduced to a crawl, and only three great powers left in existence, of which Britain was both the weakest and the one most heavily burdened with global economic, political, and military obligations. The peoples of the world were reeling under the shock of the war's savagery and destructiveness, topped off by the atomic bomb.

Order and security stood near the head of nearly everyone's want list in the West during the autumn of 1945. However, the bumps and irritations that had occurred between the USSR and the western powers during the final year of the war—ranging from Operation Sunrise to harsh Soviet occupation policies and the disputes over Poland—were not reassuring. Those tensions and troubles had been cast into an even more frightening light by the possibility of a future nuclear confrontation. For the first time, every uncertainty and irritation became subject to a possible atomic magnifier. Even before the atomic bomb had been dropped, and before the Red Army had spread out across Manchuria and Korea, Britain and the United States had linked arms to collect and share intelligence information regarding the USSR's overall power, military deployment, and intentions. Once the bomb had been detonated, such intelligence activity was bound to increase, because the Soviet Union was the only powerful non-Atlantic power with an assertive, if not aggressive, foreign policy of its own, and the capability ultimately to produce its own bomb.

The decision to extend Anglo-American cryptanalytic cooperation into the postwar era consequently bore the marks of inevitability. So many factors, ranging from mundane budgetary considerations to fears of Armageddon, played a part, that none of those involved in the decision making needed to look very far in search of a special reason to act. However, when all the preparations had been completed, and Harry Truman signed his name on 12 September 1945, a whole new round of work and worry commenced, as British and American officials tried to sort out the jumble of existing special intelligence understandings and agreements, and began to prepare a new secret charter to make Anglo-American cryptanalytic operations effective in the years to come.

CHAPTER NINE

The Making of a Permanent Agreement, 1945–47

"Parties don't make history, classes make history."
Karl Marx

If a scientific law existed covering the secret activities of modern governments, one of its basic tenets surely would be that the closer one approaches current governmental practices and procedures, the less reliable would be the relevant available evidence. Certainly there is no informative documentation now open to the public or the historical researcher regarding the system of cryptanalytic cooperation currently operating between Britain and the United States. Due to the rigid secrecy policies employed by London and Washington, the public is completely excluded from all the rules and procedures affecting cryptanalytic cooperation that have prevailed since 1946. It is highly probable that the formal U.S.–U.K. code- and cipher-breaking agreement was signed in 1948, although precisely when in that year cannot now be established. The agreement seems to have included in its embrace the code- and cipher-breaking activities of Canada, New Zealand, and Australia, as well as those of Britain and the United States, but there is no conclusive proof that these provisions are still in force.[1]

Although the terms and the precise timing of the postwar U.S.–U.K. cryptanalytic agreement remain secret, it is possible to identify the main features of the negotiating process that produced that agreement, as well as many significant factors that helped to shape its final provisions. The negotiations actually began in Washington during the autumn of 1945, with Sir Edward Travis and Dr. Harry Hinsley speaking for Britain, and a joint Op-20-G and army Signal Security Agency team representing the United States. Trouble over who should be parties to the agreement erupted almost immediately. Travis and Hinsley visited Ottawa in mid-October 1945 and persuaded the Canadian Joint Intelligence Committee on 22 October that a British-Canadian cryptanalytic agreement should be concluded immediately, allowing Britain to speak for both itself and Canada in subsequent negotiations with the United States. When the British pair returned to Washington, however, they found the American negotiators violently opposed to such an arrangement. Washington strongly favored full bilateral agreements with the Canadians on all intelligence matters. A December 1945 memo prepared for the director of MIS, G-2, stated that due to "Canada's strategic position with respect to the United States and Russia, it is believed that all consideration of U.S. intelligence relations with that nation should be made independently."[2]

Similar complications in the Anglo-American cryptanalytic discussions arose regarding the position of New Zealand and Australia. The British claimed to speak for all their Dominions, whereas the Americans, citing wartime arrangements in which they had formed special intelligence links with Australia and New Zealand, insisted that the Dominions, as well as Britain and the United States, should be full and independent parties in the negotiations. The British produced one draft agreement after another attempting to bridge this gap and others, but all of them were rejected or sharply modified by the Americans. Consequently the negotiations dragged on for well over a year, beginning in the United States during the last months of 1945 and continuing throughout 1946 on Duke Street in London. The haggling was so protracted and acrimonious that the American government apparently established a cryptanalytic liaison office in London in order to provide its delegation with a strong organizational base camp for this knock-down-and-drag-out campaign in the British capital.[3]

In addition to the conflict over the role the Dominions should play in the negotiations and the agreement, there were also problems over whether intelligence relating to all countries should be included in the final sharing arrangement. During the early stages of the negotiations, Washington put an embargo on some categories of intelligence it had collected regarding China. By late 1946 the United States also refused to include information on the Philippines in any intelligence exchanges with Britain or the Dominions. Throughout the entire negotiation period, and in the final agreement, the Americans refused to provide their cryptanalytic partners with intelligence of any kind regarding Latin America.[4]

Despite Washington's rigidities, the Americans' desires seemed far from clear during much of the negotiation period. This lack of clarity and consistency apparently arose at least in part because the American organizational system for cryptanalysis, indeed for all aspects of intelligence activity, was repeatedly changing during the early postwar period. In December 1945 the State Department was added to the Army-Navy Communications Intelligence Board, which was then renamed the State-Army-Navy Communications Intelligence Board (SANCIB). In June 1946 the FBI joined this cryptanalytic oversight group, which then was retitled the U.S. Communications Intelligence Board. At the same time that the FBI was added to the cryptanalytic policy board, the first major move was made to partially centralize the entire American intelligence community. In 1946 the Central Intelligence Group (CIG), a nearly toothless tiger, was created to perform liaison duties between the various American intelligence organizations and at the same time to provide the president with "consensus" intelligence estimates applicable to important foreign policy matters. In June 1946 the CIG also became a member of the U.S. Communications Intelligence Board.[5]

The American evolution toward intelligence centralization was hampered and disturbed by a number of factors, of which bureaucratic lethargy and interdepartmental rivalries were among the most important. Throughout the American intelligence community, every department fought for its privileges and could always count on an active cadre of veterans and retirees, whether composed of soldiers, sailors, or FBI men, ready to rally sections of public opinion to the cause if important prerogatives were threatened. In addition, jurisdictional conflicts within some of the major departments erected obstacles to any move in the direction of centralization, cooperation, or increased efficiency. In January 1946 a comparatively polite squabble erupted within the U.S. Navy Department over the role of cryptanalysis and the need for centralization in naval intelligence. As frequently occurred in such battles, this one pitted ONI against the naval communications sections. After a few spirited exchanges, the squabble finally trailed off with no serious casualties.

One important fact central to the history of postwar American intelligence, and U.S. relations with the British, was revealed during this naval intramural squabbling, namely that U.S. Navy cryptanalysis (recently renamed U.S. Naval Communications Supplementary Activities) had provided "disappointingly little of real value" since V-J Day, as even the navy cryptanalysts admitted. That deficiency suggests that a major reason why the British and American governments took so long ironing out their cryptanalytic differences was that neither country had made much headway against high-grade Soviet codes and ciphers in the immediate postwar period. If it is correct that none of the Anglo-American cryptanalysts was producing Soviet decrypts of great value, as a number of hints from unofficial investigations suggest, then the two governments were free to dawdle over the negotiations as long as they wished, because there was little or nothing to gain by speed.[6]

In any event, it is certainly true that American intelligence relations with Britain had ups and downs during the first two years after the war. United States intelligence cooperation with Britain was called into question in April 1946 (put "under review" is the official phrase), and again late in 1947, when every aspect of technical cooperation with London was put on hold following a sale of British jet aircraft to the Soviet Union. Even in the best of times, the Washington authorities would not permit disclosure to Britain of the "source[s] of [American] intelligence" information, "the methods of acquisition," or "any information pertaining to cryptography and cryptographic devices, except that necessary to implement communications agreements with the United Kingdom."[7]

However, cryptanalysis cooperation was not a one-way street on which all traffic moved in a westerly direction and all power was concentrated at the American stop line. In sharp contrast to what happened regarding cooperation on the atomic bomb—where Britain was squeezed out because she had no firm wartime agreement with the Americans (except one concerning the supply of uranium) and had no direct control over the vital bomb production facilities, all of which were in the United States—London had important assets in the cryptanalytic game. The British had more extensive and long-lasting experience in this field than did the Americans: Their code- and cipher-breaking operations were more effectively centralized, they had a worldwide radio and cable interception network that girdled the USSR, and they had already been engaged with the Americans in secret intelligence operations directed at the Soviet Union well before the end of World War II.[8]

Some of the latter operations did not miss a beat after V-J Day. The U.S. and Royal navies hammered out a comprehensive exchange system between 24 August and 8 October 1945 regarding Red Navy intelligence. This particular agreement focused on such purely naval matters as ship construction, dockyards, "training and readiness," as well as "naval aviation, gunnery, engineering and electronic data," but it eschewed the exchange of information on Soviet political, economic, army, and air force information to avoid jurisdictional conflicts with other departments in London and Washington. Even so, the arrangement did not elude all traditional territorial struggles. The ONI successfully insisted that all information must pass only between itself and the DNI in London, with Op-20-G and Bletchley Park left out of the transmission loop, even though the intelligence involved was to be graded "Top Secret Ultra," or as all U.S. Navy intelligence from agents and cryptanalysis was relabeled in January 1946, "Covert."[9]

An important factor that helped smooth the way for such arrangements, and would ultimately assist in the conclusion of an Anglo-American postwar cryptanalytic agreement, was a nucleus of links between the British and American military services that had managed to survive the formal demise of the Combined Chiefs of Staff after V-J Day. In December 1945 the Combined Communications Board was still functioning, and an interim plan for secret communications between the chiefs of staff of the two countries had already been developed, with the U.S. Navy preparing the "key lists, indicator tables, etc." for the participants on both sides of the Atlantic. The British Chiefs did fail in their February 1946 attempt to secure acceptance by the American Chiefs of a formal revival of the entire Combined Chiefs of Staff system, but as Brig. A. T. Cornwall-Jones of the British Joint Staff Mission in Washington consoled himself on 5 February 1946, collaboration between the armed forces of the two countries regarding training and intelligence was "in fact already continuing."[10]

During the critical last months of 1945 and the first months of 1946, in the shadow zone that followed the end of the war, British and American leaders were highly prone to alarmist worries, because after having become accustomed to directing huge armies and navies, they discovered that their populations were determined to enjoy a bit of peace and prosperity, leaving the governments with few instruments of power to affect international events. In many areas of the world outside Britain and the United States, suffering and despair were nearly universal, and there was considerable political instability and border conflict. In this tense atmosphere the actions of the Soviet Union provided Washington and London with much to ponder and worry about. The Red Army stripped central and eastern Europe in 1945 and clamped down highly repressive Communist regimes on Poland, Romania, and Bulgaria, while demanding only moderately less repressive ones in Hungary and Czechoslovakia. The Red Army and Navy were not much reduced in size, and the foreign secretary meetings that occurred during 1945–46 in London, Moscow, and Paris did little to establish a genteel modus operandi linking East and West. The Soviet Union's repeated vetoes in the United Nations, combined with its refusal to evacuate its occupation zone in northern Iran, further alarmed western leaders in the winter of 1945–46, prompting Churchill's "Iron Curtain" speech at Fulton, Missouri, in March. That the foreign secretaries finally did arrange peace treaties for the "minor Axis" states at Paris in October 1946 seems to have been a case of too little, too late. The western powers had conducted atomic bomb tests at Bikini in July, which Moscow considered crudely threatening gestures, and then the Anglo-Americans decided to merge their occupation zones in Germany during December 1946. The latter action not only underscored the serious trouble Britain was having in meeting her postwar international obligations, as well as her need to gain assistance from the United States, but also showed that the transatlantic powers were pulling closer together in the face of what they saw as a dangerous Soviet threat.

From the earliest days, Anglo-American apprehensions about the Soviet Union had featured a peculiar mixture of external dangers plus the threat of internal espionage and subversion. In the last stage of World War II a Soviet code clerk, Igo Gouzenko, had defected to the Canadian authorities and poured out detailed accounts of extensive Soviet espionage activities to Canadian, British, and American security officials. The resulting investigations by the three governments turned up formidable Soviet intelligence operations in the western countries, which helped unleash a great Red scare, and also increased western fears about Soviet international intentions and capabilities. In the resulting atmosphere of dread and suspicion, the Nunn, Rosenberg, and Hiss cases occurred, and in March 1947 Harry Truman drew the line overseas by announcing in the Truman Doctrine that the United States would shoulder Britain's burdens in the eastern Mediterranean and assist "free" governments threatened by internal subversion or external attack.

Anglo-American intelligence services were inevitably compelled by these events to tighten up their security procedures and expand operations directed at the USSR. The rising public and governmental belief in the existence of an imminent Red threat also provided a sharp spur to increase Anglo-American intelligence cooperation in order to measure Soviet capabilities and intentions more accurately. This situation put the British and American armies and navies in the intelligence front line. Soviet pressure had to be expected or anticipated not only in Europe, where British and American troops were stationed in Germany, Austria, and Italy, but along the southern Soviet border in the Middle East and western Asia, where British forces were trying to cope with anticolonial independence movements, and in China, where American military missions were trying to assist Chiang Kai-shek in his struggle with the Chinese Communists.

Consequently the American Army G-2 moved swiftly in December 1945 to make certain that the arrangements it had with the British army and RAF for the sharing of "factual" intelligence (order of battle, topographical, technical, et cetera) on each other's land and air forces, as well as those of other powerful countries around the world, would continue and, if possible, be expanded. G-2 was especially anxious to maintain the wartime sharing arrangement with Britain because "the British have superior facilities and coverage of the European and Middle Eastern areas," and G-2 believed that between them, "the United States and Great Britain control the majority of the strategic positions around the world (Gibraltar, the Middle East, Australasia, the Pacific islands, and Panama)." Therefore, "a continuation of the policy for the full and free exchange of factual military information and intelligence with British agencies" would, in the view of G-2, "enable both nations to be the best informed in the world."[11]

By February 1946 the belief that Anglo-American intelligence cooperation would increase defensive strength had been translated by the American army in Europe into a three-tiered system for sharing with the nations the U.S. Army now characterized as "our former allies" the intelligence that the Americans gained from their study of German technology and captured Wehrmacht records. Local American army commanders were authorized to provide British authorities routinely with any of this information classified "Secret" or below. However, such exchanges with the French were only to be carried out "with caution," whereas in respect to the Soviets, "no exchanges" of any kind were permitted regarding "military intelligence reports and publications," or "information likely to develop into military intelligence," unless specifically authorized by higher headquarters.[12]

United States Navy planning during 1946 also pointed in the direction of ever closer cooperation with the British amid rising apprehension about security dangers in far corners of the world. For the Navy Department, the fundamental issue was the coverage its network of radio intercept stations could provide, because in 1946 all naval cryptanalytic work had been concentrated in Washington, and the Pacific Supplementary Radio Unit (the cryptanalytic unit on Oahu) had been closed down. By August 1946 the U.S. Navy intercept stations in the Pacific were located on Guam, Samoa, Okinawa, Adak in the Aleutians, and Wahiawa in Hawaii, with an additional station planned for Kwajalein. In the Atlantic, navy intercept stations were located at San Juan in Puerto Rico, Toro Point in the Panama Canal Zone, Recife in Brazil, and in the Mediterranean at Port Lyautey in French Morocco. However, U.S. Navy authorities were worried that they would be denied long-term use of the Port Lyautey installation, and in August 1946 they urged the State Department to make an all-out effort in the current negotiations with Portugal to secure for the navy an intercept base at Terceira in the Azores.[13]

Despite the wide scope of these intercept arrangements in the southern and western Atlantic as well as the northern, southern, and central Pacific, there were serious holes in the U.S. Navy's radio intercept coverage. No American stations existed in the eastern Mediterranean, the Red Sea, the Indian Ocean, or in the Pacific below the equator. Another important gap in coverage lay in the North Atlantic, the North Sea, and the Baltic. Some of these deficiencies, especially those in northern Europe, might be made good if the U.S. Army in Germany would perform intercept activities that fitted navy needs, and, even more problematical, if the army could actually be counted on to deliver quickly the intercepted radio traffic to the naval authorities in Washington.

A far more promising and less troublesome way for the U.S. Navy to cover the holes in its intercept net, however, was to acquire the needed radio traffic from the British. The Royal Navy concentrated much of its interception activity in the very zones where the U.S. Navy had little or no coverage—the North Atlantic and North Sea area as well as from the Mediterranean through the Red Sea and the Indian Ocean to the South Pacific. The Admiralty could also be counted on to intercept the kind of material that would be of most value for U.S. Navy radio traffic analysts and cryptanalysts, and the British also would be able to make use of Canadian, Australian, New Zealand, and South African intercept operations, which, like those of Britain, tended to focus on areas where American needs were greatest.

Although the U.S. military and naval services seemed to British eyes to possess almost boundless riches in manpower, equipment, money, and technology, Washington was nonetheless coming around to the view that it alone could not bear what it saw in late 1946 as the burden of the worldwide containment of the Soviet Union. Allies were needed, especially in critical strategic areas, but before new multinational security arrangements could be created—such as the North Atlantic Treaty Organization, which did not appear until 1949—Washington had to look toward Britain and the Dominions as the first line of an expanding American defense system.

Predictably, general intelligence cooperation between the two countries was one of the areas where the urgent sense of a developing common interest first manifested itself. In September 1946, two months prior to the conclusion of a technical cooperation agreement between London and Washington, and three months prior to the merging of the British and American zones of occupation in Germany, which is frequently seen as an important way station on the road to the close postwar partnership of the Atlantic powers, a tentative intelligence-sharing agreement was concluded between Sir Stewart Menzies ("C") of MI 6 and the deputy chief of the new U.S. organization to coordinate and centralize intelligence, the Central Intelligence Group (CIG). The arrangement called for an exchange of intelligence between the CIG and the new British Joint Intelligence Board (the successor of the Joint Intelligence Committee), which would act as a counterpart to the American CIG, and covered a "complete exchange of information from all sources and on all subjects except commercial." The exchanges of intelligence were scheduled to begin before the end of 1946 in London, with the American side of the partnership represented by a CIG Liaison Group permanently stationed in the British capital.[14]

With that agreement, transatlantic intelligence cooperation was back on track to meet what London and Washington saw as the fundamental challenges of the cold war era. The cryptanalytic intelligence agreement that was finalized in the following year was, in actuality, simply an expansion and extension of a series of intelligence cooperation arrangements between London and Washington whose central component was the CIG–Joint Intelligence Board agreement of September 1946.

All of these various British-American intelligence-sharing arrangements, the last of which was finally concluded in 1948, obviously arose in some degree or another from the West's all-pervading fear of the USSR. But every step taken toward Anglo-American intelligence cooperation also awakened memories of the wartime transatlantic intelligence partnership and the common experience of the Combined Chiefs of Staff system. Nostalgia for what came to be seen as the grand days of common purpose, which had prevailed from 1942 to 1945, apparently played at least a supporting role in the attitudes of many senior officers and officials. Though most of the top American leaders who had created the important wartime partnerships, such as the BRUSA agreement, were no longer in control of affairs in Washington during 1946 and 1947, Travis and Menzies continued to play significant roles on the British side, and their experience and prestige in regard to the more delicate aspects of Anglo-American relations certainly helped once again to bind the two governments together in a secret special partnership.[15]

Ideology may also have done its bit. Although America was too far to the right for a good many Britons, and the Labour government too much to the left for many in the United States, when compared with the Soviet Union, these differences seemed minor, for the two peoples shared a common commitment to representative government, civil rights, and at least some form of free-enterprise economics. The two governments also shared deep common interests in the immediate postwar period. Britain was overextended and in decline, while the United States was still rising both in political and military power, but both countries were actually satiated states with little inclination to radical change. They both needed and wanted worldwide stability, economic recovery, increased output, expanded trade, and an open path for international investment. When compared with an aggressive and apparently expanding Soviet empire covering much of the heartland of Europe and Asia, any differences that existed between Britain and the United States looked miniscule.

Yet all these factors would probably not have been able to quickly smooth the way for creation of comprehensive Anglo-American intelligence-sharing agreements between 1945 and 1947 if the cold war crisis had not occurred in the immediate shadow of the broad and deep intelligence cooperation arrangements that united the two countries between 1942 and 1945. Because a host of obstacles ranging from security difficulties to the need for reciprocity had been successfully surmounted, and a series of highly secret agreements had actually been concluded just a few years earlier, it was comparatively easy to grasp that the process could be repeated in 1946–47, even though the balance of power had shifted decisively in America's favor. Both governments were fully aware of the substantial benefits they had secured from the earlier arrangements, and despite much grumbling there was mutual respect. On the lower rungs of the ladder in Bletchley, Arlington, ONI, and Op-20-G, hundreds of officials knew from their own experience that intelligence cooperation could work, and pay handsome dividends to those bold enough to attempt it.

Thus on every scale of cause and effect that one may wish to contemplate, the secret special relationship was virtually destined to be extended into the chilly postwar world of 1946–47. It was not the result of any secret tricks played on the people or governments of the two countries by shadowy figures who huddled in dark doorways practicing the arts of secret chicanery. The important cause-and-effect relations that operate in clandestine secret politics do not differ much from those that operate "above the line." Invisible men, with or without trenchcoats, did not create the postwar secret special relationship that continues to bind together Britain and the United States, for the documentary record shows that the combination of governmental self-interest, wartime precedent, and the force of circumstance came together at just the right moment to offer the secret special relationship the opportunity for an extended life.

Once the massive and powerful general factors had done their work, however, then new circumstances were created in which invisible men could ply their trade in ways the public at large, and most government leaders, could not see or understand. This applied not only to those Americans and Britons busily exchanging official secrets, but also to their opponents in the employ of the Soviet Union. In August 1946, as the negotiations to create the CIG–British Joint Intelligence Board sharing agreement were drawing to a conclusion, the U.S. Navy was extremely anxious to prove to the British that American intelligence departments were producing valuable intelligence on the Soviet Union. The ONI was especially proud of a recent monograph it had produced on the "Soviet Intelligence Services," and one copy (number 9) was alloted to British MI 6. In order to produce the maximum effect, that copy was sent to Cdr. Peter Belin in the offices of the Commander, U.S. Naval Forces Europe, London, so he could deliver it by hand to the appropriate office in Broadway. But in a casual conversation with an MI 6 acquaintance, Belin discovered to his horror that even before he delivered the document the MI 6 man already knew about the monograph. An exchange of worried messages passed back and forth between Belin and the security officers in the chief of Naval Operations headquarters in Washington trying to account for this strange occurrence, and checking whether there had been a serious breach of security. No one could account for the incident unless, as a security officer in Washington blithely noted, the report had reached the British prematurely through "some special method" of transmittal "not currently in use by ONI."

The inquiries stopped there, and the matter was forgotten. But the report had indeed been distributed by a "special method not currently in use by ONI." The MI 6 officer in question was none other than Kim Philby, practicing his regular trade of redistributing highly secret western intelligence documents, and ultimately sending them on to Moscow. Philby obviously had gotten in on the ground floor of the new intelligence-exchange system being arranged between London and Washington, and he therefore was able to pass on detailed accounts of that system to Soviet authorities.[16]

Through Philby, and perhaps other moles in the western intelligence services, Moscow knew from the very beginning what the Germans and Japanese had failed to discover during four years of war: Washington and London had linked arms to carry through a massive attack on their opponent's communications and informational systems in order to make intelligence serve them better than it did their totalitarian foe. Learning that a modified version of the Ultra-Magic partnership was back in business and aimed at them would certainly have made the Soviets double their guard, and may well have nullified some of the positive effects that London and Washington had hoped to net from their partnership.

Philby's actions in this incident, and presumably in others, epitomize the popular book-jacket fact that secret agents can make a difference, and it is appropriate that the best-known spy of the cold war era should make an appearance in this study of the most secret special relationship. But as Marx was fond of noting, ephemera does not cause truly significant change, and this judgment is as appropriate to the history of modern intelligence partnerships as it is to many other phenomena. The vital changes in the history of intelligence that have occurred in this century involved technological advances, improvements in organization, and innovations in cooperation between the intelligence systems of differing countries.

The most secret special relationship caused some of these important developments and was itself the product of powerful political, economic, and strategic forces that linked the United States and Great Britain between 1941 and 1945, and then reunited them in the postwar period. As such, it, rather than the likes of Kim Philby, should have the greatest claim on our interest and attention, because to adapt Marx to a post-Marxist world, the most secret special relationship, far more than Kim Philby, made fundamentally important contributions to the history of our times.

ARCHIVE KEY TO NOTES

Great Britain, Public Record Office, Kew Surrey (PRO)

ADM 1	Admiralty and Secretariat Papers
ADM 53	Ships' Logs
ADM 116	Admiralty and Secretariat Cases
ADM 204	Admiralty Research and Laboratory Reports
ADM 205	First Sea Lord
ADM 223	Naval Intelligence
CAB 21	Cabinet Offices, Registered Files
CAB 69	War Cabinet Defence Committee, Operations
CAB 79	War Cabinet Chiefs of Staff
CAB 103	Historical Section, Registered Files
CAB 105	War Cabinet Telegrams
CAB 118	Various Ministries
CAB 120	Minister of Defence Secretariat
CAB 122	Joint Staff Mission
CAB 138	BSC, Minutes and Memoranda
DEFE 1	Postal and Telegraph Censorship
FO 371	Foreign Office General Correspondence
FO 850	General Correspondence, Communications
FO 954	Eden Papers
PREM 3	Prime Minister, Operations
WO 106	Directorate of Military Operations and Intelligence
WO 165	World War II, War Diaries
WO 193	Directorate of Military Operations, Collation Files
WO 208	Directorate of Military Intelligence

United States, National Archives and Records Service

NA National Archives, Washington
MR Military Reference Branch, Washington
Diplomatic Diplomatic Branch, Washington
Suitland Federal Record Center, Suitland, Maryland

Eisenhower Library   Dwight D. Eisenhower Presidential Library, Abilene, Kansas

Roosevelt Library   Franklin D. Roosevelt Presidential Library, Hyde Park, New York

Truman Library   Harry S. Truman Presidential Library, Independence, Missouri

NOTES

Chapter 1: The Anglo-American Setting

1. Donald C. Watt, *Succeeding John Bull: America in Britain's Place* (Cambridge: Cambridge University Press, 1984), IX. Durand to Grey, 9 July 1906, FO 371/158/23258, PRO.
2. Durand to Grey, 25 January 1906, Attaché memo; 17 August 1906, FO 371/158/4297 and FO 371/160/30712, PRO; Donald C. Watt, *Succeeding John Bull*, 24–29.
3. John Ferris, "The British Army and Signals Intelligence in the Field during the First World War," *Intelligence and National Security*, III, no. 4 (Oct. 1988), 42.
4. Robert M. Hathaway, *Ambiguous Partnership: Britain and America, 1944–47* (New York, New York: Columbia University Press, 1981), 9; Robin Edmonds, *Setting the Mold: The United States and Britain, 1945–50* (Oxford: Oxford University Press, 1986), 12; Christopher Thorne, *Allies of a Kind* (London: Hamilton, 1978), 20f.
5. F. H. Hinsley, E. E. Thomas, et al., *History of British Intelligence in the Second World War* (London: HMSO, 1979ff.), Vol. I, 311; Malcom Murfett, *Foolproof Relations* (Singapore: Singapore University Press, 1984), passim.
6. Bradley F. Smith, *The Shadow Warriors* (New York: Basic Books, 1983), 24.
7. *Ibid.*, 21. Foreign Office note, 11 August 1940, FO 371324256/A3692, PRO. Throughout the war British authorities were deeply concerned about U.S. public and press opinion. See Terry H. Anderson, *The United States, Great Britain and the Coldwar* (Columbia, Missouri: University of Missouri Press, 1981), 3–5; Henry Butterfield Ryan, *Visions of Anglo-America* (Cambridge: Cambridge University Press, 1987), 21–39.
8. Bradley F. Smith, *The Shadow Warriors*, 24.
9. *Ibid.*, 11–12.
10. *Ibid.*, 21.
11. *Ibid.*
12. *Ibid.*, 25.
13. Diary of Henry L. Stimson, 18 December 1940, Yale University.

14. Papers of Harold Smith, 11 April 1940, Franklin D. Roosevelt Library.
15. Admiral Godfrey memoir, MLBE, 1/6 and 1/7, Churchill College, Cambridge. A recent book by authors not enamored with Churchill is James Rusbridger and Eric Nave, *Betrayal at Pearl Harbor: How Churchill Lured Roosevelt into War* (London: Michael O'Mara, 1991).

Chapter 2: The Intelligence Setting

1. FO 371/247241/F3406, PRO.
2. FO 371/20649/A5649 and FO 371/21023/F9947, PRO. See also ADM 116/4302, PRO.
3. Eden to Alexander, 22 November 1944, ADM 1/15687, PRO.
4. F. H. Hinsley, E. E. Thomas, et al., *History of British Intelligence in the Second World War* (London: HMSO, 1979ff.), Vol. I, 36. But matters were far from perfect. In 1935 "Y" intercept material was not teleprinted to GC & CS, but sent by registered mail. ADM 116/4088, PRO.
5. Bradley F. Smith, *Shadow Warriors* (New York, New York: Basic Books, 1983), 369.
6. Robert Cecil, " 'C' 's War," *Intelligence and National Security*, I, no. 2 (1986), 170–83. The various PREM series in the PRO, especially PREM 7, have a healthy sprinkling of papers on Morton's activities.
7. On Menzies, Robert Cecil, " 'C' 's War," *Intelligence and National Security*, I, no. 2 (May 1986); interview with R. Cecil, December 1990; diary of F. H. N. Davidson, "O" series, 18 December 1940, and 13 and 18 March 1941, Liddell Hart Centre, King's College, London.
8. Denniston papers, 1/4, Churchill College, Cambridge.
9. Hinsley, et al., *British Intelligence*, Vol. I, 312–13; Gordon Welchman, "From Polish Bomba to British Bombe: The Birth of Ultra," *Intelligence and National Security*, I, no. 1 (January 1986), 71–110; Ralph Erskine, "Naval Enigma: The Breaking of Heimisch and Triton," *Intelligence and National Security*, III, no. 1 (January 1988), 162-83; David Kahn, *Seizing the Enigma* (Boston: Houghton Mifflin, 1991), 48-126. For general material on Enigma and Bletchley there are two journals—*Cryptologia* in the United States and *The Enigma Bulletin*, Cracow, Poland—devoted to the subject.

10. Hinsley, et al., *British Intelligence*, Vol. I, 109, 137, 213.
11. *Ibid.*, 117; Gordon Welchman, *The Hut Six Story* (New York, New York: McGraw Hill, 1982), 119; Gordon Welchman, "From Polish Bomba to British Bombe," *Intelligence and National Security*, I, no. 1 (January 1986), 98–99; interviews with Sir Herbert Marchant, 9390/3/3, Roll I, Imperial War Museum.
12. Robert Cecil, " 'C' 's War," *Intelligence and National Security*, I, no. 2 (May 1986), 170–83.
13. Hinsley, et al., *British Intelligence*, Vol. I, 53; 6 December 1940, London Messages, September 1938–December 1940 file, Box 1, Entry NAC-76, COMNAV Europe, RG 38, MR, NA.
14. Godfrey report, CAB 122/1021; Bradley F. Smith, "Admiral Godfrey's Mission to America," *Intelligence and National Security*, I, no. 3 (September 1986), 440–50.
15. 5 August 1940 memo, (20) Communications Intelligence (AHM) file, Box 1, ONI, RG 38, MR, NA.
16. Where Op-20-G stood on the Japanese navy's JN 25 system is still a mystery; see James Rusbridger and Eric Nave, *Betrayal at Pearl Harbor* (London: Michael O'Mara, 1991), passim; SRH 152, RG 457, MR, NA; 4 October 1940 Safford memo for Op-20-A, Box 225, Entry Sec. Nav/CNO TS, RG 80, MR, NA.
17. *Ibid.*
18. Bidwell-Friedman exchanges, 1954, CMH Background papers, Box 52B, RG 319, MR, NA.
19. Sinkov interview, Carlisle Barracks; Sinkov interview, 19–20 October 1990 by B. F. Smith; SRH 001, Vol. III, RG 457, MR, NA; 5 August 1940 (20) memo, Communications Intelligence (A-H-M) file, Box 1, RG 38, MR, NA.
20. James Bamford, *Puzzle Palace* (Boston, Massachusetts: Houghton Mifflin, 1982), 35; Preliminary Historical Report, SRH-159, RG 457, MR, NA: Declassified NSA Cryptologic History in the papers of the author, deposited in the Hoover Institution, Stanford.
21. Marshall to Bryden, 25 October 1940, Folder 47, Box 63, Selected Marshall Papers, Marshall Library, Lexington, Virginia.
22. Memo, 5 March 1942, FW 841.20211/36, Diplomatic Branch, NA; 820.00 Series records, confidential, Foreign Service Posts, London, RG 84, Suitland/NA; Hinsley, et al., *British Intelligence*, Vol. II, 55; Bradley F. Smith, *Shadow Warriors*, 21ff.
23. Godfrey report, ADM 223/84, PRO.

24. B.C. (J) 6th Mtg., 23 September 1940, CAB 122/159, PRO. Stark to Knox, 4 November 1940, PSF, Roosevelt Library.
25. Kirk to G-2, 10 July 1941, Corr. A83-EE13, July–Sept 1941 file, Sec. Nav/CNO, RG 80, MR, NA; October 1940 conference, CAB 122/159, PRO.
26. London Messages, 6 December 1940, September 1938–December 1940 file, Box 1, Entry NHC-76, COMNAV Europe, RG 38, MR, NA.
27. Admiral Pott message, 14 January 1941, ADM 223/84, PRO; Eden comment, 15 January 1941, FO 371/26516/C345, PRO.

Chapter 3: Broken Deal, 1940–41

1. COS (40) 289, Mtg. 31, CAB 79/6, PRO. Interestingly, another copy of this COS minute is in a U.S. Navy file, Subject File A, Anglo-American Standardization, 1940, Vol. I, Entry NHC-76, RG 38, MR, NA.
2. F. H. Hinsley, E. E. Thomas, et al., *History of British Intelligence in the Second World War* (London: HMSO), Vol. I, 312–13.
3. SRH 149, RG 457, MR, NA. Published in Dandus P. Tucker, "Rhapsody in Purple," *Cryptologia*, VI, no. 3 (July 1982), 193–228.
4. NSA Cryptologic History, 114. (A "sanitized" copy of this volume is in the author's papers, deposited in the Hoover Institution, Stanford, California.)
5. Henry Stimson diary, 16 July 1940, Yale University; PM Minute, 20 May 1940, FO 371/24255/A2961, PRO.
6. Tizard Mission file, A-8-3/EF-13 to A-8/QQ, Sec. Nav/CNO Sec. sec. corr. RG 80, MR, NA.
7. *Ibid.* Henry Stimson diary, 7 September 1940, Yale.
8. Martin Gilbert, *Winston Churchill: Finest Hour*, Vol. 6 (Boston, Massachusetts: Houghton Mifflin, 1983), 682; 13 December 1940 draft summary of instructions for private secretary, CAB 21/2739, PRO.
9. Ronald Clark, *The Man Who Broke Purple* (Boston, Massachusetts: Little Brown, 1977), 154; NSA Cryptologic History, 114; 9 September 1940, Miles to COS, WPD, 4340-1, Box 213, MR, NA [this document source comes from David Kahn, *Seizing the Enigma* (Boston, Massachusetts: Houghton Mifflin, 1991)].
10. Ghormley report, 22 October 1940, Ghormley correspondence file, Box 20, Entry NH-C-76, RG 38, MR, NA.

11. Safford memo, SRH 149, RG 457, MR, NA.
12. Henry Stimson diary, 23–24 October 1940, Yale.
13. Henry Stimson diary, 12 December 1940, Yale; SRH 149, RG 457, MR, NA; Ralph Erskine, "Naval Enigma: the Breaking of Heimisch and Triton," *Intelligence and National Security*, III, no. 1 (January 1988), 163; Friedman to Bidwell, 8 November 1954, CMH Background papers, Box 53B, RG 319, MR, NA. It should be noted that General Mauborgne remembered the story differently and stated that the army mission had been sent "since we feared the navy was about to send over one of these machines and steal our thunder." But Mauborgne granted that "Mr. Friedman can give the entire story," and Friedman's version has been followed in the text. Bidwell to Friedman, 2 November 1954, CMH Background papers, Box 53B, RG 319, MR, NA.
14. 15 November 1940 memo, A-6-2/CA 44-A6-2QS, Box 224, Entry Sec. Nav/CNO, Box 224, RG 80, MR, NA.
15. NSA Cryptologic History, 115.
16. SRH 149, RG 457, MR, NA: Ralph Erskine, "Naval Enigma," 163–83.
17. Henry Stimson diary, 16 May 1941, Yale.
18. SRH 145, RG 457, MR, NA.
19. Hinsley, et al., *British Intelligence*, Vol. I, 313.
20. ADM 53/1145001, PRO; David Kahn, *Seizing the Enigma*; SRH 149, RG 457, MR, NA; Sinkov interview, Carlisle Barracks, and 29 October 1990 interview by author.
21. Sinkov interviews and author's correspondence with Sinkov (in Hoover Library); Hinsley, et al., *British Intelligence*, Vol. I, 413–14, 454.
22. Mitchell to Stewart, MLBE 2/13, Churchill College; Sir Herbert Marchant, 9390/3/3, Reel 2, Imperial War Museum. For a later period, William P. Bundy, "Some of My Wartime Experiences," *Cryptologia*, XI, no. 1 (April 1988), 73. For the navy parallel system, see David Kahn, *Seizing the Enigma*, 233–34.
23. Sinkov interview, 29 October 1990.
24. Diary of Gen. F. H. N. Davidson, "O" Series, 28 January 1941, Liddell Hart Centre, King's College, London.
25. Ralph Erskine, "Naval Enigma," *Intelligence and National Security*, III, no. 1 (1988), 163; Sinkov, 11 April 1941 Report, SRH 145, RG 457, MR, NA.

26. Sinkov interviews and letters, 1990–91; Mitchell to Stewart, MLBE, 2/3, Churchill College; SRH 145, RG 457, MR, NA. Much controversy has surrounded the issue of what the British provided: see Louis Kruh, "Why was Safford pessimistic about breaking the German Enigma cipher machine in 1942?" *Cryptologia*, XIV, no. 3/4 (July 1990), and Burke and Erskine replies, *Cryptologia*, XV, no. 2 (1991). David Kahn in *Seizing the Enigma* (Boston, Massachusetts: Houghton Mifflin, 1991), using some but not all the material cited in this note, inclines more toward British openhandedness, but Sinkov's statement that the mission neither saw nor was told about a bombe tips the evidence strongly in the other direction.

27. Ismay to the prime minister, 12 December 1940, CAB 120/744, PRO; Hinsley, et al., *British Intelligence*, Vol. I, 264.

28. General Hollis report, 8 December 1940, CAB 120/744, PRO; H. Johnson to Foreign Office, December 1940, FO 371/242631/A5017, PRO.

29. SRH 145, RG 457, MR, NA.

30. SRH 149, RG 457, MR, NA. The same idea was later present in American SIS, interview with retired WO Joseph Richard, 19 October 1990.

31. Robert Cecil, " 'C' 's War," *Intelligence and National Security*, I, no. 2, (May 1986), 170–83; interview with Robert Cecil, 7 December 1990; letter from P. Reilly, 17 December 1990, diary of F. H. N. Davidson, "O" Series, 18 December 1940, 13 and 18 March 1941, Liddell Hart Centre, King's College, London; COS 440th, 30 December 1941, WO 193/306, PRO; interview with Robin Denniston, October 1990; John Ferris, "From Broadway House to Bletchley Park: The Diary of Captain Malcolm D. Kennedy, 1934–1946," *Intelligence and National Security*, IV, no. 3 (July 1989), 440.

32. Citations in the previous note and Robin Denniston, "A. G. Denniston, The Government Code and Cipher School Between the Wars," *Intelligence and National Security*, I, no. 1 (January 1986), 48–70.

Chapter 4: Edging Closer in 1941

1. 7 July 1941 report, CAB 122/1021, PRO.

2. J. E. Hoover memo, 21 June 1941, Box 225, Entry Sec. Nav/CNO,

RG 80, MR, NA; Lee to Hoover, 19 January 1942, file l-13-42 to 2-6-42, Box 456, 311.5, Entry 47, Suitland, NA.

3. George A. Brownell, *The Origin and Development of the National Security Agency*, (Laguna Park, California: Aegean Press, 1981), 11.

4. 27 June 1941 War Department Orders for General Lee, WO 193/305, PRO; 25 April 1941, Halifax to FO, FO 371/26253/A3031, PRO.

5. 17 May 1941 memo, 119/1299 Diplomatic Branch, NA.

6. 13 June 1941 memo, Communications Procedures file, Box 25, Entry NHC-76, RG 38, MR, NA.

7. 10 May 1941 report, Great Britain, Box 563, 311.5, Entry 47, RG 319, Suitland, NA.

8. *Ibid.*

9. Air attaché report, 19 August 1941, file 9540, Box 1455, Entry 77, RG 165, Suitland, NA.

10. 27 March 1941, B.U.S. (J) (41) 3, CAB 122/15, PRO; Folder H, F. H. N. Davidson papers, Liddell Hart Centre, King's College, London.

11. 6 May and 9 May 1941 reports, CAB 105/36 and CAB 105/37, PRO; 7 May 1941 memo, CAB 122/78, and CAB 122/1021, PRO. Godfrey was very doubtful about intelligence exchanges with the United States even before his visit: See ADM 116/4302 for his views in May 1940.

12. F. H. Hinsley, et al., *History of British Intelligence in the Second World War* (London: HMSO, 1979), Vol. I, 413–14, 454, 468, 472, 478; Martin Gilbert, *Winston S. Churchill: Finest Hour*, (Boston, Massachusetts: Houghton Mifflin, 1983), 1117 and 1260.

13. Memos, 16th numerical decimal file, 1941, Box 6, Entry ONI, RG 38, MR, NA; 14 May 1946 memo, file A 8-2EF 37, Box 42, Entry CNO/TS, RG 80, MR, NA.

14. Eden to Halifax, 13 June 1941, CAB 122/1030, PRO; Edwin Layton, *And I Was There* (New York, New York: Morrow, 1987), 207. Ambassador Halifax appears to have overstated the degree of cooperation agreed in his discussion with Sumner Welles on 16 June. 800.20200/2 PS/BUH, DB, NA. (My thanks to Professor James Burrows, University of Toronto, for this reference.)

15. Halifax to FO, 23 April 1941, FO 371/26220, and 25 April 1941, FO 371/26253/A3031, PRO.

16. Hinsley, et al., *British Intelligence*, Vol. I, 271; Naval Signals Reorganization, May 1941, ADM 1/17745, PRO.
17. Hinsley, et al., *British Intelligence*, Vol. I, 339.
18. *Ibid.*, 336–39; Ralph Erskine, "Naval Enigma: The Breaking of Heimisch and Triton," *Intelligence and National Security*, III, no. 1 (January 1988), 162–83.
19. Winn was appointed 2 January 1941, "British Intelligence System" memo, Box 80, Donovan papers, Carlisle Barracks; comments in MLBE 1/1, and Godfrey to Beesly, MLBE, 2/41, Churchill College, Cambridge; author's talks with Beesly, 1984–85.
20. Pott to Kirk, 30 April 1941, A8-3/EF-13 to A8-5QQ, Box 230, Sec. Nav/CNO Secret Correspondence, RG 80, MR, NA.
21. 17 June 1941, Admiralty to Safford, A6-3/EF28-A6-6, Box 225, Sec. Nav/CNO Secret Correspondence, RG 80, MR, NA.
22. John Winton, *Victory at Sea* (London: Leo Cooper, 1988), 94–95.
23. Hinsley, et al., *British Intelligence*, Vol. I, 346.
24. Memo, 9 December 1941, file 10/19/41 to 11/30/41 350.5 (10/18/41)-350.05 (1/31/42), Entry 47, RG 319, Suitland, NA; JPS Staff Conclusion, 23 June 1941, CAB.122/100, PRO; Knox to Alexander, 16 October 1941, ADM 1/14994, PRO.
25. 17 October 1941 memo, Box 718, Entry 47, RG 319, Suitland, NA.
26. 15 December 1941–1 February 1942 exchanges, 311.5 (12/13/41), Box 183, Entry 360, RG 407, MR, NA.
27. Memo, 17 October 1941, Box 718, Entry 47, RG 319, Suitland, NA. Hinsley, et al., *British Intelligence*, Vol. II, 635–66; D. M. Horner, *Australia and Allied Intelligence in the Pacific in the Second World War* (Canberra: Australian National University, 1980), 4; Naval Cryptologic Veterans Association, *Intercept Station C* (Denver, Colorado: no publisher listed; n/d), 66.
28. Memo, 22 November 1941, 10/17/41 to 12/14/41 file, Box 456, Entry 47, RG 319, Suitland, NA.
29. Three Secretaries meeting, 29 December 1942, Book 7, Box 42, Entry 422, RG 165, MR, NA; Pearl Harbor Investigation Files, FO 115 4294, PRO.
30. POW reports, WO 208/4201, PRO; Admiralty Organization, Subject file "A," Box 17, CINCUS NAVE, Entry NHC-76, RG 38, NA; Hinsley, et al., *British Intelligence*, Vol. I, 47.
31. U.S. Navy Daily Situation Maps, July–August 1941, Operational Archives, U.S. Naval Historical Center, Washington; Hinsley, et al., *British Intelligence*, Vol. II, 55.

32. *Ibid.*
33. COMINCH File of Messages on U-boats, October 1941–September 1942, SRMN-033, RG 457, MR, NA.
34. Coded dispatch traffic, British–U.S. Navy, November–December 1941, Pearl Harbor Liaison Office, Box 55, RG 80. See also NAC CINCUS CON NAVEU, Subject file A, Adm. Conferences, Box 17, Entry 76, RG 38, MR, NA.
35. Hinsley, et al., *British Intelligence*, Vol. II, 174.
36. OIC Summary, 20 December 1941, ADM 223/15, PRO.
37. "ESF War Diary," July 1942, Part 1, Section 5, 27, Operational Archives, Naval Historical Center, Washington. Michael Gannon, *Operation Drumbeat* (New York, New York: Harpers, 1990), quotes this line omitting the lead-in phrase, "the British had developed the use of RDF to such an extent . . ." Obviously "RDF" was used here in large part as a cover to disguise Ultra and other secret sources, but the omission is misleading.
38. U.S. Navy Daily Situation Map, 18 September 1941, Operational Archives, Naval Historical Center, Washington. Kahn's account of Bletchley Park's work in this period is especially useful: David Kahn, *Seizing the Enigma* (Boston, Massachusetts: Houghton Mifflin, 1991) 90–194.
39. 19 October 1941, Lee to Washington, file 10/16/41, Box 247, Entry 59, RG 319, Suitland, NA; SRH 117, RG 457, MR, NA.
40. Jeffrey T. Richardson and Desmond Ball, *The Ties that Bind* (Boston, Massachusetts: Houghton Mifflin, 1985), 3.
41. Commander Denniston's diary, kindly loaned by Robin Denniston.
42. Denniston to Friedman, 19 June 1945, and Friedman to Denniston, 12 April 1945, Denn 6/6, Churchill College, Cambridge.
43. Hinsley, et al., *British Intelligence*, Vol. II, 55; 17 October 1943 report no. 9540, Box 1455, Entry 77, RG 165, Suitland, NA.
44. State Department memo, 7 July 1941, 110.72/98, Diplomatic Branch, NA; British worries about American security were long-lasting; see William P. Bundy, "Some of My Wartime Experiences," *Cryptologia*, XI, no. 1, (April 1988), 69.
45. F. W. Winterbotham, *The Ultra Secret* (London: Weidenfeld & Nicholson, 1974), 129; Churchill to Roosevelt, 23 February 1942, Warren F. Kimball (ed.), *Churchill and Roosevelt*, Vol.1 (Princeton: Princeton University Press, 1984), 371. Note than even Martin Gilbert could find no documentation in Churchill's papers for the claim that the prime minister sent the president Ultra-Enigma messages,

even on the Far East, in 1941, and could refer only to a "private communication" as the source of the possibility, or probability, that this had happened. Martin Gilbert, *Winston Churchill: Finest Hour* (Boston, Massachusetts: Houghton Mifflin, 1983), 1260.

46. Ronald Spector (ed.), *Listening to the Enemy* (Wilmington, Delaware: Scholarly Resources Press, 1988), 172 (SRH 035, RG 457, MR, NA).

47. NSA, U.S. Cryptologic History, 6, 10. SRH 141, RG 457, MR, NA.

48. Ronald Lewin, *Ultra Goes to War* (New York, New York: Farrar Straus, 1978), 245–46; Lee to Hoover, 19 January 1942, file 1/13/42, 311.5, Entry 47, RG 319, Suitland, NA.

49. Army codes and ciphers, 23 December 1941, file 12/15/41 to 1/12/42, Entry 47, RG 319, Suitland, NA.

50. FDR to Donovan, Welles, et cetera, 12/30/1941, OF 4485, OSS files, Roosevelt Library.

51. Hinsley, et al., *British Intelligence*, Vol. II, 748; Andrew Hodges, *The Turing Enigma* (London: Unwin, 1985), 219–22.

52. David Kahn, *Seizing the Enigma* (Boston, Massachusetts: Houghton Mifflin, 1991), 186–89; P. S. Milner Barry, "Action This Day," *Intelligence and National Security*, I, no. 2 (May, 1986), 272–76. Patrick Beesly, *Very Special Intelligence* (London: Hamilton, 1985), 10; Filby to Lewin, 11 April 1979, DENN 2/3, Churchill College; Brigadier Tiltman to Robin Denniston, 4 March 1942 (kindly loaned to the author by Robin Denniston); interviews, September–December 1990 with Sir Harry Hinsley, Peter Calvocoressi, Robin Denniston, Robert Cecil; letter from Telford Taylor, 3 May 1990; Hinsley, et al., *British Intelligence*, Vol. II, 657.

53. On Travis, interviews cited in immediately preceding note, plus Taylor letter of May 1990. Patrick Beesly, *Very Special Intelligence*, 11; James Bamford, *The Puzzle Palace* (Boston, Massachusetts: Houghton Mifflin, 1982), 313.

54. Gordon Welchman, *The Hut Six Story* (New York: McGraw Hill, 1982), 121, 204, 220–21, 365. Robert Cecil interview; F. H. N. Davidson diary, 28 January 1941, Liddell Hart Center, King's College, London; John Ferris, "From Broadway House to Bletchley Park," *Intelligence and National Security*, IV, no. 3 (July 1989), 442.

55. On Tiltman: interviews and Taylor letter cited in note 52, plus Alan Stripp, *Codebreaker in the Far East* (London: Frank Cass, 1989), 14–16; Welchman, *The Hut Six Story*, 204; interviews with Mrs. M. Blythe and Lady Marchant, 11 January 1991. The confiden-

tial navy list carries only Hastings, not Denniston or Travis. On de Grey, William P. Filby, "Bletchley Park and Berkeley Street," *Intelligence and National Security*, III, no. 2 (April 1988), 271–84; NID List, October 1941, ADM 223/257, PRO.

56. Admiral Little to First Sea Lord, 2 December 1941, ADM 205/9, PRO; interview with Sir Harry Hinsley, 6 August 1990.

57. DNI to vice chief of naval staff, 19 December 1941, ADM 205/9, PRO.

58. Hinsley, et al., *British Intelligence*, Vol. II, 5; COS 440th, 30 December 1941, WO 193/306, PRO.

Chapter 5: Toward the Navy Cryptanalytic Agreement

1. Britain lost Y stations in Hong Kong, Penang, Kuching, Singapore (2), ADM 1/21145, PRO; John B. Lundstrom, *The First South Pacific Campaign* (Annapolis, Maryland: Naval Institute Press, 1975), 76.

2. *Ibid.*, 76–77; Richard B. Frank, *Guadalcanal* (New York, New York: Random House, 1990), 38ff.

3. 20 February and 3 April 1942, Japanese Intelligence, no. 63, Map Room, Roosevelt Library; Lundstrom, *The First South Pacific Campaign*, 77; See also, Edward J. Drea, *MacArthur's Ultra: Codebreaking and the War Against Japan* (Lawrence, Kansas: University of Kansas, 1992).

4. Ted Wildman, *The Expendables* (Clearwater, Florida: self published, 1983), 128–29; regarding Enigma machines, see A8-3EF, Box 22, CNO/TS RG 80, MR, NA, and a statement to the author by Professor John Chapman, July 1991.

5. 22 May 1942, BAD to First Sea Lord, CAB 105/29, PRO.

6. Commander U.S. Naval Forces Europe Messages, June–October 1942, Series 1, Box 11, NHC 76, RG 38, MR, NA.

7. Ronald Lewin, "A Signal Intelligence War," *Journal of Contemporary History*, XVI, no. 3 (July, 1981), 506; 1942 materials, file A6-2A8, Box 287, Sec. Nav/CNO, RG 80, MR, NA.

8. 15–17 August 1942 materials, Series I, Box 2, King papers, Operational Records, Naval Historical Center, Washington. Robert McCormack file, Box 13, King Papers, Library of Congress; 26 July 1942, Strong to OWI, File 7/21/42 to 8/15/42, Box 455, 311.5, Entry 47, RG 319, Suitland, NA; 8 June 1942 Report, CAB 122/242, PRO.

9. Desmond Ball, *A Suitable Piece of Real Estate: American Installations in Australia* (Sydney: Hale and Iremonyer, 1980), 27–31; D. M. Horner, *Australia and Allied Intelligence in the Pacific in the Second World War* (Canberra: Australian National University, 1980), 8–11.

10. *Ibid.* Sinkov interview, Carlisle Barracks; Herbert C. Merrilat, "The Ultra Began at Guadalcanal," *Marine Corps Gazette*, LXVI, no. 9 (September 1982), 44–49; Richard B. Frank, *Guadalcanal* (New York, New York: Random House, 1990), 38ff.

11. Alan Stripp, *Codebreaker in the Far East* (London: Frank Cass, 1989), 72; Edward J. Drea, *MacArthur's Ultra: Codebreaking and the War Against Japan, 1942–45* (Lawrence, Kansas: University of Kansas, 1992), p. 76.

12. SRH-116, RG 457, MR, NA; letter from Telford Taylor, 3 May 1990; Report, 22 April 1942, 1–30 April 1942 file, 311.5, Entry 47, RG 319, Suitland, NA; Kroner to 3rd Army, 30 March 1942, Box 176, 311.23, RG 407, MR, NA.

13. SRH 141, SRH 117, RG 457, MR, NA.

14. 26 May 1942, 1 May–10 June, file, Box 456, Entry 47, RG 319, Suitland, NA; SRH 116, RG 457, MR, NA; Jeffrey Dorwart, *Conflict of Duty* (Annapolis, Maryland: Naval Institute Press, 1983), 160–61.

15. J. E. Hoover Report, 24 November 1942, File 11/18/42 to 12/15/42, Box 455, 311.5, Entry 47, RG 319, Suitland, NA; SRH-364, RG 457, MR, NA; 8 April 1942, Signal Corps memo, File, 1–30 April, 1942, Box 456, 311.5, Entry 47, RG 319, Suitland, NA.

16. 3 April 1942, Strong to Berle, File A6-2/EF—28-21-A6-2VZ, Box 287, Sec. Nav/CNO, RG 80, MR, NA; Marshall to the president, 18 June 1942 (1942–45), RG 218, JCS, MR, NA.

17. 29 November 1942 Report, File A6-3EF 13 (AR 42)-A6-4, Box 289, RG 80, Sec. Nav/CNO, 1942, MR, NA; OSS Memos, Box 4, Goodfellow Papers, Hoover Institution, Stanford.

18. 23 October 1942, CCS 334 (5/4/42) JIC, Main Decimal, RG 218, MR, NA: 13 January 1943, Donovan to Strong, Folder 80, Box 120, Donovan Papers, Carlisle Barracks.

19. Memo, 1/6/43—1.26.43, Box 455, RG 311.5, Entry 47, RG 319, Suitland, NA; FDR order, etc., 8 and 25 July 1942, 311.5 (6/18/42), Box 87, RG 218, MR, NA; 3 March

20. 27 July 1943, Strong to Dykes, file 7/24/42 to 8/15/42, Box 455,

311.5, Entry 47, RG, 319, Suitland, NA; 20 July 1943, Strong memo, CCS 311.51, JCS 65/1 (7/4/42), Box 87, RG 218, MR, NA; Bern to State, 24 July 1942, 119.25/1398, Diplomatic Branch, NA.

21. 27 July 1942, Bratton to MIS, Box 781, Entry 203, G-2, RG 165, MR, NA; Joseph Eachus letter to author, 27 April 1991. An indication of a U.S. Navy officer at Bletchley Park, apparently in 1944, is in SRH 110, RG 457, 34, MR, NA. NSA, United States Cryptologic History, 11; F. H. Hinsley, E. E. Thomas, et al., *History of British Intelligence in the Second World War* (London: HMSO), Vol. II, 48; F. W. Winterbotham, *The Ultra Secret* (London: Weidenfeld & Nicholson, 1974), 131; interview with Sir Harry Hinsley, 6 August 1990.

22. Alex Danchev, *Establishing the Anglo-American Alliance* (London: Brassey's, 1990), 151–52.

23. J. R. Lovell memo, File G-2 Teletype Net, Box 792, Entry 203 (G-2), RG 165, MR, NA; Hinsley, et al., *British Intelligence*, Vol. II, 49.

24. Hinsley, et al., *British Intelligence*, Vol. II, 47; 15 May 1942 Canadian Report, WO 165/45, PRO; 10 April 1942, Stoner to G-2, 311.5, Entry 47, RG 319, Suitland, NA.

25. 22 July 1942, Report, CAB 122/21, PRO; Hinsley, et al., *British Intelligence*, Vol. II, 56; JSM to COS, 12 October 1942, CAB 105/40, PRO.

26. 17 February 1942 Kirkman memo, WO 193-306, PRO; Diane Putney, *Ultra and the American Air Force in World War II* (Washington: Office of the Air Forces, 1987), 74; Hinsley, et al., *British Intelligence*, Vol. II, 56.

27. Godfrey Minute, November 1941, ADM 1/18895, PRO.

28. Alex Danchev, *Establishing the Anglo-American Alliance*, 10, 214; COS (42) 319 (O) PREM 3/365/1, PRO.

29. JSM Summary, 22 July 1942, CAB 122/21, PRO; Strong to Marshall, 9 July 1942, 311.52, Box 63, Entry 13, RG 165, MR, NA; Marshall to FDR, 11 July 1942, Communications File, Map Room, Box 162, Roosevelt Library (published by Louis Kruh, "British-American Cryptanalytic Cooperation," *Cryptologia*, IV, no. 2 (July 1989), 123–34.

30. President Roosevelt to Admiral King, 7 July 1942, FDR file, Box 14, King Papers, Library of Congress.

31. 3 March 1942ff., Enemy Subm. Sighting, Map Room, Box 40, Roosevelt Library; 2 May 1942, Nazi Subs, no. 27, Map Room,

Box 41, Roosevelt Library; Hinsley, et al., *British Intelligence*, Vol. II, 47. Information from Timothy Mulligan, National Archives.

32. NSA, United States Cryptologic History, 117.
33. February–July 1942 reports, FO 371/30698/A3908, PRO. A 1952 U.S. Navy study casts doubt on the overall significance of the B Dienst break-in, SRH 368, RG 457, MR, NA.
34. The minutes of the meeting are in file A-6-2/A8 (6–17 April 1942), Box 287, Sec. Nav/CNO, RG 80, MR, NA. See also COS to JSM, 30 September 1942, CAB 105/30; SRH 197, RG 457, MR, NA. Captain Sandwith was chief of NID 9, October 1941 NID list, ADM 223, 257, PRO.
35. 6 April 1942, Ghormley to King, King Papers, Box 2, Operational Archives, Naval Historical Center, Washington. (Professor Alan Wilt kindly drew my attention to this item.) Hinsley, et al., *British Intelligence*, Vol. II, 56.
36. On the April/May date for the Winn visit, Welles to King, King papers, Box 3, Series 1, Correspondence, December 1942 file, Operational Archives, Naval Historical Center, Washington; Thomas Parrish, *The Ultra Americans* (New York: Stein and Day, 1985), 156; Winn's commendation, October 1943, ADM 1/14207, PRO. Also, see Ronald Lewin, *Ultra Goes to War* (New York, New York: McGraw Hill, 1978), 243–44, and especially Winn's 3 June 1942 report, ADM 223, 107, PRO.
37. Hinsley, et al., *British Intelligence*, Vol. II, 171; SRMN-031, 035, 036, RG 457, MR, NA.
38. Eastern Sea Frontier War Diary, June–August 1942 file, Box 332, Operational Archives, Naval Historical Center, Washington.
39. SRMN-038, MR, NA; Ralph Erskine, "Naval Enigma: the Breaking of Heimisch and Triton," *Intelligence and National Security*, III, no. 1 (January 1988), 170ff.
40. Hinsley, et al., *British Intelligence*, Vol. II, 638–39. Don Seilor seems to have been the man who designed the adapter: Ralph Anderson, "If I Remember," *Cryptologia*, VI, no. 1 (January 1982), 40–44.
41. Alex Danchev, *Establishing the Anglo-American Alliance* (London: Brassey's, 1990), 138, 222.
42. Note from First Sea Lord, 7 October 1942, ADM 205/21, PRO; Hinsley, et al., *British Intelligence*, Vol. II, 479; 28 September 1942 report, WO 204/4499, PRO. On the Merchant navy, ADM 1/12785,

PRO and ADM to ADM Delegation, Washington, 8 August 1942, ADM 1/11749, PRO.
43. 11 March 1942, Forbes to DNI, ADM 205/23, PRO.
44. Churchill to First Sea Lord, 22 September 1942, ADM 205/14, PRO.
45. Hinsley, et al., *British Intelligence*, Vol. II, 57, 748–49.
46. On Tiltman coming by sea, Index to *General Correspondence of the Foreign Office*, 1942.
47. Interview with Sir Harry Hinsley, 6 August 1990. NSA, United States Cryptologic History, 118.
48. Diary notes of Professor McVittie, courtesy of Robin Denniston.
49. NSA, United States Cryptologic History, 119. Professor Hinsley's estimate that the U.S. Navy planned to have 360 bombes by the end of 1942 seems well wide of the mark: Hinsley, et al., *British Intelligence*, Vol. II, 57.
50. Interview with Sir Harry Hinsley, 6 August 1990. On the timing of Travis' arrival, CAB 105/30 and 54, PRO; on the date of the agreement, NSA, United States Cryptologic History, 119. See also Stone to Op-20, 23 June 1943, SRH 200, Part 2, Section 2, RG 457, MR, NA.
51. Interview with Sir Harry Hinsley, 6 August 1990; SRMN 038, RG 457, MR, NA. Hinsley, et al., *British Intelligence*, Vol. II, 57, Vol. III, 460; Kahn provides a graphic account of the operation of the joint system: David Kahn, *Seizing the Enigma* (Boston, Massachusetts: Houghton Mifflin, 1991), 239–42.
52. 24 November 1942 meeting, Enemy Communications Committee, CCS 334 (9/11/42), RG 218, MR, NA.

Chapter 6: BRUSA

1. F. H. Hinsley, E. E. Thomas, et al., *History of British Intelligence in the Second World War* (London: HMSO, 1979–1988), Vol. II, 478–79; 13 October 1942 report, WO 106/2778, PRO; Richard Frank, *Guadalcanal* (New York: Random House, 1990), 598f.
2. Marshall to the president, 80/34, Correspondence Selected, Marshall papers, Marshall Library, Lexington, Virginia; COMINCH, 8 January 1943, OPD 311.5, C and C (Section IV), classes 132–209, Box 517, Entry 418, RG 165, MR, NA.
3. NSA, United States Cryptologic History, 44.

4. February 1943 rules, CCS 385 (2/4/43), Section 1, RG 218, MR, NA; 24 January 1943, "Magic," CAB 118/90, PRO.
5. 20 February 1943, Marshall to the president (also 5 August 1942 and 8 November 1943), 80/34, Correspondence Selected, Marshall papers, Marshall Library, Lexington, Virginia; COMINCH, 8 January 1943, OPD, 311.5, C and C (Section IV), classes 132–209, Box 517, Entry 418, RG 165, MR, NA.
6. Hinsley, et al., *British Intelligence*, Vol. II, 50.
7. 16 December 1942, mtg., CCS 311 (1/10/42), Section 3, Box 74, RG 218, MR, NA; 21 November 1942, Report, CAB 105/30, PRO; General Reports, 1942–43, WO 165/81, PRO. Material on "Y" and cryptanalytic cooperation with the USSR from a forthcoming volume by the author; see especially 6 July 1941 to 30 Mission, WO 193/ 649; September exchanges in WO 32/15548, War Diaries in WO 178 and ADM 199/1102, PRO.
8. Andrew Hodges, *The Turing Enigma* (London: Unwin, 1985), 242– 55, and notes, 552–53; see also Derek Jacobi's play or script, "Breaking the Code."
9. 15 January 1942, Chief Signals Officer Directive, Correspondence Selected, 65/35, Marshall Papers, Marshall Library, Lexington, Virginia.
10. 2 and 9 December 1942, Marshall-Dill exchanges, CAB 122/14, PRO.
11. King to McNarney, 29 December 1942, Box 82, COS, 350.05, Entry 15, MR, NA; Tiltman memo and Marshall-Dill exchanges plus Hastings' memos, CAB 122/14, PRO.
12. NSA, Cryptologic History, 121; Marshall-Dill exchange, CAB 122/ 14, PRO.
13. NSA, Cryptologic History, 121–22; Dill memo, 7 January 1943, CAB 122/14; Marshall note, on 7 January 1943 document, and Strong to Marshall,1 January 1943, Box 82, 350.05, Entry 15, COS, RG 165, MR, NA.
14. 17 February 1943, Air Ministry to Britman, CAB 105/31; JSM to War Cabinet, 28 April 1943, CAB 105/42; JSM to COS, 20 February 1943, CAB 122/561; 26 March 1943 Bletchley Report, CAB 120/768, PRO.
15. David Kahn, *The Codebreakers* (New York, New York: Macmillan, 1967), 556; Warren F. Kimball (ed.), *Churchill and Roosevelt*, Vol. II (Princeton: Princeton University Press, 1984), 336. John Ferris

kindly provided references to scrambler phone development; see John Ferris, "The British Enigma: British Signals Security and Cipher Machines," *Defence Analysis*, Vol. 3, no. 2 (June 1987). Also on the scrambler phone see CAB 122/554 and 561, PRO.

16. NSA, Cryptologic History, 120; Dill to Marshall, 20 February 1943, Folder 31, Box 64, Marshall Papers, Marshall Library, Lexington, Virginia.

17. NSA, Cryptologic History, 120–21; William Bundy, "Some of My Wartime Experiences," *Cryptologia*, XI, 1 (April 1988), 67–68.

18. NSA, Cryptologic History, 122, 127; Hinsley, et al., *British Intelligence*, Vol. II, 57.

19. NSA Cryptologic History, 123.

20. *Ibid.*; the "Y" station was operating in northern Russia at least as late as 24 November 1943, AIR 20/8059. Both the Germans and the West could break low-level Soviet crypto systems with relative ease, but not the Soviet high-level systems. David Kahn, *The Codebreakers*, 644–65; 13 December 1943, Martel to Slavin, WO 178/27, PRO.

21. NSA, Cryptologic History, 123; Robert Cecil, "The Cambridge Spies," in Christopher Andrew and David Dilles (eds)., *The Missing Dimension* (London: Macmillan, 1984), 186.

22. *Ibid.*

23. *Ibid.*, CCS 334, (9/22/42), RG 218, MR, NA.

24. NSA, Cryptologic History, 121.

25. D. M. Horner, *Australia and Allied Intelligence in the Pacific* (Canberra, Australia: Australian National University, 1980), 14, 15; Wilkinson comments, File 3/2, Wilkinson Papers, Churchill College, Cambridge.

26. W. J. Holmes, *Double Edged Secrets* (Annapolis, Maryland: Naval Institute Press, 1979), 126; Alan Stripp, *Codebreaker in the Far East* (London: Frank Cass, 1989), 70.

27. John Costello, *The Pacific War* (New York, New York: Rawson Wade, 1985), 398; Ronald Lewin, *American Magic* (New York, New York: Farrar Straus, 1982), 196; interview and written statement by Joseph Richard, October 1990.

28. SRH, 141, 219 confirms the Water Transport Code break-in; SRH 035 states that it did not occur until June (both RG 457, MR, NA). Joseph Richard is emphatic about the earlier date (see note 27, immediately above). See also Edward J. Drea, *MacArthur's Ul-*

tra: Codebreaking and the War Against Japan, 1942–45 (Lawrence, Kansas: University of Kansas, 1992), passim.

29. SRH 160, RG 457, MR, NA.
30. 31 March 1943, CNO, CINCUS, Series 1, Box 12, COMNAVEU, RG 38, MR, NA; C. M. Cooke Memo, File January 1943–44, Double Zero, 1941–46, Box 39, Operational Archives, Naval Historical Center, Washington.
31. 11 May 1943, memo, 350.05, Box 82, Entry 13, RG 165, MR, NA.
32. Summary memo, and 31 March 1943 report, Box 782, Entry 203, RG 165, MR, NA.
33. F. H. Hinsley and C. A. Simkins, *British Intelligence*, Vol. IV (London: HMSO 1990), 187; 22 April 1943 (2/8/42) Section 1, Part 5, RG 218, MR, NA. Additional information from Timothy Neftali, Harvard University.
34. 8 April 1943 memo, SRH-145, RG 457, MR, NA.
35. Telford Taylor interview, 17 October 1990.
36. Clarke note, April 1943; records of Civil Service, 1919–43; Friedman papers, Marshall Library, Lexington, Virginia.
37. NSA, Cryptologic History, 125; E. R. Vincent correspondence, B-8/F29, Friedman papers, Marshall Library, Lexington, Virginia.
38. NSA, Cryptologic History, 125.
39. *Ibid.*
40. *Ibid.* 126–27. For the British bombe arrangement at this time see David Kahn, *Seizing the Enigma* (Boston, Massachusetts: Houghton Mifflin, 1991), 231–32.
41. NSA, Cryptologic History, 126.
42. SRH 110, RG 457, MR, NA.
43. Thomas Parrish, *The Ultra Americans* (New York, New York: Stein & Day, 1985), 98–99; SRH 110, RG 457, MR, NA.
44. Diane Putney, *Ultra and the American Air Forces in World War II* (Washington, D.C., Office of the Air Force, 1987), 81.
45. NSA, Cryptologic History, 171ff.; SRH-110, RG 457, MR, NA; Diane Putney, *Ultra and the American Air Forces*, 81ff.
46. Strong to Marshall, 10 June 1943, COS, 350.05, Entry 13, RG 165, MR, NA.
47. 21 May 1943, SRH 110, RG 457, MR, NA.
48. See above, p. 144.
49. Hinsley, et al., *British Intelligence*, Vol. II, 752.
50. McCloy to McNarney, 9 June 1943, and Nelson to G-2, 11 June

1943. Box 346, Entry 175, RG 165, MR, NA; 14 May 1943, Nelson to G-2, Box 22, 350.05, Entry 47, Assistant Secretary of War, RG 165, MR, NA.

51. SRH 035, RG 457, MR, NA.

52. *Ibid.*

53. *Ibid.* McCormack to Corderman, 1 September 1943 (9/1/43 to 10/18/43) file, Box 454, 311.5, Entry 47, RG 319, Suitland, NA.

54. 9 November 1943, Marshall to McNarney, Correspondence Selected, Box 65/41, Marshall papers, Marshall Library, Lexington, Virginia; MID Report, 311.5, Box 426, RG 319, Suitland, NA.

55. NSA, Cryptologic History, 6.

56. *Ibid.* 125ff.

57. SRH 110 and SRH 141 (p. 178), RG 457, MR, NA; William P. Filby, "Bletchley Park and Berkeley Street," *Intelligence and National Security*, III, no. 2 (April 1988), 271–84; John Ferris, "From Broadway House to Bletchley Park," *Intelligence and National Security*, IV, no. 3 (July 1989), 428ff.; January 1944 and January 1945 memos, Boxes 68242-3, Acc. 46A-0445, RG 111, Suitland, NA; general materials in ADM 116/5437, PRO.

58. NSA, Cryptologic History, 128; general materials in Denn 6/6, Churchill College; Sir Herbert Marchant interview, 9390/3/, Reel 3, Imperial War Museum.

59. Alan Stripp, *Codebreaker in the Far East* (London: Frank Cass, 1989), 22; Gordon Welchman, *The Hut Six Story* (New York, New York: McGraw Hill, 1982), 135; Peter Calvocoressi, *Top Secret Ultra* (New York: Pantheon, 1980), 63; Peter Calvocoressi interview, autumn 1990; interview, 11 January 1991, Mrs. Margaret Blythe and Lady Marchant; SRH-110, RG 457, MR, NA.

60. Denniston to Friedman, 4 October 1943, B-3/F-16, Friedman papers, Marshall Library, Lexington, Virginia; William Bundy, "Some of My Wartime Experiences," *Cryptologia*, XI, no. 1 (April 1988), 68ff.; William Bundy letter to author, 18 March 1991.

61. Thomas Parrish, *The Ultra Americans*, 182; interview with Telford Taylor, 17 October 1990.

62. SRH 141, 183ff., and SRH 110, RG 457, MR, NA; NSA, Cryptologic History, 128.

63. Diane Putney, *Ultra and the American Air Forces*, 85.

64. SRH 034, RG 457, MR, NA; NSA, Cryptologic History, 128.

65. Telford Taylor letter, 3 May 1990; SRH 141, 185ff., RG 457, MR, NA.

66. SRH 110, RG 457, MR, NA: Dunn memo, 24 February 1944, 41/ 171, RG 226, MR, NA. (Thanks to Timothy Naftali for this reference.)
67. NSA, Cryptologic History, 125, 127–28; Joseph Eachus letter, 27 April 1991; William Bundy letters, 18 March and 4 May 1991; William P. Bundy, "Some of My Wartime Experiences, *Cryptologia*, XI, no. 1 (April 1988), 68–75.
68. NSA, Cryptologic History, 127–28; Thomas Parrish, *The Ultra Americans*, 116–21.
69. July 1943 materials, CCS (Spain 3/26/43), Section 1, RG 218, MR, NA; SRH 113, RG 457, MR, NA.
70. *Ibid.*
71. *Ibid.*
72. *Ibid.*
73. SRH 200, Part 2, Section 2, 25 May 1943, 172, MR, NA.
74. SRMN 032, RG 457 (30 March 1943), MR, NA.
75. SRH 200, RG 457, MR, NA.
76. (23 June 1943), SRH 200, Part 2, Section 2, RG 457, MR, NA.
77. 12 August 1943 memo, "to Admiral" file, January 1943–September 1944 file, Double Zero, 1941–46, Box 39, Operational Archives, Naval Historical Center, Washington.
78. SRH 141, 283ff., RG 457, MR, NA.
79. *Ibid.*
80. SRH 200, Part 2, Section 2, RG 457, MR, NA.
81. *Ibid.*

Chapter 7: Highways and Byways in SIGINT Cooperation

1. March 1943 Admiralty messages, CAB 122/265, PRO; for the bureaucracy, see CCS 334, CCB (6/25/42)ff., RG 218, MR, NA. Failure by the Italian decryption service may well be a scholarly convention based on minimal research. There are some signs of Italian successes; see, for example, ADM 223/260/286, PRO.
2. 13 May 1943, note of DNI to DSD, ADM 1/13481; Rushbrooke to First Sea Lord, 17 January 1944, ADM 1/16606 (also DEFE 1/ 391), PRO.
3. Gordon Welchman, *The Hut Six Story* (New York, New York:

McGraw Hill, 1982), 173–75; COS (W) 1108, March 1944, CAB 105/58, PRO.

4. Roosevelt Order, 10 May 1944, Case 354, Box 519, Entry 418, RG 165, MR, NA; Hoechst to State Department, 28 July 1945, 119.25/ 7-2845, Diplomatic Branch, NA.

5. Diane Putney, *Ultra and the American Air Forces* (Washington: Office of the Air Force, 1987), 82; Gordon Welchman, *The Hut Six Story*, 173–75. For coding machines in 1943, FO 850/132 and John Ferris, "The British Enigma: British, Signals Security and Cipher Machines, 1906–46," *Defence Analysis*, III, June no. 2 (1987), passim.

6. JSM to War Cabinet, 15 December 1944, CAB 122/561, PRO; Gordon Welchman, *The Hut Six Story*, 176.

7. Churchill to Ismay, 8 August 1943, CAB 21/1479, PRO; Marshall to G-2 and OPD, 1 September 1943, Box 3, 311.55, Entry 15, COS, RG 165, MR, NA.

8. 9 October 1943, Campbell to Cadogan, CAB 122/561, PRO.

9. 2 February 1944, Hoover to President Roosevelt, and related documents, Box: 81, Folder 9, Marshall papers, Marshall Library, Lexington, Virginia.

10. November 1944 incident and the OSA, ADM 1/15666, PRO.

11. Gordon Welchman, *The Hut Six Story*, 179; Welchman to Friedman (no day, but 1944), Friedman Correspondence, B-9/F-4, Marshall Library. On Travis see General Index of Foreign Correspondence, 1944. Routine arrival of two British army captains (Manson and Farmery) at Arlington, 20 June 1944, CAB 122/1347, PRO; Travis to O'Conner, 26 August 1944, 311.00, Box 6, Entry 15, COS, RG 165, MR, NA. Op-20 to Op-16, 29 September 1944, A6-1 (10), Box 1, CNO/TS, RG 80, MR, NA.

12. Gordon Welchman, *The Hut Six Story*, 179; German changes, F. H. Hinsley, E. E. Thomas, et al., *History of British Intelligence in the Second World War*, Vol. III, Part 1 (London: HMSO, 1979-1988) 51–52; Alan Stripp, *Codebreaker in the Far East* (London: Frank Cass, 1989), 26; NSA, United States Cryptographic History, 131.

13. G-2 Study, 12th Army Group, Box 43, Walter B. Smith papers, Eisenhower Library, Abilene, Kansas; Factual intelligence, G-2 and DMI agreement, 5 October 1944, "British Participation" file, Box 782, Entry 203, RG 165, MR, NA.

14. Alan Stripp, *Codebreaker in the Far East*, 119; Hinsley, et al., *British Intelligence*, Vol. III, Part 1, 319, note.
15. Bletchley totals, 15 March 1945, COS (45) 181 (O), CAB 80/92, PRO; U.S. Navy totals, 21 November 1944 memos for MIS and Nelson, Box 6, 311.00, Entry 15, RG 165, COS, MR, NA; Marshall to Dill and McCarthy to G-2, 23 June 1944, Folder 40, Box 64, Marshall Papers, Marshall Library, Lexington, Virginia; see Wilkinson papers, 23 June 1944, for an example of British officials slipping such items to Americans, File 1/3, Churchill College, Cambridge.
16. 25 March 1945 list, Richard Collins papers, SHAEF file, Carlisle Barracks, Pennsylvania; NSA, United States Cryptologic History, 129.
17. Combined Japanese Intelligence file, Box 782-3, Entry 203, RG 165, MR, NA; SRH 035, RG 457, MR, NA; James Bamford, *Puzzle Palace,* 315; Abraham Sinkov letter, 23 March 1991.
18. Alan Stripp, *Codebreaker in the Far East*, 71; COS (O) mtg, 23 September 1944, CAB 122/1020, PRO; JIC item, 28 September 1944, and M. M. (s) (44), 40th mtg., 5 October 1944, CAB 122/1417, PRO; Hinsley, et al., *British Intelligence*, Vol. III, Part 1, 341; 29 May 1944 memo, SRH 200, Part 2, Section 2, RG 457, MR, NA.
19. SRMN-0-39, RG 457, MR, NA; Somerville to King, 8 March 1945, Double Zero files, Operational Archives, Naval Historical Center, Washington; W. J. Holmes, *Double Edged Secrets* (Annapolis, Maryland: Naval Institute Press, 1979), 204; British Participation file, Box 782, Entry 203, RG 165, MR, NA; 28 November 1944, King order, A3-1EN3-10, Box 1, CNO/TS, RG 80, MR, NA; JSM to King, 28 February 1945, Box 28, File A8, Entry 32-J, RG 38, MR, NA; CNO memo, Box 28, Entry J, RG 38, MR, NA.
20. Sinkov interview, Carlisle Barracks, Pennsylvania; Ronald Spector (ed), *Listening to the Enemy* (Wilmington, Delaware: Scholarly Resources, 1988), (SRH 127, RG 457, MR, NA); D. M. Horner, *Australia and Allied Intelligence in the Pacific in the Second World War* (Canberra, Australia: Australian National University, 1980), 38–41; Ronald Lewin, *Ultra Goes to War* (New York, New York: McGraw Hill, 1978), 245–47; Ronald Lewin, *American Magic* (New York, New York: Farrar Straus, 1982), 148–52; SRH 197, RG 457, MR, NA; June–August 1944 exchange, A6-2/A8, Box 1, CNO/TS, RG 80, MR, NA; transcript, Jewett-Sinkov telephone conversation,

2 December 1944, Conversations file, Box 68245, Entry 46A-0445, RG 111, Suitland, NA.

21. Sommerville to Cunningham, 21 June 1944, Rushbrooke to Cunningham, 14 July 1944, ADM 205/42, PRO; USAAC proposal, 6 June 1944, Box 9, 350.05, COS, Entry 15, RD 165, MR, NA.

22. King to CO Pacific Fleet, 23 December 1944, Hq. COMINCH Top Secret Correspondence, 1945, A6 file, Box 27, Records of the CNO, RG 38, MR, NA. (Thanks to Timothy Nenninger for this reference.)

23. Brown Books, 30 December 1943, 110.72/94, Diplomatic Branch, NA; British items to President Roosevelt, Naval Aides Intelligence files, Map Room, Box 163, Roosevelt Library; Reforms, 12 February 1944, Box 81, folder 9; McCarthy to Leahy, 14 February 1944, Box 74, folder 8; Marshall papers, Marshall Library, Lexington, Virginia.

24. History of Special Branch, SRH 117, RD 457, MR, NA.

25. Ronald Lewin, *Ultra Goes to War*, 260; SRH 117, SRH 131, and SRH 146, MR, NA; SRH 035 in Ronald Spector, *Listening to the Enemy*; June situation, Box 348, Entry 175, RG 165, MR, NA.

26. George A. Brownell, *The Origin and Development of the National Security Agency* (Laguna Park, California: Aegean Press, 1981), 13; 12 December 1944 order, Box 6, 311.00, Entry 15, COS, RG 165, MR, NA.

27. SRH 117, RG 457, MR, NA.

28. George A. Brownell, *The Origin and Development of the National Security Agency*, 13; 12 December 1944 order, Box 6, Entry 15, COS, RG 165, MR, NA.

29. McCormack statement, 3 August 1943, SRH-141, Part 2, RG 457, MR, NA.

30. 22 February 1944, U.S. restrictions regarding China, A2 file, 820.02, London Embassy files, RG 84, Suitland, NA; June–August 1944, British arrangements in China, and Hayes to MI 2, 22 March 1945, WO 208/471, PRO; 13 January 1945 system, "Canadian Joint Staff," file, Box 782, Entry 203, RG 165, MR, NA; Op-20-G to Admiral Thebaud, Box 21, CNO/TS, RG 80, MR, NA; Corderman to Carter, January 1944, January 1943 file, Box 426, MID, 311, RG 319, Suitland, NA.

31. 17 February 1944, COS (W) 1108 and related materials, CAB 105/58 and CAB 122/1347, PRO; "C" message, 21 April 1944 and 3 May 1944 British CCS message, CCS 474/4 and 5, ABC 311.5

(25.1.44), RG 165, MR, NA; Op-20-G to COMINCH, 15 August 1944. File A6-2/A8, CNO/TS, and 9 October 1944 CNO message, A7-2(3) file, Entry 32-5, CNO/TS, RG 80, MR, NA.

32. JSM message, 9 March 1945, CAB 105/189; 4 May 1944, COS (W) 32 to JSM, CAB105/60, PRO.

Chapter 8: The Last Phase of the War and Continuation of Cryptanalytic Cooperation

1. Roosevelt to Stettinius, 17 January 1945, Memos for Secretary file (October to February), Box 733, Stettinius papers, University of Virginia; Bradley F. Smith, *The Shadow Warriors* (New York, New York: Basic Books, 1983), 400.

2. Lt. (jg) John Cannarton, 9 June 1944, SRH 016, RG 457, MR, NA; Leahy to Three Secretaries, 22 August 1944, Box 6, 311.5, Entry 15, RG 165, MR, NA; 28 August 1944, JCS 4193, A 16-2/ A-8, Box 1, CNO/TS, RG 80, MR, NA; CCS 311.5 (7/1/44), RG 218, MR, NA.

3. DNC to Marshall, 7 April 1945, and Admiral Redman message, 10 March 1945, A6-3 (10), Box 21, CNO/TS, RG 80; 10 March 1945 King-Marshall exchange, 32-J, File A6, Box 27, RG 38, MR, NA; SRH 200, Part 2, Section 2, RG 457, MR, NA; Memo, 73/30 Marshall papers, Marshall Library, Lexington, Virginia.

4. Marshall to President Truman, 17 April 1945, 81/33, Marshall papers, Marshall Library, Lexington, Virginia.

5. On the handling of Ultra-Magic in the Truman White House: Leahy to Marshall, 14 May 1945, 74/18, Marshall papers, Marshall Library, Lexington, Virginia; Map Room Log, 17 April 1945, Roosevelt Library; "Gestapo" reference, 4 May and 15 June 1945 entries, Intelligence Service file, Box 7, Eben Ayers papers, Harry S. Truman Library.

6. Bissell-Marshall, 16 June 1945, Box 9, 350.05, Entry 15, COS, RG 165, MR, NA; Edwards and King memos, 10 July 1945, Box 28, Entry 32-J, RG 38, MR, NA.

7. 31 August 1944, J. F. Carter report, Carter files, PSF, Roosevelt Library.

8. Hinsley, et al., *British Intelligence,* Vol. III, Part 2, 20; on OB meetings

with USSR, see for example February 1943–April 1944 weekly OB meeting minutes, Boxes 1044–1045, 350.0511, Entry 47, RG 319, Suitland, NA. Also British Military Mission records beginning with 15 March 1943, WO 178/27, PRO. Military Mission input to Red Army OB, 23 February 1944, WO 208/1850, PRO; USAF in Soviet Union, on Red Air Force OB, 16 May 1944, RG 334, "Air Intelligence File," Box 1, MR, NA; retrospective comment, 13 August 1972, Alan Brooke, 3/A/VI, Liddell Hart Centre, King's College, London. (Thanks to Professor A. Wilt for this reference.)

9. 15 February 1944, Memo, Box 805, 4–15 February Summaries, Entry 182, RG 165; "Conferences Russia" file, Box 783, Entry 203, RG 165, MR, NA.

10. McCormack-O'Brien exchanges, "British Participation" file, Box 782, Entry 203, RG 165, MR, NA; Diane Putney, *Ultra and the American Air Forces,* 61–62; Hinsley, et al., *British Intelligence,* Vol. II, 59, 69f., 619; Vol. III, Part 1, 18.

11. Marshall to Antonov, 10 April 1945, Anglo-Soviet Planning file, Box 2, RG 334, MR, NA; Bradley F. Smith and Elena Agarossi, *Operation Sunrise* (New York: Basic Books, 1979), 101–124.

12. McMahan to Wenger, 25 May 1945, SRH 200 (Section 2), RG 457, MR, NA; 6 September 1944 memo, Admiral Stark file, King Double Zero files, 1941–46, Box 38, Operational Archives, Naval Historical Center, Washington; 4 June 1945, Naval attaché reports file, COM, Navy Europe Reporting, Box 8, Entry 98C, RG 38, MR, NA; 22 February 1945 memo, Folder: Technical Office, 5 March 1945 memo, Folder: Technical Info., both Box 31; 11 April 1945 memo, Folder: Germany, Box 9, RG 334, Moscow Mission, MR, NA.

13. Rattan, 5 June 1945, Marshall to King, etc. 73/35, Marshall Papers, Marshall Library, Lexington, Virginia.

14. McCormack-O'Brien exchanges, "British Participation" file, Box 782, Entry 203, RG 165, MR, NA.

15. June 1945 JSM cipher policy review, CAB 122/548, PRO; Stark to Horne and reply, 3 March 1945, File A8-3/EF13, Box 22, CNO/TS, RG 80, MR, NA.

16. McCormack-O'Brien exchanges, "British Participation" file, Box 782, Entry 203, RG 165, MR, NA.

17. James Bamford, *The Puzzle Palace* (Boston, Massachusetts: Houghton Mifflin, 1982), 44; George A. Brownell, *The Origin and Devel-*

opment of the National Security Agency (Laguna Park, California: Aegean Press, 1981), Vol. II, 20–21; COS to JCS, 15 August 1945, CAB 122/1340, PRO.

18. Eden to Alexander, 22 November 1944, ADM 1/15687, PRO. In 1947 Clement Attlee was minister in charge of MI 5 (as well as PM), CAB 103/256, PRO; Bradley F. Smith, *Shadow Warriors,* 396 and notes.

19. CCS 350.05 (8/5/45) RG 218, MR, NA; Nimitz order, 19 December 1945, Box 21, A8-2, 1945, CNO/TS, RG 80, MR, NA; Norman Denning's statement on revealing information, 25 February 1965, Godfrey Papers, MLBE 1/2, Churchill College, Cambridge; 7 January 1946, Forrestal Memo, A-8-2, Box 42, 1946, CNO/TS, RG 80, MR, NA.

20. Marshall-King exchange, 18–22 August 1945, SRH 200, Part 2, Section 2, RG 457, MR, NA (other copies in 18 August 1945 Admiral King, Double Zero files, 1942–47, Operational Archives, Naval Historical Center, Washington, 350.09, COS, Entry 15, RG 165, MR, NA; Marshall papers 73/36, Marshall Library, Lexington, Virginia).

21. 28 August 1945, Truman order, 311.5, Box 519, Entry 418, RG 165, and ABC 311.51 (10/25/42), RG 165, MR, NA.

22. George A. Brownell, *The Origin and Development of the National Security Agency*, Vol. II, 38; SRH-169, RG 457, MR, NA.

23. See source references in note 20.

24. "Establishment of a Central Intelligence Service," JCS 1181 Series, CCS 334, CIA (12/6/42), Section 1, RG 218, MR, NA.

25. 5 September 1945, Conferences with the President file, Box 15, Harold Smith papers, Harry S. Truman Library.

26. On Friedman, the security Questionnaire (828.8) and correspondence under names of Travis, Tiltman, Denniston, etc. Friedman papers, Marshall Library, Lexington, Virginia.

27. Three Secretaries memorandum, which was initiated by the War Department (it is on a War Department letterhead), Naval Aide Files, Truman Library.

28. Leahy to Secretary of the Navy, 12 September 1945, Forrestal to Admiral King, etc., Entry 32-J, NND, 813002, RG 38, MR, NA. Bradley F. Smith, "A Note on the OSS, Ultra, and World War II's Intelligence Legacy for America," *Defence Analysis*, III, no. 2 (April 1987), 184–89.

29. CCS instructions, Admiralty to COMINCH, 16 September 1945, Naval Aide Files, Truman Library.
30. 13 September 1945, "Conferences with the President" file, Box 15, Harold Smith papers, Truman Library; Bradley F. Smith, *Shadow Warriors*, 406–47.
31. 20 September 1945 report, "Intelligence and Security Activities," R and I files, Box 7, Panuch papers, Truman Library.

Chapter 9: The Making of a Permanent Agreement, 1945–47

1. James Bamford, *The Puzzle Palace* (Boston, Massachusetts: Houghton Mifflin, 1982), 309ff.
2. Interview with Sir Harry Hinsley, 6 August 1990; 8 October 1945 report, file 2503, Box 9, CNO, Entry 98C, RG 38, MR, NA; 19 December 1945, Summary, 350.051, Entry 47, RG 319, Suitland, NA. Wesley K. Wark, "Cryptologic Innocence: The Origins of Signals Intelligence in Canada," *Journal of Contemporary History*, XXII, no. 4, (October 1987), 659.
3. Interview with Sir Harry Hinsley, 6 August 1990; Ronald Clark, *The Man Who Broke Purple* (Boston, Massachusetts: Little Brown, 1977), 208.
4. 24 June 1946 memo, 350.0511, Entry 47, RG 319, Suitland, NA; 3 October 1947 memo for Secretary of the Navy, File A7-A8, Box 51, CNO/TS, RG 80, MR, NA; 18 July 1946, M.M. (s) (46) 54, CAB 138/7, PRO.
5. George A. Brownell, *The Origin and Development of the National Security Agency* (Laguna Park, California: Aegean Press, 1981), Vol. II, 15–16.
6. 28 December 1945 to 16 January 1946 papers, File A-8, Box 42, CNO/TS, RG 80, MR, NA.
7. 25 April 1946, Paige memo, 171/47/226, MR, NA. (Thanks to T. Naftali for this reference.) 8 December 1947, Nimitz to Secretary of the Navy, A-7 to A-8 file, Box 51, CNO/TS, RG 80, MR, NA; 3 October 1947 to Secretary of the Navy, A-7 to A-8 file, Box 51, RG 80, MR, NA.
8. Jonathan E. Helmreich, *Gathering Rare Ores: The Diplomacy of Uranium Acquisition*, 1943–54 (Princeton, New Jersey: Princeton University Press, 1986), 97–101; Jill Edwards, "Roger Makins: Mr.

Atom" in John Zametica (ed.), *British Officials and British Foreign Policy, 1945–50* (Leicester: Leicester University Press, 1990), 8–38.

9. 8 October 1945, Shelley to Inglis and related documents, file 2503, Box 9, CNO/TS, Entry 98C, RG 38, MR, NA; 29 January 1946, CNO to Fleet Commanders, File A8-3, Box 42, CNO/TS, RG 80, MR, NA.

10. 7 February 1946, A. T. Cornwall-Jones Note, CAB 138/7, PRO; 18 December 1945, Conway CCB, CAB 122/548, PRO.

11. 19 December 1945, Memo for Chief MIS, 350.0511, Entry 47, RG 319, Suitland, NA.

12. 15 February 1946, Com. Nav. Eu. Report, File 2662, Box 9, Entry 98C, CNO, RG 38, MR, NA.

13. 23 August 1946, Op-20 to Op-23 and related memos, Box 41, 1946, CNO/TS, RG 80, MR, NA.

14. Technical Cooperation file, FO 115/4258, PRO, CNO to COUSNFE, 19 September 1946, File A8-3, EF/3, CNO/TS, RG 80, MR, NA.

15. See Friedman papers for evidence of these continuations, such as Travis to 8 April 1946, 828.6, Marshall Library, Lexington, Virginia.

16. Espe to Belin, 20 September 1946, File A8-3, EF/3, CNO/TS, RG 80, MR, NA.

BIBLIOGRAPHY

Manuscript Collections, in addition to the Public Record Office (Kew Surrey) and the National Archives, Washington, D.C.

1. Carlisle Barracks, Carlisle, Pennsylvania
   Richard Collins
   William J. Donovan
   Abraham Sinkov
2. Churchill Library, Cambridge
   A. Denniston
   Lewin/Beesly
   G. H. Wilkinson
3. Eisenhower Library, Abilene, Kansas
   W. B. Smith Collection of World War II Documents
4. Imperial War Museum, London
   Sir Herbert Marchant (tapes)
   F. W. Winterbottom
5. Library of Congress
   Ernest King
6. Liddell Hart Centre, King's College, London
   F. H. N. Davidson
7. George Marshall Library, Lexington, Virginia
   William Friedman
   George Marshall
8. Operational Archives, Naval Historical Center, Washington Navy Yard
   ESF War Diary
   Admiral King Papers
   Situational Maps
9. Franklin D. Roosevelt Library, Hyde Park, New York
   Map Room
   Official Files (OF)
   OSS Files (Map Room)
   President's Secretary's Files (PSF)
   Harold Smith
10. Harry S. Truman Library, Independence, Missouri
    Eben Ayres
    J. A. Panuch

Harold Smith
Naval Aide Files
11. University of Virginia, Charlottesville, Virginia
Edward Stettinius
12. Yale University, New Haven, Connecticut
Henry L. Stimson Manuscripts and Archives

Interviews and/or letters to the author
Patrick Beesly
Mrs. Margaret Blythe
William Bundy
Peter Calvocoressi
Robert Cecil
Robin Denniston
Joseph Eachus
Sir Harry Hinsley
Lady Marchant
Professor McVittie's diary entries (loaned by Robin Denniston)
Timothy Mulligan
Mrs. Mary Pain
Joseph Richard
Frank Rowlett
Abraham Sinkov
Telford Taylor

Books
Anderson, Terry H. *The United States, Great Britain and the Coldwar.* Columbia, Missouri: University of Missouri, 1981.
Andrew, Christopher and David Dilles (eds). *The Missing Dimension.* London: Macmillan, 1984.
Ball, Desmond. *A Suitable Piece of Real Estate: American Installations in Australia.* Sydney: Hale and Iremonyer, 1980.
Bamford, James. *The Puzzle Palace.* Boston, Massachusetts: Houghton Mifflin, 1982.
Beesly, Patrick. *Very Special Intelligence.* London: Hamilton, 1985.
Brown, Anthony Cave. *Bodyguard of Lies.* New York, New York: Harper, 1967.
Brownell, George A. *The Origin and Development of the National Security Agency.* Laguna Park, California: Aegean Press, 1981.

Calvocoressi, Peter. *Top Secret Ultra*. New York, New York: Pantheon, 1980.

Clark, Ronald. *The Man Who Broke Purple*. Boston, Massachusetts: Little, Brown, 1977.

Constantinides, George C. *Intelligence and Espionage: An Analytical Bibliography*. Boulder, Colorado: Westview Press, 1983.

Costello, John. *The Pacific War*. New York, New York: Rawson and Wade, 1985.

Danchev, Alex. *Establishing the Anglo-American Alliance*. London: Brassey's, 1990.

Dorwart, Jeffrey M. *Conflict of Duty: The U.S. Navy's Intelligence Dilemma*. Annapolis, Maryland: Naval Institute Press, 1983.

Drea, Edward J. *MacArthur's Ultra: Codebreaking and the War Against Japan, 1942–45*. Lawrence, Kansas: University of Kansas, 1992.

Edmonds, Robin. *Setting the Mold: The United States and Britain, 1945–50*. Oxford: Oxford University Press, 1986.

Frank, Richard B. *Guadalcanal*. New York, New York: Random House, 1990.

Gannon, Michael. *Operation Drumbeat*. New York, New York: Harpers, 1990.

Gilbert, Martin. *Winston Churchill: Finest Hour*. Boston, Massachusetts: Houghton Mifflin, 1983.

Hathaway, Robert M. *Ambiguous Partnership: Britain and America, 1944–47*. New York, New York: Columbia University Press, 1981.

Heinrichs, Waldo. *Threshold of War*. New York, New York: Oxford: 1988.

Helmreich, Jonathan E. *Gathering Rare Ores: The Diplomacy of Uranium Acquisition, 1943–54*. Princeton, New Jersey: Princeton University Press, 1986.

Hinsley, F. H. and C. A. Simkins. *British Intelligence in the Second World War*. Vol. IV. London: HMSO, 1990.

Hinsley, F. H., E. E. Thomas, et al. *History of British Intelligence in the Second World War*. III Vols (Vol. III in two parts). London: HMSO 3, 1979–1988.

Hodges, Andrew. *The Turing Enigma*. London: Unwin, 1985.

Hodgson Godfrey. *The Colonel: The Life and Wars of Henry Stimson*. New York, New York: Knopf, 1990.

Holmes, W. J. *Double Edged Secrets*. Annapolis, Maryland: Naval Institute Press, 1979.

Horner, D. M. *Australia and Allied Intelligence in the Pacific in the Second World War*. Canberra, Australia: Australian National University, 1980.

Kahn, David. *The Codebreakers*. New York, New York: Macmillan, 1967.

————. *Seizing the Enigma*. Boston, Massachusetts: Houghton Mifflin, 1991.

Kimball, Warren F. (ed.). *Churchill and Roosevelt*. Vol. I. Princeton, New Jersey: Princeton University Press, 1984.

Kozaczuk, Wladyslaw. *Enigma*. London: Arms and Armour, 1984.

Layton, Edwin T. (with Roger Pineau and John Costello). *And I Was There*. New York, New York: Morrow, 1987.

Lewin, Ronald. *American Magic*. New York, New York: Farrar Straus, 1982.

————. *Ultra Goes to War*. New York, New York: Farrar Straus, 1978.

Lundstrom, John B. *The First South Pacific Campaign*. Annapolis, Maryland: Naval Institute Press, 1975.

Murfett, Malcolm. *Foolproof Relations, 1937–1940*. Singapore: Singapore University Press, 1984.

Naval Cryptologic Veterans Association. *Intercept Station C*. Denver, Colorado: privately printed, no date.

Parrish, Thomas. *The Ultra Americans*. New York, New York: Stein & Day, 1985.

Putney, Diane. *Ultra and the American Air Forces in World War II*. Washington, D.C.: Office of the Air Force, 1987.

Richardson, Jeffrey T. and Desmond Ball. *The Ties That Bind*. Boston, Massachusetts: Houghton Mifflin, 1985.

Rusbridger, James and Eric Nave. *Betrayal at Pearl Harbor: How Churchill Lured Roosevelt into War*. London: Michael O'Mara, 1991.

Ryan, Henry Butterfield. *Visions of Anglo-America*. Cambridge: Cambridge University Press, 1987.

Smith, Bradley F. *Shadow Warriors*. New York, New York: Basic Books, 1983.

Smith, Bradley F. and Elena Agarossi. *Operation Sunrise*. New York, New York: Basic Books, 1979.

Spector, Ronald (ed.). *Listening to the Enemy*. Wilmington, Delaware: Scholarly Resources Press, 1988.

Stevenson, William. *A Man Called Intrepid*. New York, New York: Harcourt Brace, 1976.

Stripp, Alan. *Codebreaker in the Far East*. London: Frank Cass, 1989.

Thorne, Christopher. *Allies of a Kind*. London: Hamilton, 1978.

Watt, Donald C. *Succeeding John Bull: America in Britain's Place*. Cambridge: Cambridge University Press, 1984.

Welchman, Gordon. *The Hut Six Story*. New York, New York: McGraw Hill, 1982.

West, Nigel. *The Sigint Secrets*. New York, New York: Morrow, 1988.

Wildman, Ted. *The Expendables*. Clearwater, Florida: privately printed, 1983.

Winterbotham, F. W. *The Ultra Secret*. London: Weidenfeld & Nicholson, 1974.

Winton, John. *Victory at Sea*. London: Leo Cooper, 1988.

Woods, Randall Bennett. *A Changing of the Guard: Anglo-American Relations, 1941–1946*. Charlotte, North Carolina: University of North Carolina, 1990.

ARTICLES

Anderson, Ralph. "If I Remember." *Cryptologia*. VI, no. 1 (January 1982), 40-44.

Bundy, William P. "Some of My Wartime Experiences." *Cryptologia*. XI, no. 1 (April 1988), 65-76.

Andrew, C. M. "The Growth of the Australian Intelligence Community and the Anglo-American Connection." Intelligence and National Security IV, no. 2 (April 1989).

Cecil, Robert. " 'C' 's War." *Intelligence and National Security*. I, no. 2 (May 1986), 170-183.

Denniston, Robin. "A. G. Denniston, and the Government Code and Cipher School Between the Wars." *Intelligence and National Security*. I, no. 1 (January 1986), 48-70.

Edwards, Jill. "Roger Makins: Mr. Atom." In John Zametica (ed.), *British Officials and British Foreign Policy, 1945–50*. Leicester: Leicester University Press, 1990.

Erskine, Ralph. "Naval Enigma: The Breaking of Heimisch and Triton." *Intelligence and National Security*. III, no. 1 (January 1988), 162-183.

Ferris, John. "The British Army and Signals Intelligence in the Field During the First World War." *Intelligence and National Security*. III, no. 4 (October 1988), 23-48.

———. "The British Enigma: British Signals Security and Cipher Machines." *Defence Analysis*. III, no. 2 (June 1987), 153-165.

———. "From Broadway House to Bletchley Park: The Diary of Captain Malcolm D. Kennedy 1934–1946." *Intelligence and National Security*. IV, no. 3 (July 1989), 421-450.

Filby, William P. "Bletchley Park and Berkeley Street." *Intelligence and National Security*. III, no. 2 (April 1988), 272-284.

Kruh, Louis. "Why Was Safford Pessimistic About Breaking the German Enigma Cipher Machine in 1942?" *Cryptologia*. XIV, no. 3 and 4 (July 1990), 253-257. (Replies in Vol. XV, no. 2.)

Lewin, Ronald. "A Signal Intelligence War." *Journal of Contemporary History*. XVI, no. 3 (July 1981), 501-512.

Merrilat, Herbert C. "The Ultra Began at Guadalcanal." *Marine Corps Gazette*. LXVI, no. 9 (September 1982), 44-49.

Milner Barry, P. S. "Action This Day." *Intelligence and National Security*. I, no. 2, (May 1986), 272-276.

Smith, Bradley F. "Admiral Godfrey's Mission to America." *Intelligence and National Security*. I, no. 3, (September 1986), 441-450.

———. "A Note on the OSS, Ultra and World War II's Intelligence Legacy for America." *Defence Analysis*. III, no. 2, (April 1987), 184-189.

Tucker, Dandus P. "Rhapsody in Purple." *Cryptologia*. VI, no. 3 (July 1982), 193-228.

Wark, Wesley K. "Cryptologic Innocence: The Origins of Signals Intelligence in Canada." *Journal of Contemporary History*. XXII, no. 4, (October 1987), 639-667.

Welchman, Gordon. "From Polish Bomba to British Bombe. The Birth of Ultra." *Intelligence and National Security*. I, no. 1, (January 1986), 71-110.

INDEX

ABC-1 agreements, 54, 71, 74
Abwehr (German), 154
Acheson, Dean, 211
Addis Ababa, Ethiopia, 65
Africa, 65, 83, 115, 134
Afrika Korps, 131
Air Intelligence Division, AID (U.S. Army Air Corps), 20
Air reconnaissance, 122
Alaska, 33, 224
Alba, Duke of, 134
Aleutian Islands, 107, 224
Algeria, 131, 146, 190
Allied Convoy Code, 121
Allied Intelligence Bureau, 107
Allies (in World War I and 1939–41), 4–8
Allies of a Kind by Christopher Thorpe, 172
American Military Attache Codes, 111
Anderson (British Headquarters, Colombo), 185
Anderson, Admiral Walter, 50
Ankara, Turkey 175
Arabia, 121
Arcadia Conference, 91–92, 94–95, 103
American Occupation of Japan, 205
Argentina, 178
Arlington Hall, 138, 142–45, 147, 149–52, 156–61, 165, 167, 171, 179, 183, 186–88, 198, 210, 227
Army-Navy Communications Intelligence Committee and Board (US), 187, 195–96, 208, 213, 219
Asia, 5, 81, 83, 91, 94, 100, 102, 114, 133, 190, 193, 205, 209
Atlantic cables, 160
Atlantic Charter, 83, 173
Atlantic, Ocean and Battle of, 3, 34, 78–81, 83–84, 86–88, 91, 101–02, 117–18, 124–25, 127–29, 132, 147, 177, 180, 188, 192, 224
Atomic bomb, 204, 206, 209, 212, 215–16, 220
Attlee, Clement, 192, 215

Australia, 94, 105–07, 143, 183, 217–18, 223, 225
Austria, 34, 193, 209, 223
Axis (Nazi Germany and Fascist Italy), 6, 21, 37, 78, 111, 133, 144, 154, 178–79
Azores, 224

B Dienst (German), 84, 118, 173–75
Bainbridge Island, Washington, 120
Balkans, 65–66
Baltic Sea, 224
Bamford, James, 35
Barbarossa (June 1941), 67, 81
Bataan, 91
Battle of Britain, 28, 67
Battle of the Bulge, 193
"Beechnut," 165
Beesly, Patrick, 78
Belgium, 7, 9
Belin, Commander Peter, 228
Bell Laboratories, 136–40, 142, 175–76
Bentinck, Cavendish, 102
Berkeley Street branch of GC and CS, 98, 151, 155, 160–62, 165, 210
Berle, Adolf, 17
Berne, Switzerland, 175
Bexley, Kent, 165
Bicher, Colonel George A., 145, 165
Bikini atomic tests, 223
Bismarck, 78
Bissell, General Clayton, 171, 183, 197
Black Books, 186
Black Chamber (U.S.), 20, 32, 50
Bletchley Park (Station X), 23, 27–30, 35, 48, 56–57, 62, 67, 72, 77–81, 86, 88–89, 94, 96, 98, 100, 102, 108, 113, 116, 118, 121, 123, 125–28, 136–38, 140–41, 144–45, 149–54, 156–64, 166–67, 169, 178–83, 188, 206, 210, 215, 221, 227. *See also* Government Code and Cipher School.
Blitz, 1940, 16, 38, 39, 58